P9-DVV-840

Onward!

In this book Todd Starnes combines his signature humor and award-winning investigative journalism skills to expose the Left's war on religious liberty.

—SEAN HANNITY

Seasoned journalist and valiant culture warrior Todd Starnes has sounded an alarm in his newest book that every American should listen to. Starnes's unique insights, seasoned with his trademark wit, make *God Less America* a must-read for every American who cherishes his freedom to worship God.

—DR. ROBERT JEFFRESS
PASTOR, FIRST BAPTIST CHURCH, DALLAS

In *God Less America* Todd Starnes captures the greatest threat currently facing our nation: an attack on our first freedom by governmental, educational, and Hollywood elites. Upon the outcome of this struggle over religious freedom hinges every other freedom Americans hold dear. Every American who values liberty should read this book. It is my hope that this book will embolden you to stand uncompromisingly for our most valuable freedom—our freedom of religion, the freedom upon which all other freedoms rest.

—TONY PERKINS
PRESIDENT, FAMILY RESEARCH COUNCIL

This is a wake-up call! Todd Starnes has sounded a rather loud alarm in *God Less America*. While most are only dealing with the "what" of our current state of affairs, Todd digs deeper into the "why" and points to our only remedy. There is hope, and it's not too late—if we don't give in, don't give up, and don't give out in the culture war swirling around us. Read this book and reap!

—DR. O. S. HAWKINS
FORMER PASTOR, FIRST BAPTIST CHURCH, DALLAS, TX
PRESIDENT, GUIDESTONE FINANCIAL RESOURCES

Thanks to the Left's relentless attack on religious freedom, it's now considered by many to be a mere suggestion rather than a bedrock principle of essential human liberty. Todd Starnes turns this pathology on its head—and reminds us of a critical truth: an America without true freedom of speech, assembly, and religion is actually not America at all. Starnes sounds the alarm—and cleverly and wittily tells us how to restore this central pillar of American exceptionalism.

—MONICA CROWLEY, PhD
NATIONALLY SYNDICATED RADIO HOST, FOX NEWS CHANNEL

Todd Starnes does what the great authors have always done—he paints pictures in your mind with words. He's a master storyteller. Don't get me wrong. *God Less America* is very much a book about the great clash in twenty-first-century America between good and evil. Todd has thoroughly researched and documented the great moral conflict in our country. He gives details you've never heard before and calls you to action. His biting wit skewers the absurdity of liberal dogma.

But this book is so much more than that. Interspersed between descriptions of the war between adherents of God's law and man's preferences are the bittersweet, poignant remembrances of a man who grew up with buttermilk biscuits, sweet tea, and a home full of warm Christian love. His words paint the pictures of covered dish "dinner on the grounds" after church in rural Mississippi. Todd does what the great storytellers have always done. He takes you there. Read *God Less America*...and be blessed.

—Doc Washburn
Host, *The Doc Washburn Show*

In *God Less America* Todd Starnes has gathered a comprehensive collection of specific examples in which traditional values and the people who hold them are coming under fire.

Whether it be in small towns such as Muldrow, Oklahoma; Frisco, Texas; or Mount Dora, Florida; or large cities such as Atlanta, New York City, and Washington DC, no person devoted to the teachings and applications of the Bible is immune to these attacks. *God Less America* is virtually a training manual on what to expect and, more importantly, how others have handled these assaults on faith.

The best offense is a good defense, and 1 Peter 3:15 commands believers to "be ready always to give an answer." From the words in *God Less America* we find those answers and are given strength because of the knowledge that fighting for righteousness is not in vain. The various examples Starnes uses show that those of faith are not alone in their fight to save our communities and our country from the immorality and wickedness of modern-day evil.

—Scottie Nell Hughes
News director, Tea Party News Network

For such a time as this Todd Starnes sounds the siren of alarm one unbelievable story after another. Read this book!

—Karen Kingsbury,
#1 *New York Times* best-selling author of *Fifteen Minutes*

GOD LESS AMERICA

TODD STARNES

FRONT
LINE

Most CHARISMA HOUSE BOOK GROUP products are available at special quantity discounts for bulk purchase for sales promotions, premiums, fund-raising, and educational needs. For details, write Charisma House Book Group, 600 Rinehart Road, Lake Mary, Florida 32746, or telephone (407) 333-0600.

GOD LESS AMERICA by Todd Starnes
Published by FrontLine
Charisma Media/Charisma House Book Group
600 Rinehart Road
Lake Mary, Florida 32746
www.charismahouse.com

This book or parts thereof may not be reproduced in any form, stored in a retrieval system, or transmitted in any form by any means—electronic, mechanical, photocopy, recording, or otherwise—without prior written permission of the publisher, except as provided by United States of America copyright law.

Unless otherwise noted, all Scripture quotations are from the New King James Version of the Bible. Copyright © 1979, 1980, 1982 by Thomas Nelson, Inc., publishers. Used by permission.

Scripture quotations marked NAS are from the New American Standard Bible, copyright © 1960, 1962, 1963, 1968, 1971, 1972, 1973, 1975, 1977, 1995 by The Lockman Foundation. Used by permission. (www.Lockman.org)

Scripture quotations marked NIV are from the Holy Bible, New International Version. Copyright © 1973, 1978, 1984, International Bible Society. Used by permission.

Copyright © 2014 by Todd Starnes
All rights reserved

Cover design by Justin Evans
Design Director: Bill Johnson

Visit the author's website at www.toddstarnes.com.

Library of Congress Cataloging-in-Publication Data:
An application to register this book for cataloging has been submitted to the Library of Congress.
International Standard Book Number: 978-1-62136-591-4
E-book ISBN: 978-1-62136-592-1

While the author has made every effort to provide accurate telephone numbers and Internet addresses at the time of publication, neither the publisher nor the author assumes any responsibility for errors or for changes that occur after publication.

Todd Starnes's articles and reporting from Fox News and Fox News Radio are used herein with permission. All such articles and reporting are the sole property of Fox News Network LLC. All rights reserved.

First edition

14 15 16 17 18 — 9 8 7 6 5 4 3 2 1
Printed in the United States of America

CONTENTS

ACKNOWLEDGMENTS

IT TAKES THE support of a lot of godly people to write a book about a godless country. And I've been blessed to work with so many wonderful folks on this project.

To my colleagues at Fox News Channel—thank you for your friendship. It's been an honor to work alongside you at the Fox News Corner of the World for all these years.

I'm so thankful for my sweet family. We've shared many laughs, tears, jugs of sweet tea, and more barbecue than we care to disclose. I'm blessed with a wonderful family tree—firmly planted alongside living waters. A special thank-you to Aunt Lynn, Cousin Bill, Uncle Jerry, Amy, Saundra, Aunt Norma, Uncle Bob, Uncle Don and Aunt Sarah, and Cousin Clint. I just hope you can accept my sincere apologies if you are subjected to an Internal Revenue Service audit.

To my researchers, Chicago Garrett and New York City Garrett—you are the brain trust! Your work was herculean. NYC Garrett, your take on pop culture was spot-on—and your analysis of twerking was deft. You are gentlemen and scholars.

To Caleb, my assistant—thank you for the long hours and tremendous work you've done on this project. You've been a good colleague and friend on this journey. Along the way you've experienced the pleasure of sipping sweet tea and you've learned the proper usage of the phrase "bless your heart."

I'd be remiss if I didn't mention Kenton, Tonya, Cory, Kellen, Sarah, and the Liberty Belles—great friends and patriots.

To my sweet friends Joni, Michelle, and Paul—thank you for the late-night readings. Your advice and guidance made this a better book. Dalton, your work on our Facebook page has made it a special community. Thank you for your hard work, your dedication, and your faithfulness.

It's been an honor to work with the team at Charisma House. Their staff bathed this project in prayer and worked fiercely to get this book published. A huge, huge thank-you to Steve, Tessie, Debbie, Adrienne, Woodley, Althea, Jason, and Leigh. Tessie, that meeting in Nashville really did turn out to be a divine appointment.

I'm also blessed to have one of the finest literary agents in the business. Frank Breeden, thank you for your wisdom, your guidance, and your encouragement. I'd also like to thank the spectacular team at Premiere Speakers for giving me a platform to share my work. And a huge thanks to Bryce—the best attorney a writer could have.

I've also been blessed to know some of the great warriors of the faith—Tony Perkins, Retired Lieutenant General Jerry Boykin, J. P. Duffy, Tim Wildmon, Jim Stanley, Robert Jeffress, Hiram Sasser, Jay Sekulow, Sarah Palin, Ron Crews, Craig and Janet Parshall, and Jerry Johnson, just to name a few. These men and women are on the front lines fighting for our freedom.

Finally, a special thank-you to my readers, listeners, and viewers. You are the ones who make all this possible. Thank you for putting your trust in me to tell our stories. Some of the finest radio stations in the nation carry my daily commentaries. Thank you to the program directors, producers, and hosts for bringing our stories to life on the nation's airwaves. And how about our Facebook and Twitter communities! Sweet mercy! It's such an honor to hang out with so many gun-toting, Bible-clinging great Americans. Your friendship is something I cherish.

But most of all, I give glory to the author of my salvation—my Lord and Savior, Jesus Christ.

Onward, Christian soldiers!

FOREWORD

MERICA IS A nation at war. This is not a war being fought with guns and bombs; it's being fought with words and ideas. We aren't sending armies to face off with our enemy, but there are definitely opposing sides in a confrontation. The battle isn't taking place on foreign soil; it's right at our doorstep. And the casualties are mounting daily.

The war I'm speaking of is a culture war. It's a battle for the religious freedom our forefathers embedded into the very first amendment of our nation's Bill of Rights.

Those of us on the front lines of this war see its effects on a daily basis. We learn of the stories of Chick-fil-A and *Duck Dynasty* and share them with you every day. But there is more at stake than the chicken sandwiches and duck calls these stories contain. Our very religious liberties are in question, and they are being chiseled away one chip at a time.

In recent years militant special interest groups have made it their goal to co-opt our religious liberties and force industry and government to go beyond tolerance of their views and demand full approval of them. Anyone who believes otherwise is told to shut up. We've become a society that obsesses over tolerance and acceptance of everyone—except God.

Thankfully there are people like Todd Starnes who are not afraid to join me on the front lines of America's culture war. I've known Todd for years as we have worked together at Fox News. We're trench buddies in this war to uphold the traditional family values and biblical principles that have been at our nation's core foundation since its birth. In *God Less America* Todd shares stories from the front lines with his distinctly recognizable brand of homespun humor. But he also very clearly sounds a wake-up call to American Christians. It's time to stand together against the barrage of liberal media and special interest groups who seek to eliminate all tolerance of anyone whose worldview doesn't line up with theirs.

"Not on my watch" is a slogan we hear often. It comes from the military concept of one person being on watch—standing guard—while others sleep. When you're on watch, you're responsible for what happens. When you're standing guard, it's your job to recognize the threat, wake others up, and initiate a plan of action that allows them to defend themselves from attack.

We're living at a crucial point in history. Many around us are sleeping. They aren't aware of the plan that is already underway to steal our freedoms right out from underneath us. I am not over-dramatizing the agendas of many special interest groups when I call them an attack. If our generation stays asleep or chooses to stand by and do nothing in this battle, the America our children and grand-children inherit from us will be completely unrecognizable to us, let alone to our country's Founding Fathers.

Todd Starnes has earned a national reputation for providing fair and balanced coverage of the culture war. His dispatches from the front lines of the war on religious liberty have become must-read material for Americans disturbed about the direction of our nation. Todd combines Southern story-telling with investigative journalism to craft a book that will not only entertain but also inform the nation about the extent of the culture's decay. I read Todd's books, and you should too!

As you read this book, you'll be moved—sometimes to laughter and other times to soberness at the reality of the state of our country. Let it motivate you to do something. Let it wake you up to join those of us taking a stand regardless of the price. We cannot allow our Christian beliefs to be marginalized or legislated out of our society.

Not while we are alive and able to do something to stop it. It's time for us to rally together and determine, "Not on our watch!"

—MIKE HUCKABEE

Mike Huckabee, former Arkansas governor and former Republican presidential nominee, is the host of *Huckabee*, which airs on Fox News Channel. He is the author of nine books, including the *New York Times* best sellers *A Simple Government*, *Do the Right Thing*, *A Simple Christmas*, and *Can't Wait Till Christmas*.

If we ever forget that we're one nation under God, then we will be a nation gone under.[1]
—RONALD WILSON REAGAN

Introduction

GOD BLESS AMERICA?

I FEEL LIKE A *Duck Dynasty* guy living in a Miley Cyrus world. And to be perfectly honest with you, I feel like I'm getting twerked on by Washington DC.

It's really no surprise that I identify with Mr. Phil and Miss Kay and Uncle Si. We're all Southern. And like the Robertsons, I'm proud to call myself a gun-toting, sweet-tea-drinking, Bible-clinging American.

President Obama calls us bitter, but I prefer to be called blessed. Besides, the only reason we're clinging to our guns and our Bibles and our jugs of sweet tea is because we're afraid he's going to take them away from us.

We're a peculiar people. That's how the Bible describes us. My Uncle Jerry, from Coldwater, Mississippi, fancies himself to be an armchair theologian. He said the literal interpretation of that passage means, "I'm an odd duck."

Well, quack, quack, quack, baby.

I grew up in a much simpler time—when blackberry was a pie and dirty dancing meant somebody forgot to clean out the barn for the square dance. It was a time when father still knew best—when the girls were girls and the men were men. I grew up in a time when a rainbow was a sign of God's promise, not gay rights.

When I grew up, spam was something you ate and a hard drive was the twelve-hour trip to grandma's house without any bathroom breaks. It was a time when a virus was cleared up with a bowl of chicken soup, not the Geek Squad from Best Buy. It was a time when Doobie was a brother and hip-hop was something a bunny rabbit did. It was a time when a grill was used for burgers, not a hood ornament for your face.

But my, how the times have changed.

It seems like only yesterday when President Obama promised his legion of followers that he would fundamentally transform the nation.

As it turned out, he's lived up to that promise.

It wasn't too long after his election that the president distanced himself from the Judeo-Christian foundation of our nation.

"We do not consider ourselves a Christian nation," President Obama told a gathering in Turkey.[1]

It was not the first time he had made such a declaration. In 2008 he infamously told the Christian Broadcasting Network that "America is no longer just a Christian nation."[2]

In the early days of his presidency Obama considered removing the Nativity from the East Room of the White House,[3] omitted the traditional phrase "in the year of our Lord" on a presidential proclamation,[4] and once forgot to issue an Easter proclamation.[5]

He told the *New York Times* the Muslim call to prayer was "one of the prettiest sounds on Earth."[6] (On a personal note, I believe the recitation of the sinner's prayer at a Billy Graham crusade is the prettiest sound on Earth.) The Obama administration briefly banned Bibles at Walter Reed Medical Center[7] and Christian prayers at the National Cemetery in Houston.[8] Military chaplains were told they could no longer pray in the name of Jesus,[9] and airmen were punished for opposing gay marriage.[10]

The administration's behavior has been a bit unsettling and downright puzzling, especially since the president professes to be a Christian.

Then again, maybe we shouldn't be terribly surprised. President Obama once belonged to a church whose pastor asked God to punish America. Remember the Reverend Jeremiah Wright, the potty-mouthed preacher at Trinity United Church of Christ in Chicago?

"No, no, no, not God bless America," he thundered from the pulpit. "God damn America!"[11]

It's beginning to feel like the Almighty may have answered Pastor Jeremiah Wright's prayer. Instead of God bless America, it's God less America.

In the words of the Reverend Wright, the chickens are coming home to roost.

Rick Warren was recently in my office in the far right side of the Fox News Corner of the World. He told me something that caused the hair on my arms to frizzle.

"I believe religious liberty will become the civil rights issue of our generation," he said.

The civil rights issue of our generation. Let that sink in for a moment. Imagine the implications. Imagine what the future might look like for people of faith.

Could it be that one day the pastor of the local First Baptist Church will be arrested for preaching hate? Could it be that one day police will turn hoses on little Christian boys and girls as they sing "Jesus Loves Me" at vacation Bible school? Is it possible that Christian business owners could one day be forced to close down for refusing to violate the tenets of their faith?

Will evangelical college students be denied entry into science and psychology programs because they believe in creationism? Will chaplains be thrown out of the armed forces if they pray in the name of Jesus? Will evangelical organizations be labeled domestic hate groups for defending the traditional definition of marriage?

The perfect storm is brewing. The White House is waging an all-out assault on religious liberty. Public schools are indoctrinating our children with the gospel of secularism. Hollywood is spewing toxins into our homes. The soundtrack of our lives is a pulsating mix of sex and violence and filth. The American family is in ruins. What was once wrong is now right and what was once right is now wrong.

Sadly, I believe the day Pastor Warren warned me about is already upon us. In these pages you will read stories of modern-day persecution. You will be introduced to fellow brothers and sisters in the Lord—patriots who have taken a stand for Christ and paid a price.

What the nation needs is a prophetic voice. But even our churches have been corrupted by the culture—turned into trendy nightclubs where good looks trump good character. Some preachers have traded the Word of God for pithy, self-help gimmickry.

And in those rare instances when some pastors have taken to their bully pulpits to rail against anti-Christian bigotry, their outrage rings hollow. They issue utterances of condemnation, telling us it's once again time to draw a line in the sand. Unfortunately, it's too late. We're already knee-deep in the ocean.

Richard Land, president of Southern Evangelical Seminary, brilliantly laid bare the impotence of some modern evangelical churches.

"Sadly, too often modern evangelical churches haven't even been thermometers, recording the actual temperature, but just mirrors reflecting a carefully constructed image that camouflages the darker spiritual reality behind the mask in the mirror," Land wrote.[12]

"We do not live in a neutral world," Land told a gathering in Charlotte, North Carolina. "We live in a world that is wracked with demonic activity, and evil and malignant satanic intent. We need to understand that. We are engaged in spiritual warfare. And once we become believers of the Lord Jesus Christ, we begin to march in the opposite direction of the devil."[13]

I once heard a Chicago-area pastor put it this way: we don't need more Americans bowing down to the Democrat donkey or the Republican elephant. We need more Americans bowing down to the Lion of Judah.

As the great patriot Thomas Paine wrote, "These are the times that try men's souls. The summer soldier and the sunshine patriot will, in this crisis, shrink from the service of his country; but he that stands it now, deserves the love and thanks of man and woman."[14]

One of my favorite presidents is Ronald Reagan. He understood the American dream. He understood the source of our nation's power and might. He understood that morning in America could only happen because of the bright Morningstar.

"Freedom is a fragile thing and is never more than one generation away from extinction," he declared. "It is not ours by inheritance; it must be fought for and defended constantly by each generation, for it comes only once to a people. Those who have known freedom and then lost it have never known it again."[15]

On April 18, 1775, Paul Revere mounted a horse and took off on his historic midnight ride, warning the patriots that the British were fast approaching. As Henry Wadsworth Longfellow put it in his poem about that famous night:

> For, borne on the night-wind of the Past,
> Through all our history, to the last,
> In the hour of darkness and peril and need,
> The people will waken and listen to hear
> The hurrying hoof-beats of that steed,
> And the midnight message of Paul Revere.[16]

I have neither a horse nor a lantern. But I do have a keyboard and a microphone. I pray you heed my midnight message. The secularists are coming! The secularists are coming! These are the stories of our fellow countrymen—men and women, boys and girls, teachers and bakers, soldiers and airmen. These are the stories the mainstream media doesn't want you to read.

So hunker down and grab a jug of sweet tea. You're about to jump into a bunker on the front lines of the war on religious liberty.

Chapter 1

THE WAR ON CHRISTIANITY

THE UNITED STATES is no longer just a Christian nation." Those are the words of Barack Hussein Obama. Many Americans were rightfully stunned when he announced the demise of Christianity: "Whatever we once were, we're no longer just a Christian nation; we are also a Jewish nation, a Muslim nation, a Buddhist nation, a Hindu nation, and a nation of nonbelievers," the president said in that now-infamous interview with David Brody of the Christian Broadcasting Network.[1]

It was a puzzling statement, considering the president publicly professes to be a follower of Christ. And yet in his speeches and his politics the president has gone out of his way to marginalize Christianity.

In 1995 the future president agreed to an interview with Hank De Zutter, a writer for the *Chicago Reader*. In the article Obama accused the Christian right of hijacking the moral high ground. "It's always easier to organize around intolerance, narrow-mindedness and false nostalgia," he said to De Zutter. "And they also have hijacked the higher moral ground with this language of family values and moral responsibility."[2]

In 2007 then-US Sen. Barack Obama unleashed on conservative Christians again, this time at a national meeting of the United Church of Christ, one of the most left-wing denominations in the country. Obama accused evangelical leaders of exploiting and politicizing religious beliefs in an effort to divide the nation.

"But somehow, somewhere along the way, faith stopped being used to bring us together and faith started being used to drive us apart," he said in remarks covered by CBS News. "Faith got hijacked, partly because of the so-called leaders of the Christian Right, all too eager to exploit what divides us."[3]

But Obama was just getting warmed up. "At every opportunity, they've told evangelical Christians that Democrats disrespect their values and dislike their church," he continued, "while suggesting to the rest of the country that religious Americans care only about issues like abortion and gay marriage, school prayer and intelligent design."[4]

Now, whatever would give us the impression that the Democrats disrespect church? It's not like they tried to vote God out of their party platform.[5] It's certainly not that they booed God at the 2012 Democratic National Convention.[6] Oh, wait. They did.

And how can we forget his private comments to a group of elitists in San Francisco, where he declared people who cling to their guns and their religion are bitter Americans?[7] That's a taste of Barack Obama unplugged. And he has governed accordingly.

Since he was sworn into office, President Obama has waged a massive assault on the Christian faith with the intent to marginalize Christianity and silence those who follow the teachings of Christ. I believe the end goal is to eradicate the Christian faith from the public marketplace of ideas.

Under this president's leadership, a US military training brief labeled Catholics and evangelical Christians as religious extremists,[8] churches and Christian organizations were forced to violate the tenets of their faith, and schoolchildren were ordered to sing government-approved Christmas carols.[9]

The Internal Revenue Service launched a widespread series of attacks on Christian ministries and pro-life groups—all deemed enemies of the Obama administration. The IRS even set its sights on one of the most famous evangelical Christians in the world: America's pastor, Billy Graham.

The Billy Graham Evangelistic Association and Samaritan's Purse were hit with IRS audits not too long after they ran full-page ads supporting North Carolina's marriage amendment. The ad concluded with these words: "Vote for biblical values this November 6, and pray with me [Billy Graham] that America will remain one nation under God."

Franklin Graham, the evangelist's son, said the audit was "morally wrong and unethical—indeed some would call it 'un-American.'"[10] The IRS eventually cleared the ministries of any wrongdoing, but the message they sent was crystal clear: enemies of the Obama administration's policies will suffer the consequences.

The *Biblical Recorder*, the official news journal for the North Carolina Baptist State Convention, was also hit with an audit. The newspaper had run a copy of Graham's advertisement. They too were cleared—but only after spending more than $15,000 in legal fees.[11]

"There seems to be a very anti-Christian bias that has flowed into a lot of government agencies—oppression literally against Christian organizations and groups," editor Allan Blume told me. "It makes you wonder what's going on."

IRS agents ordered two pro-life groups to reveal the content of their prayers and prayer meetings, "as if they were engaged in highly offensive or criminal behavior," the Thomas More Society charged. Another pro-life group was told they could not picket or protest abortion clinics. An attorney representing the pro-life groups called the IRS actions "intimidating" and "heavy-handed." One IRS agent went so far as to tell a pro-life group it had to remain neutral on the issue of abortion and lectured the group's president about forcing its religious beliefs on others. "You have to know your boundaries," IRS agent Sherry Wan can be heard saying in a recording. "You have to know your limits. You have to respect other people's beliefs."[12]

Perhaps Ms. Wan could show us where that edict is located in the US Constitution? And while she's at it, maybe she could also tell us when the IRS became assigned with the task of policing Christian speech.

Frank Page, president of the Southern Baptist Convention Executive Committee, warned of a bleak future for Christians in America. "I'm not a conspiracy theorist, but I do believe the day is coming when churches will see outright persecution as well as a continued pattern of harassment and marginalization in this culture," he told me. "Churches better gear up and realize that day is coming."

Over the past few years, I've documented hundreds of instances of religious persecution, including:

- A North Carolina pastor who was fired from his duties as an honorary chaplain for the state House of Representatives after he invoked the name of Jesus in a prayer;[13]

- A senior citizens' center in Port Wentworth, Georgia, that told elderly guests they could no longer pray over their meals;[14]

- A federal judge who ordered a Texas school district to prohibit public prayer at the Medina Valley Independent School District graduation ceremony. The judge also forbade students from using religious words such as *prayer* and *amen*;[15]

- A Massachusetts eight-year-old boy who was sent home from school and ordered to undergo a psychiatric evaluation after he drew a picture of Jesus on a cross;[16]

- A professor at the University of Kentucky who applied for a job directing the university's observatory but was turned down after the hiring committee found out he was a Christian;[17]

- Bibles and other religious materials that were briefly banned from Walter Reed Medical Center;[18]

- A New York public school teacher who was ordered to remove inspirational Bible verses from her classroom. The teacher was also told to remove a quote from former President Ronald Reagan. Ironically, the quote read, "If we ever forget that we are one nation under God, then we will be a nation gone under."[19]

Dr. Page said the culture is moving rapidly toward an intolerance for people who have a biblical worldview. He called the pace mind-boggling and nerve-rattling. And he made a bone-chilling prediction.

"There will be active and open persecution because of the biblical worldview of churches.... When you have national leaders who say Baptists and other evangelicals are guilty of hate speech because of our recitation of simple scripture, then you are going to see the alienation and active persecution of churches in the United States."[20]

As you read the following pages, I'm afraid you'll see that Dr. Page's greatest fears are already being realized.

Banning Prayers

A widow who lives in a Minnesota apartment complex funded by the Department of Housing and Urban Development (HUD) was told she could not pray, read her Bible, or have private discussions of a religious nature in the commons area of the complex.[21]

The incident occurred at the Osborne Apartments in Spring Lake Park, Minnesota, near Minneapolis. Ruth Sweats was having a casual conversation with another resident about the Bible when a social worker interrupted their conversation and told her she could not talk about religion or the Bible in the commons area.

The social worker then told the widow the apartment complex receives funding from the federal government and therefore she did not have First Amendment rights because HUD does not allow religious discussions in public areas of the complex.

Sweats contacted Alliance Defending Freedom (ADF), a legal advocacy group, who immediately dispatched a letter to the senior living complex urging them to reconsider their actions. "Government funding should not be misused to ban a widow's prayers," said ADF legal counsel Matt Sharp. "The private decision of senior citizens to discuss their faith, read the Bible, and pray is private speech, and no law requires this privately owned independent living facility to restrict the religious expression of these members of America's greatest generation."[22]

The letter explained that "HUD does not prohibit discussion about religion in the facilities to which it provides funding" and that federal court precedent has established that "simply because the government provides a benefit with public funds does not mean that all 'mention of religion or prayers' must be whitewashed from the use of the benefit."[23]

Alliance Defending Freedom also suggested the facility's actions may have violated federal and state anti-discrimination laws. "The right thing to do out of respect for the senior citizens—many of whom fought or saw their spouses fight in wars to defend our nation and the freedoms upon which it is built—is to remove the ban on religious expression in the commons area," the letter states. "We hope that this letter will clear up these issues and that you will do away with this terrible policy."[24]

College Shuts Down Dorm Room Bible Study

Officials at Rollins College in Florida ordered a group of students to shut down a Bible study they were holding in the privacy of a dorm room because, they said, it violated the rules. The incident occurred in the midst of a campus battle over whether religious groups that require their leaders to adhere to specific religious beliefs are violating the school's non-discrimination policies.

Four students affiliated with InterVarsity Christian Fellowship were holding an informal Bible study in the common area of a dorm suite. Midway through the study a resident hall assistant entered the room and asked the student leading the study to step outside.

"He was told they were no longer allowed inside the dorm, even with the express consent of the students to do Bible studies," said Greg Jao, InterVarsity's national field director. "They said it was because InterVarsity was no longer a registered student group on campus."

The well-known Christian ministry was de-recognized as an official campus organization after it refused to comply with the college's non-discrimination policy. This is a common practice among public universities that are hostile to Christian students.

While InterVarsity welcomes all students and faculty to join its group, it requires leaders to be followers of Christ. The college maintained that requirement is a violation of its non-discrimination policy.

One student who was inside the dorm room when the Bible study was shut down told me it was a confusing moment. "It was really sad," the student said. "One of the students in our group called it frightening." The student asked not to be identified due to fears of backlash from the college.

"I'm so disappointed in the decision that was made to do that," the student said. "We do love this campus. That's why we are involved in student ministry here. There's a great feeling of disappointment because we do feel like this decision is not in the spirit of open dialogue and diversity that we know Rollins upholds as a core belief."

Jao said the students took their concerns to Student Affairs. He said they compared it to kicking a fraternity off campus but still allowing it to sponsor parties. "We pointed out that Christian students holding a Bible study is a little bit different than a fraternity sponsoring a kegger in a dorm," Jao said. "If students want to have a Bible study, they should be free to do so."

But Jao said the college was sending a message to Christian students that they are not welcome. "The challenge is that InterVarsity students are feeling somewhat targeted in ways that no other religious group would be," he said. "You don't get much more quiet than four students meeting together to study the Bible."

And in the aftermath of the college's decision not to exempt religious groups from its non-discrimination policy, other Christian organizations were getting nervous. "Christian students certainly feel marginalized and unwelcome," Jao said. "Whether it's intended or not, that's the message the students have received."

Jao also said at least one other Christian group had been de-recognized, and the college's Catholic student group was also worried about the ruling. "They want to know how it will affect Catholic students," Jao said. "I think they see it's in the cards."

"This kind of policy leaves open the door for lots of further consequences as far as expulsion and demands on ministries," the anonymous student said. "The non-discrimination policy is turning into an exclusionary policy in their hands, and we're hoping the college will see the irony in what's happening."

So why not just change InterVarsity's policy and comply with the college's demands? The student who reached out to me said that just can't happen. "To change our policy would be to say anyone with any set of values can lead," the student said.

I spoke with several other students at the school, and they said they love Rollins College but are very concerned about the future of Christian student ministry. "With decisions like this, it makes the claim that whatever group is being removed off campus isn't worthy of having that voice," one student said. "They are not valued by the college."

"By and large, they are saying this group of students isn't wanted in the greater conversation on campus," another student added.

And so the underground church is alive and well in Florida.

Wounded Warrior Rejects Church's Donations

Elsewhere in Florida, a Christian church and school were devastated after the Wounded Warrior Project refused to accept their fundraising effort because, they were told, it was "religious in nature."

"We were heartbroken," said Wallace Cooley, pastor of Liberty Baptist Church and Academy in Fort Pierce, Florida.

Cooley said they had already paid a $100 registration fee to raise money for the Wounded Warrior Project and were about to launch the campaign when they received an e-mail from the organization. The church had planned on taking up a special offering on the last Sunday in February 2013, and students were collecting money from family and friends.

"We must decline the opportunity to be the beneficiary of your event due to our fundraising event criteria, which doesn't allow community events to be religious in nature," read the e-mail from the Wounded Warrior Project community events team. "Please note your registration fee will be refunded within the next 7-10 business days."

The project said that as a nonpartisan organization, it cannot accept event fundraising from companies "in which the product or message is religious in nature."

Pastor Cooley said the church and school were so shocked that the school secretary called the Wounded Warrior Project to make sure there hadn't been a mistake. He said a representative assured her that "religious" was indeed on their banned list. "We had to tell our children and parents we can't give to the Wounded Warrior Project," Pastor Cooley told me. "We are second-class citizens now because we are people of faith."

The fundraising project was a joint effort by the 400-member church and the 460 students who attend the academy. The pastor said he first learned about the project by watching Fox News Channel. "We appreciate the freedoms we enjoy in this country and the fact that our soldiers have fought for freedom of religion," he said. "We teach patriotism in our school."

The pastor said they expected to raise as much as $50,000 for the veterans. "We are not a wealthy congregation," he said. "But they are generous. We could tell as we began to talk to our people that it stirred their hearts." He said the idea of giving sacrificially to help someone else struck a chord with students in the academy.

Ted and Cherilyn Mein have two young daughters who attend the school. Cherilyn said their girls were simply devastated by the news the fundraising effort had been cancelled. "Our school is all about patriotism," she told me. "We teach that our country was founded for religious freedom—and then to find out that we couldn't even support the Wounded Warriors because we are Christians? It was hard to explain it to them."

Kindergarten teacher Tanya Sue Albritton posted a note on the Wounded Warrior Project Facebook page recounting what she had to tell her class. "They were very sad," Albritton wrote. "One little girl wanted to know, 'Why can't we share with the soldiers?'"

"I was at a loss as to what I should tell her because I don't understand it myself," she wrote. "Well, WWP, why can't we share with the soldiers?"

Cooley broke the news to his congregation in what he called "one of the saddest letters I have ever had to write."

"We are very disappointed that we, as a religious organization, are being discriminated against," he wrote to parents. "But they are a private organization and have and should have the freedom to make their own rules."

On the flip side, the pastor told parents, "We also have the right to make our choice as to where our support goes."

Becky Sharp teaches sixth grade at Liberty Baptist Academy. She posted a message on the Wounded Warrior Facebook page noting her extreme disappointment. She said her students had already raised $400 and that many of the boys and girls donated their lunch money in the fundraising effort. "I am deeply disappointed that an organization such as yours would reject money from American citizens who want to thank their soldiers for what they have done," she wrote.

Pastor Cooley said they returned donations that had been collected and were looking for another veterans group to help.

Police Chaplain Told to Stop Praying in the Name of Jesus

For more than seven years pastor Terry Sartain ministered to police officers and their families in Charlotte, North Carolina. Whenever the Charlotte-Mecklenburg Police Department invited him to deliver an invocation, he prayed "in the name of Jesus."

But not anymore. Volunteer chaplains in the Charlotte-Mecklenburg Police Department are no longer allowed to invoke the name of Jesus in prayers at public events held on government property. Major John Diggs, who oversees the chaplain program, told television station WSOC the policy is a "matter of respecting that people may have different faiths and that it is not aimed at any one religion or denomination."[25]

Sartain, the pastor of Horizon Christian Fellowship, told me he first learned of the change when he was scheduled to give an invocation at a promotion ceremony. Before the event, he received a telephone call from his superior major. "I was told chaplains can no longer invoke the name of Jesus on government property," Sartain said. "[He said] if I could refrain from that during the invocation, he would appreciate that."

Sartain said he was surprised by the telephone call. The pastor said he's prayed "consistently" in the name of Jesus at past police department events without any issues. "I'm very sad about it," he said. "I'm a pastor, and Jesus is the only thing I have to offer to bless people—His life and His person.

"It brings about a very real concern about where we are heading as a nation," he continued. "I serve a God who loves people unconditionally, who died for their sins on the cross, who wants to reconcile Himself to them and love them where they are at—and now I'm told I can't bless people as a result of that."

The police department said Sartain could still pray—just not to Jesus. So to whom was the Christian minister supposed to pray? "That was my question," Sartain said. "If I'm going to pray, what should I pray?"

Sartain said the police department wanted him to deliver a "secular prayer." But he said, "Even when I wasn't a Christian, in my past, I didn't even know what a secular prayer was. Why even pray if it's to the one who's in the room? That could be anybody." So Sartain asked the police department to withdraw his name from consideration for future public prayers.

Sartain said it's apparent that "Christians, for the most part, are targeted in these days that we exist in." He said Christians just want the same rights and privileges as everybody else. "Let the playing field remain level," he said.

Churches Banned From Public Spaces

In 2011 an evangelical Christian church was told by New York City officials it could no longer rent a community room in a federally funded housing project named after Supreme Court Justice Sonia Sotomayor.

An attorney representing the Bronx Bible Church said the congregation was notified that Christmas Day would be the last day the church could worship at the housing project. "It does present a very ugly picture of the state of religious liberties in New York City," said Jordan Lorence, senior counsel with the Alliance Defending Freedom. "It's the height of irony that the housing authority would violate the First Amendment at a place named after a Supreme Court justice."

Lorence said the New York City Housing Authority based its decision on a recent court case that said New York City has a constitutional right to bar churches from renting schools during non-school hours for worship services. The Supreme Court declined to review the case—meaning dozens of Christian churches were then forced to find other places to hold their services. "What's next—Central Park?" Lorence asked. "Religious groups can't meet there? Where is this all going to stop?"

A spokesperson for the Housing Authority declined to comment but did offer the following statement: "The terms of this lease have expired, and the New York City Housing Authority is reviewing the renewal of all of its leases."

The only trouble is, Lorence told me there was no expiration date on the lease and that when the pastor of Bronx Bible Church was contacted by the Housing Authority, there was no mention of the end-of-the-year expiration of the lease. "This is an arbitrary and unconstitutional decision," Lorence told me shortly after the church was banned. "Even if they adopt an anti-worship-service policy, they haven't done so yet. So there's no reason why they should be kicking out a church—especially during the holidays."

Lorence said the decision to evict the church sends a dangerous message to the city's Christian community. "They're suggesting that religion is something dangerous that people shouldn't be exposed to, and that is an extreme and wrong understanding of the Establishment Clause," he said, referring to the clause in the First Amendment that prevents the government from declaring a specific church or religion to be the official religion or church of the government. "Religious expression is being driven away, prohibited in public buildings that are open to all other community groups to meet."

Jailed for Hosting a Bible Study

A Phoenix man who violated city zoning laws by hosting a Bible study in the privacy of his home was sentenced to sixty days in jail. Michael Salman was found guilty in the city of Phoenix court of sixty-seven code violations. He was sentenced to sixty days in jail along with three years of probation and a $12,180 fine.[26]

Members of Salman's Bible study group posted a video of their teacher as he self-reported to the Maricopa County Sheriff's Office. It was an emotional scene. "We believe that people should not be prohibiting other people from having Bible studies in their homes," Salman said outside the jail. "We believe what they are doing is wrong. It's private property. It's our home."

Salman embraced some of his Bible study members before offering final remarks. "At the very end, after all is said and done, God will ultimately have glory in this," he said. "We do this for the glory of the Lord."

Someone off camera could be heard remarking, "I love you, pastor."

Salman's incarceration is the result of a long-running feud between the ordained pastor and the city of Phoenix over weekly Bible studies that Salman and his wife hosted in their home. City officials determined that the weekly gatherings constituted a church—and therefore violated a number of code regulations.

The controversy erupted in 2009, when nearly a dozen police officers raided the Salmans' home and a two-thousand-square-foot building in their backyard. The family had moved their Bible study into the building after the group outgrew the home's living room.

The charges that sent Salman to jail were a result of that raid, ranging from not posting exit lights above the doors to not having handicap ramps or handicap parking.

Salman told me the attacks on his family were nothing more than a crackdown on religious liberty. "They're attacking what I, as a Christian, do in the privacy of my home," he said. "At what point does the government have the right to state that you cannot have family and friends over at your home three times a week?"

But city officials said it was a matter of zoning and proper permitting, not religious freedom. They said he was given a permit to convert a garage into a game room, not a church. "Any other occupancy or use—business, commercial, assembly, church, etc.—is expressly prohibited pursuant to the city of Phoenix building code and ordinances," said Vicki Hill, the chief assistant city prosecutor.

The irony of that rule was not lost on Salman. "If I had people coming to my home on a regular basis for poker night or Monday Night Football, it would be permitted," he said. "But when someone says to us we are not allowed to gather because of religious purposes, that is when you have discrimination."

The city of Phoenix argued otherwise. They put out a fact sheet to back up their assertion that he was operating a church on his property. They released a damning memorandum detailing a mountain of evidence. They said that Salman filed for tax-exempt status annually and had as many as eighty people attending services. They also said he collected a tithe.[27]

But perhaps the most disturbing evidence was found inside the family's home. City officials allege they found chairs—and they were "aligned in a pew formation." Well, that settles it. I'm surprised they didn't tie the man to a pole and burn him at the stake.

Tony Perkins, president of the Family Research Council, said the attack against Salman should serve as a wake-up call to Christians across the nation. "Any time religious freedom or the freedom of speech is infringed upon, Americans should be concerned," Perkins said. "We are seeing jurisdictions using zoning ordinances to crack down [on] the exercise of religious freedom."

Perkins said there is a movement in recent years for churches to move back to an early church model, where Christians met in private homes rather than church facilities. As a result, he said some communities are, in fact, cracking down on what people do in the privacy of their homes.

"We're seeing more Bible studies, home-based churches, small groups meeting together," he said, "and people are not able to do with their own property that which is an exercise of their religious freedom." Perkins also took issue with the city of Phoenix deciding what constitutes a church. "The definition is nebulous," he said. "A family of more than eight people who gather for prayer could meet the definition of a church."

"It goes back to religious freedom," Perkins continued. "As long as it's not posing a threat or a nuisance to the surrounding property owners, people should be free to do with their property as they see fit."

No Jesus in the Graveyard

The family of a Colorado preacher's wife is still fuming after the director of the city-owned cemetery refused to engrave her final resting place with the name *Jesus* because it might offend people. The city eventually reversed course under public pressure.

"We were in disbelief," said Stacy Adams, the daughter-in-law of Linda Baker. "Who tries to censor Jesus from a cemetery?" Linda Baker lost her battle with cancer in October 2013. She was the wife of Mark Baker, the pastor of Harvest Baptist Church in Ovid. Adams said her mother-in-law was passionate about her Christian faith and her family. Her final wish was to have her cemetery marker engraved with the ichthus, a symbol of early Christianity. She also wanted the word *Jesus* written inside the fish.

"At first they told us it wouldn't fit," Adams told me. "But after we kept pushing them, the cemetery director told us that it might offend somebody. They weren't going to allow it."

The family was devastated and asked the cemetery director to reconsider. He refused. "He said, 'What if somebody wanted to put a swastika?'" Adams recounted. "My reply was, 'So what if they do?' It's not my business how they want to be remembered."

The family then took their concerns to the Sterling city manager—but once again, they were rebuffed. "He refused to work with us," Adams said. "He said he would have to take it to the city attorney. They were being difficult."

Adams said city officials kept telling them people would be offended by the name of Christ. "We weren't asking for a six-foot neon sign," she said. "We did not want to put a cross on everyone's tombstone. It's a six-inch fish with the name *Jesus* on it."

So the family decided to post their plight on Facebook—and that's when the city had a change of heart. "We gave them fair warning," Adams said. "We gave them time to do the right thing."

Sterling city manager Joe Kiolbasa told 9news.com they would no longer censor religious references on headstones and cemetery markers. He said the cemetery manager made a mistake. "This gentleman thought it may have been objectionable to someone because of the Christian connotation," Kiolbasa told the television station. "It will be allowed in the future."[28]

Adams tells me the family was incredibly distraught and disturbed by the incident. "As an American and as a Christian, we have this thing called freedom of speech, freedom of expression," she said. "We weren't trying to stop anybody from putting anything up. We just wanted the same freedom others have."

Besides, the cemetery is filled with tombstones that have Bible verses and angels and other religious symbols.

Adams can't help but wonder why "people are so fearful of one name that they would go to such lengths to try and eliminate it."

"If it can happen in a small country town like this, it makes you wonder what's happening in other parts of the nation," she said.

She raises a valid question. It's outrageous that a grieving American family had to fight and cajole a city government to allow them to engage in their constitutional rights. I say the city of Sterling,

Colorado, owes the family of Linda Baker a sincere apology—and it should probably be delivered from the pulpit of Pastor Baker's church.

As for the cemetery manager—comparing the name of Jesus to a swastika? Really, sir? My only wish is that on Judgment Day, Mrs. Baker is standing at the pearly gates watching you explain yourself to Saint Peter.

You Can't Have Your Cheese and Jesus Too

A Florida ministry that feeds the poor said a state agriculture department official told them they would not be allowed to receive USDA food unless they removed from their facility portraits of Christ and the Ten Commandments and a banner that reads "Jesus is Lord," and stopped giving Bibles to the needy.

For the past thirty-one years the Christian Service Center has been providing food to the hungry in Lake City, Florida, without any problems. But all that changed when it said a state government worker showed up to negotiate a new contract.

"The [person] told us there was a slight change in the contract," said executive director Kay Daly. "They said we could no longer have religious information where the USDA food is being distributed. They told us we had to take that stuff down."

Daly said it's no secret that the Christian Service Center is a Christian ministry. "We've got pictures of Christ on more than one wall," she told me. "It's very clear we are not social services. We are a Christian ministry."

But Daly and her staff sat in stunned disbelief as the government agents also informed them the Christian Service Center could no longer pray or provide Bibles to those in need. The government contract also forbade any references to the ministry's chapel.

"We asked if we had to change the name of the organization, but they said we could leave that," Daly said. "But we had to take our religious stuff down."

She said they were told they could continue distributing USDA food so long as it was somewhere else on the property—away from anything that could be considered religious. In other words, the Christian Service Center had a choice: choose God or the government cheese.

So in a spirit of Christian love and fellowship, Daly politely told the government what they could do with their cheese. "We decided to eliminate the USDA food, and we're going to trust God to provide," she told me. "If God can multiply fish and loaves for ten thousand people, He can certainly bring in food for our food pantry so we can continue to feed the hungry."

In a nutshell, Daly said the Christian Service Center would not compromise. "We are a Christian ministry," she said. "Our purpose is to help people in need and to share the gospel of Jesus Christ. We are going to pray with them. We are going to offer them a Bible. We are going to counsel them in Christian help. We are going to use our chapel."

Churches across Lake City have stepped up to the challenge, filling the void left when the government took away their cheese. "I'm called to do what the Lord tells me to do," Daly said. "I'm not called to worry about it. I pray about it. The Lord answers our prayers, and we move forward one day at a time, one person at a time."

Baptisms Banned in Public Rivers

For as far back as anyone can remember, Missouri Baptists have gathered on riverbanks for Sunday afternoon baptisms. The preacher leads the new believers into the water, draped in white robes as a choir sings "Shall We Gather at the River." It's the way it's been done for generations—baptizing in creeks, lakes, and rivers "in the name of the Father, the Son, and the Holy Spirit." But now the long-cherished tradition of taking the plunge has been drawn into a controversy with the federal government.

Many Christians believe the Bible commands new followers of Christ to be baptized immediately after their conversion. It's a public expression and celebration of their newfound faith in Christ. But the National Park Service began enforcing a policy that required churches to obtain special use permits in order to baptize in public waters.

As part of the same permit process, the National Park Service also mandated churches give forty-eight hours advance notice of pending baptisms. But as any Baptist or Pentecostal in good standing knows, that's a problem. "If the Holy Spirit is working on Sunday morning, you're going to baptize Sunday afternoon," Dennis Purcell told the *Salem News*. "You may not know ahead of time."[29]

The National Park Service told local churches the permits were needed to "maintain park natural/cultural resources and quality visitor experiences" and that "specific terms and conditions have been established."[30]

The feds also closed vehicle access to a sandbar along a popular creek in the Ozark Mountains, meaning churches could no longer drive their elderly members to the outdoor baptisms. And to make sure the Baptists behaved, they placed large boulders in the area to block car traffic.[31]

"Like the Baptists and Pentecostals are going to harm natural resources and adversely affect quality visitor experiences by occasionally baptizing new converts?" asked local resident Lewis Leonard. "I can think of a whole lot more activities along the river ways that are not conducive to maintain the natural resources."

Representative Jason Smith fired off a letter to the feds, demanding answers. "I am very troubled by any federal rule that requires churches to apply for a permit for the purpose of baptism, especially when these traditional activities have been done in the rivers and streams of this nation since its founding," the congressman wrote.

Smith pointed out the National Park Service does not require a forty-eight-hour notification from fisherman or swimmers—so why churches? "One would hope that the answer is not 'because the National Park Service wants to limit the number of baptisms performed on the river,'" he said.

The Park Service responded within twenty-four hours. They said the reason they needed two days' notice was to "give the park staff adequate time to prepare the permit."[32]

But based on local outrage—and Smith's promise to bring the matter before Congress—the Park Service had a change of heart. "As of today, the park's policy has been clarified to state that no permit will be required for baptisms within the Riverways," Superintendent William Black wrote in a letter to the congressman. "I can assure you the National Park Service has no intention of limiting the number of baptisms performed within the park."[33]

Smith called the decision a "victory for common sense. The notion that permits would be required for baptisms on our riverways is ridiculous," he said.[34]

But it's not the first time government officials have tried to discourage public baptisms. In 2011 a church in Olympia, Washington, was denied a permit to hold a baptism at Heritage Park, on the grounds of the state capitol.[35]

The Department of General Administration, the state agency that oversees the park, turned down their request stating that the proposed baptism service was a violation of the state constitution. "We approved their permit for the barbecue, but our state constitution does not allow public grounds or funds to be used for religious ceremonies, so we got advice from our attorney general's office and we denied their permit for the baptism," GA spokesman Steve Valandra told me.

The American Center for Law and Justice filed an appeal with the state on the church's behalf, but it was denied. ACLJ attorney Jordan Sekulow said the state of Washington was treating Christians like second-class citizens.

Acting General Administration director Jane Rushford said the government was not preventing the church from exercising its religious liberty. "It's an outrage. GA [General Administration] is not precluding members of the Reality Church from exercising their First Amendment rights to express their religious beliefs or conducting a baptism ceremony at the church," Rushford wrote. "However, the use of public property for the performance of religious worship, exercise or instruction is prohibited under the Washington State Constitution."

Article One of the Washington State Constitution provides that "No public money shall be appropriated or applied to any religious worship, exercise or instruction, or the support of any religious establishment."

Sekulow claims the US Constitution prohibits the government from suppressing or excluding speech of private parties. But the state refused to back down. "So now you've got a state saying this is too much religious activity so it's not really speech anymore," Sekulow said. "This violates the US Constitution."

Rushford, however, wrote that a "baptism ceremony is a form of religious exercise and worship. And as such it would violate Article 1, Section 11 to authorize the use of state property for this purpose."

The church held their baptism service at a local YMCA instead. Sekulow said the state's decision makes it "uncomfortable for Christians to use the facility in the future."

"If they open up this property for people to use," he said, "they can't ban religious groups from being able to access it and perform something like a baptism." He said if the church were to sue the state it could set a national precedent. "Who is the state to decide what is worship and what isn't?" he asked.

But while the government cracks down on public expressions of the Christian faith, they are embracing public expressions of the Islamic faith—many times at taxpayer expense. Universities across the nation are spending thousands of dollars to install foot baths so Muslim students can wash their feet before their five-times-a-day prayers. The *New York Times* reported that the University of Michigan-Dearborn spent $25,000 to install the foot-washing stations in restrooms. The university defended the expenditure, claiming it was for health and safety measures, not religion.[36]

In 2007 officials at Minneapolis Community and Technical College banned a campus coffee cart from playing Christmas carols. But they used taxpayer dollars to construct daily prayer preparation facilities for Muslim students.[37]

Airports have made accommodations for Muslim taxi drivers by installing foot washing basins. Sky Harbor Airport in Phoenix built a cleanup station to help Islamic drivers meet their religious needs.[38]

And San Francisco International Airport renovated a building to create a house of worship for Muslim workers.[39] Airport officials declined to reveal how much tax money was spent, but a spokesman told the *San Francisco Chronicle* they just wanted to maintain "a good relationship with ground transportation providers."[40]

So there you have it, good readers. Our government increasingly affords accommodation to the Muslim faith while attempting to regulate the Christian faith.

It reminds me of something John Adams once wrote: "Nothing is more dreaded than the national government meddling with religion."[41]

City Mows Down Cross-Shaped Flower Bed

A flower bed shaped like a cross was removed from a park in Columbus, Georgia, after non-Christians raised concerns and the city's mayor determined the cross violated the law.

"We had some complaints from other citizens not of the Christian faith," Columbus mayor Teresa Tomlinson told me.

The Windsor Park Homeowners Association was responsible for upkeep of the flower bed and at the request of city officials they removed the two arms. Now the cross is shaped like a rectangle—and conforms to federal law.

The flower bed had been a part of the Heath Lake Park for decades. Large stones had been positioned to form the outline of the cross. But Mayor Tomlinson said the symbol ran afoul of a 1983 federal court ruling that she said banned Christian crosses from public land.

She cited a court case involving a fifty-foot lighted cross in Rabun County, Georgia. That particular cross had been a part of the community for forty years, she said—until someone complained. "A Christian cross or a symbol of any particular faith could not permanently rest in a park," she said. "So we had to abide by the applicable law."

According to local media accounts, a number of citizens are upset over the removal. "The satisfactory resolution is that the cross is there," resident George Wade told television station WTVM.[42] He was one of many people to attend a recent city council meeting to demand the cross be restored.

"The councilmen are beginning to understand the urgency that needs to be addressed because the people are concerned about this," he told the television station.[43]

But that's not going to happen.

Columbus is home to Fort Benning, and the area is home to a number of military retirees, the mayor said. "We have a lot of military retirees of the Jewish faith and other faiths wearing the uniform," the mayor said. "We've had a lot of those individuals come forward talking about the fact that a lot of blood has been shed to make certain that our public institutions are open to people of all faiths, of all races, of all genders."

Tomlinson did not dispute the notion that many of her constituents might disagree with the decision to remove the cross. "Whenever we have a tradition that begins to fade, that's always something that becomes very emotional for people," she said.

She did say, though, that the city would allow Christians to hold Easter sunrise services at the park and that the neighborhood association would be allowed to plant seasonal flowers in the bed, like Easter lilies.

Maybe the city could plant pansies instead.

Diner Investigated for Giving Church Discount

A family-owned restaurant in Pennsylvania is under a state discrimination investigation for offering a 10 percent discount for diners who present a church bulletin on Sundays.

The Pennsylvania Human Relations Commission confirmed there was an investigation against Prudhomme's Lost Cajun Kitchen in the town of Columbia. The complaint was filed by John Wolff, a retired electrical engineer.

"I did this not out of spite, but out of a feeling against the prevailing self-righteousness that stems from religion, particularly in Lancaster

County," Wolff told the *York Daily Record*. "I don't consider it an earth-shaking affair, but in this area in particular, we seem to have so many self-righteous religious people, so it just annoys me."[44]

According to the Pennsylvania Human Relations Act, a restaurant is classified as a public accommodation. As such, owners are not allowed to discriminate based on religion, among other things.

Sharon Prudhomme, who owns the restaurant along with her husband, said she's not discriminating against anybody and plans on fighting the charges. "What freaks me out is the state of Pennsylvania is basically agreeing with this guy," Prudhomme told me. "We're just a mom and pop. We're not some big chain like the Olive Garden."

Prudhomme said the trouble started in April 2011, when she received the first of several letters from the Freedom From Religion Foundation (FFRF). The FFRF is a Wisconsin-based organization of "more than 17,000 freethinkers, atheists, agnostics and skeptics," according to its website.[45]

The FFRF demanded the owners stop giving discounts to patrons who brought in a Sunday church bulletin. "I just filed it and blew off the other letters," Prudhomme said. "I said I have no intention of taking [the offer] off the website."

Then the restaurant was served with a sixteen-page complaint from the state of Pennsylvania accusing her of discrimination. "I'm an American," Prudhomme said. "This is America. This is my business, and we're not breaking any laws."

Prudhomme said a representative from the state suggested she compromise and sign an agreement that she would offer discounts to any civic organization in the town. "I said, 'Wait a minute—you're asking my husband and I to give anybody coming through my door a discount?'" she recounted. "They said yes."

"I said, 'Are you crazy?'" she continued. "We have taxes to pay. We have utility bills, payroll, mortgages, and they're expecting me to give everyone a discount?"

Prudhomme said that's just not going to happen. "This is our business," she said. "We're the ones paying the taxes. We need the people coming in. Our life is in this—and then to have someone come along and tell me what I can do and what I can't do?"

She then wondered if the restaurant's other discounts might be considered discriminatory too—like the one on Tuesday night, where kids under age twelve get to eat free. Or what about the senior discount? "Could someone under sixty-five complain?" she asked.

Wolff told the LancasterOnline that he discovered the church discount on the privately owned restaurant's website. "That rubbed me a bit the wrong way," he told the online publication. "It's not a big deal in itself, and I have no animosity towards Prudhomme's, but I do bear a grudge against the religious right that seems to intrude on our civil rights."[46]

The commission ultimately determined the Prudhommes could continue their promotion, but the discount must be given to bulletin holders "from any group oriented around the subject of religious faith," even atheists, whom the federal courts consider to have a religious creed.[47]

These are just some of the more egregious skirmishes in the war on Christianity. The battles are no longer limited to urban centers such as New York City and Los Angeles. The atheists and secularists and liberals have already conquered the big cities. Now, they're going after Bible Belt towns and cities. They have taken their fight to the suburbs and small towns.

I suspect at this point in our journey that you might be slightly overwhelmed. It's understandable. These stories are not covered in the daily newspapers. You won't see them on the evening newscasts. This is a war that the mainstream media has decided is not worth covering. That's because this is an unconventional war. And the Bible tells us the enemy cannot be defeated with modern day weapons: "For our struggle is not against flesh and blood, but against the rulers, against the authorities, against the powers of this dark world and against the spiritual forces of evil in the heavenly realms."[48]

Just before the start of World War II the British government produced a motivational poster intended to raise the morale of the public.

"Keep Calm and Carry On," the posters declared.[49] We had a similar saying growing up in the Deep South. It brought a smile to our faces during those rough patches of life. And perhaps it might offer you a bit of encouragement before we move on to the next chapter: Keep Calm and Butter a Biscuit.

Chapter 2

FROM THE ANNALS OF GOD-BLESSED LIVING: BAPTISTS, BAGELS, AND BROOKLYN

I AM A TRUE son of the South. I like my tea sweet, my chicken fried, and my biscuits buttered. Where I come from, the only good pork butt is a smoked pork butt. Folks say *y'all*, pickup trucks have gun racks, and there are churches on every street corner.

So you can imagine my surprise when I moved to New York City, where the tea is unsweetened, the chicken is baked, the biscuits are bagels, and if you want something smoked, you've gotta go see the guy down on the corner. Folks say *youse guys*, only the criminals are allowed to have guns, and there are Starbucks outposts on every street corner.

It is, indeed, a tale of two cities. I live among the indigenous liberal population of Brooklyn. It's a different world. The supermarkets are stocked with unusual foods such as kale chips, hummus, and an assortment of tofu. There are yoga classes, vegan restaurants, and even places that offer liver cleansings.

There are also hipsters wearing their skinny jeans and suspenders and sporting handlebar mustaches. Folks in these parts wear plaid shirts and take pride in eating meals at farm-to-table restaurants that only serve eggs delivered by an Amish midwife. It really is that kind of neighborhood.

For better or worse, I sort of ooze Republican. I tried to fit in, but it just didn't work out. It took a tub of butter and a shoe horn to get me into a pair of those skinny jeans. It just wasn't a good look for me. I did purchase a cool leather knapsack, but the family back home in Mississippi said it's really a man bag. Aunt Lynn put me on the church prayer list.

I stand out like a ham sandwich at a tofu convention. My mailman figured out I was an out-of-towner early on. It seems I'm the only person in Brooklyn who is a member of the National Rifle Association and has a subscription to *Garden & Gun* magazine.

We also have lots of advocacy groups roaming the streets of my neighborhood in search of donations—PETA, GLAAD, the ACLU, just to name a few. One day I had just walked out of the butcher's store and was confronted by an angry PETA protester.

"Sir, do you love animals?" she demanded to know.

"Only if they're deep fried," I replied.

I've noticed that ever since I started wearing my NRA ball cap, no one asks me for donations anymore. It's like the parting of the liberals as I walk down the sidewalk. I sent the NRA a thank-you note.

The biggest adjustment has been the lack of Southern provisions. There are no biscuits, for example. I was on Amtrak's Acela Express heading toward Washington DC, and the steward offered me a biscuit for breakfast. I gladly accepted his offer and began to dream of a hot, fluffy buttermilk biscuit loaded with elderberry jelly. But what he served me was a "British biscuit." It was a glorified teething cookie in wrapping paper. No wonder Amtrak is losing money.

New York City is also home to a number of "new Southern cuisine" restaurants. I've discovered these establishments are basically run by chefs who couldn't get real Southerners to eat their food. I ate at one of those restaurants once, and those folks are doing stuff to catfish and butter beans that the good Lord never intended.

And then there's the lack of sweet tea. Here in the northern states they drink something called unsweetened tea. I must confess, I do not understand their ways. Back home we were raised at an early age to believe that sweet tea is the house wine of the South. If you order unsweetened tea in Mississippi, people might think you're a liberal.

I remember a Wednesday night prayer meeting years ago in our country Baptist church. After about two dozen unspoken requests, our Sunday school superintendent's wife raised her trembling hand. She fought back tears as she asked for special prayer for her niece.

"She's done gone off to Atlanta and got herself involved in an alternative lifestyle," Miss Roberta sobbed. "She's living in sin. We caught her drinking unsweetened tea."

My buddy Kenton from Southern California had never partaken of the sweet tea, so one day we flew down to Memphis, and I made a beeline to Corky's, one of the city's fine barbecue establishments.

I tried to tell Kenton that first-time tea drinkers should start slowly. Too much sugar can throw a grown man down on the ground. But Kenton was not to be denied his sweet tea. He ordered a large glass and took a mighty impressive swig. Within seconds his cheeks clinched and his lips puckered. His body started to tremble.

The waitress was quite alarmed. "Darlin', is this his first time?"

I nodded and replied, "Yes ma'am. He's from California. They don't drink sweet tea out there."

She gave Kenton's shoulders a tight squeeze and patted him on the back. "It's all right, sugar," she said. "Just relax and let the tea do its work."

Then she whispered to the bus boy, "Go back to the pantry and get me a crowbar. We might need to pry him loose manually. I'm afraid he's just bad to drink."

I'm glad to say that Kenton regained his composure a few minutes later, and I'll be doggoned if he didn't start talking with a Southern drawl.

They don't do too many dinners-on-the-grounds up in these parts, either. Why, back in Mississippi, a Baptist church without a dinner-on-the-grounds is like a Catholic without a pope. It's just not kosher.

Back in my growing-up years, dinners-on-the-grounds were the social event of the summer—especially the ones that coincided with the Fifth Sunday Sing. Churches would plan all-day singings on the last Sunday of months that had five Sundays. There'd be an endless supply of fried chicken, potato salad, deviled eggs, sweet potato pies, pecan pies, biscuits, cornbread, ham, congealed salad, and a bag of pork rinds brought by the single guy who couldn't cook.

Church ladies considered those meals to be sacred events—and they were also competitive. You'd best believe every single one of those saintly women was judging and critiquing the other ladies' dishes as if it was a reality television show cooking competition. "Did you see Loretta's congealed salad? Lord have mercy, it was jiggling all over the place!" "Now, I know she's not coming up in here with a bucket of store-bought chicken—Lord Jesus!"

For the record, bringing store-bought chicken to a Baptist church supper is grounds for excommunication. It's in the "Baptist Faith and Message."

My favorite part of the Fifth Sunday Sings, though, was the music. I remember grabbing a big bowl of homemade banana pudding and running to the front of the makeshift stage so I could get a good look at our visiting quartets and trios. (By the way, does anyone know why Southern gospel quartets have five people instead of four?)

Anyway, there'd be guitars and banjos, a piano, and a fiddle, and then the lady who always started speaking in tongues during the preaching would haul out a tambourine. We'd sing all sorts of rowdy songs, such as "When the Roll Is Called Up Yonder," "Victory in Jesus," "I'll Fly Away," and "In the Sweet By and By." And you just knew the quartet was solid if your banana pudding shimmied in your bowl when the bass singer hit the rock-bottom notes on "Just a Little Talk With Jesus."

As the sun would set in the Mississippi sky, it was all but guaranteed that somebody would break out and start wailing on "Sweet Beulah Land." The elderly church ladies would rock back and forth in their lawn chairs, and a few of the deacons would whip out their hankies, because that's what you do when somebody sings "Sweet Beulah Land." But let's be honest—nobody can sing "Sweet Beulah Land" like Squire Parsons.

Soon the music would fade and the preacher would walk onto the stage. He would thank the singers and thank the ladies who made the chicken and the potato salad and the butter beans. And then he'd get down to business. As the fireflies danced and the crickets chirped, the preacher would tell the folks about Jesus and how He was in the business of changing lives—of saving souls. He'd preach himself into a sweat, urging people to walk the grassy aisle and turn their wretched lives over to Christ.

Those were precious moments, precious memories of a time long passed—a place long gone. But the faith I saw lived out in the lives of those church people compelled me to get what they had. And on one of those hot summer Southern days, I asked Jesus to take the crimson stain and wash it white as snow. As I grew older, I came to understand the faith that compelled ministers to plant roots in small towns and tend small flocks.

It's the same faith that compels Christian college students to spend their spring break rebuilding homes destroyed by Hurricane Sandy. It's the faith that compels teenagers to teach vacation Bible school. It's the faith that compels senior adults to volunteer at pro-life pregnancy centers. It's the faith that compels men to do home repairs for a single mom. It's the faith that compels women to clothe the needy.

And it was the faith that compelled a church choir from southeastern Tennessee to travel to New York City to share God's love with strangers. The choir in question was from First Baptist Church of Cleveland, Tennessee—a group of nearly one hundred singers made up of hair stylists and school teachers, stay-at-home moms, and a retired police chief. They flew to the Big Apple to work in soup kitchens and food pantries and fulfill God's commandment: let everything that has breath praise the Lord.

Now, if you know anything about New Yorkers, they are a brisk and brusque people. When you have 12 million folks living bumper to bumper, there's really not much time to stop and say, "Hey, y'all." Out-of-towners interpret that as rudeness. But it's really not. Folks are just trying to get where they're going.

So when I found out the choir would be performing in one of our city's parks, I told the director not to be terribly surprised if they didn't draw a crowd. Not too many Baptists in these parts, I said. And besides, we're in the middle of a heat wave.

But the choir was determined. They gathered in shorts and T-shirts in Foley Square, just in front of the United States Courthouse—a familiar scene to those who watch the television show *Law & Order*. Soon the square was filled with a soundtrack of keyboards and guitars and a horn section and drums.

There were no theatrical lights, no smoke machines, no sparkly outfits. Just a church choir from Tennessee standing on concrete steps in the middle of a park, belting out gospel songs. As predicted, the afternoon crowd was not terribly interested in listening to these out-of-towners—but then something happened, and it was something quite remarkable.

The choir began singing a new song, "Awesome." As their voices echoed through the concrete canyons of Lower Manhattan, people began to stop. There was a lady from Jamaica and a couple from Flatbush in Brooklyn. There were some teenagers from Harlem and a family from Chinatown.

I was there and marveled at the sight. Their praise song to God rose above the rumbling subway trains and police cars. I counted some two hundred people in all—Northerners and Southerners, lovers of biscuits and bagels, united as one. Maybe, just maybe, we aren't all that different after all.

And so it was on the corner of Pearl Street and Centre Street that there were blacks and whites and Latinos and Asians with hands raised, arms outstretched, worshipping God together in the shadow of where two towers once stood.

Those are my people. Good people. Sinners saved by grace. Washed in the blood of the Lamb.

I recall a certain president once described the Muslim call to prayer as "one of the prettiest sounds on earth at sunset."[1] But for me, one of the prettiest sounds on earth was a Baptist church choir from the foothills of Tennessee singing about Jesus in four-part harmony in the heart of New York City.

Chapter 3

CHICK-FIL-A:
THE GOSPEL BIRD

HERE'S SOMETHING UNSETTLING about the public flogging of Chick-fil-A by government officials hell-bent on destroying a privately owned American company simply because of the owner's personal opinions.

Democratic lawmakers in more than a half-dozen major cities have led the charge, slandering Chick-fil-A's owner and calling for all-out bans on the company's expansion efforts in places such as Chicago, Philadelphia, Boston, and San Francisco.[1]

And Chick-fil-A's only crime is being a family-owned company that ascribes to the teachings of the holy Bible—a belief that marriage is a union between one man and one woman.

Chick-fil-A's president has been called a bigot and a homophobe. The mayor of Washington DC accused the company of peddling "hate chicken."[2]

Philadelphia city councilman Jim Kenney penned a harshly worded letter to Dan Cathy, telling him that he was not welcome in the City of Brotherly Love. "Take a hike and take your intolerance with you," he wrote. "There is no place for this type of hate in our great City of Brotherly Love and Sisterly Affection."[3]

There have been efforts to shut down Chick-fil-A restaurants across the country. Student groups launched similar campaigns on university campuses.[4]

Lost in their outrage over a belief held by a majority of the

American public is the fact that Chick-fil-A employs thousands and thousands of people. And with unemployment hovering around 8 percent when the furor broke out, you have to wonder what sort of message Democrats were trying to send to the nation.

Chicago mayor Rahm Emanuel actually denounced the family-owned company. "Chick-fil-A values are not Chicago values," he declared in a statement. "They disrespect our fellow neighbors and residents."[5]

I'd be willing to bet the hundreds of people gunned down in the streets of Mayor Emanuel's city might disagree. But I digress.

The mayor went so far as to support Alderman Joe Moreno's plan to block construction of the city's second Chick-fil-A restaurant.[6] To be clear, publicly elected officials went on record trying to block an American business from doing business on American soil.

"Because of this man's ignorance, I will now be denying Chick-fil-A's permit to open a restaurant," Moreno told the *Chicago Tribune*.[7]

And because of Alderman Moreno's ignorance, several dozen people will remain in the unemployment line. Perhaps the party of President Barack Obama believes it's morally better to be unemployed than to be anti-gay marriage?

Not that it matters, but it turns out any attempt by an elected official to block a business from opening based on ideology is illegal. That's why I checked with Mat Staver, the president of Liberty Counsel. He can quote the US Constitution in his sleep.

"No city can ban Chick-fil-A because the president has his own view regarding marriage—a view that is held by much of the American public," Staver said. "To discriminate against Mr. Cathy because of his biblical view and then to extrapolate that to Chick-fil-A is illegal."

And the vitriol from Mayor Emanuel was beyond the pale, Staver added, accusing the mayor of trying to "bully them into silence."

"This is a very intolerant response by Rahm Emanuel and some of the others who are pushing back," Staver said. "It is absolutely incredible that we are at a point in history where an individual who is an owner of a company can express his views on marriage and get so much pushback."

American Christians are facing uncertain times. Our nation's values are under assault. Religious liberty has been undermined. We live in a day when right is now wrong and wrong is now right.

The vicious left-wing assault against Chick-fil-A should serve as a wake-up call to people of faith. It's not about a chicken sandwich. It's about religious liberty. It's about free speech. It's about the future of our nation.

"Individuals have the right to decide whether or not to 'Eat Mor Chikin,'" said Leith Anderson, president of the National Association of Evangelicals. "But no government leader should restrict a business or organization from expanding to their district based on the personal or political views of the owners. Such evident discrimination and attempts to marginalize those with religious values have no place in American democracy."[8]

And the discrimination and hate was vicious. Chick-fil-A restaurants were vandalized, and customers were harassed.[9] In Chicago a group of militant activists surrounded an elderly man reading his Bible outside a Chick-fil-A and screamed in his face.[10] In West Virginia a restaurant was evacuated after a bomb threat.[11] Even customers were subjected to threats and investigations. In Dallas a veteran police sergeant was investigated after two lesbian officers complained that he brought a Chick-fil-A sandwich to work.[12] The incident occurred on "National Chick-fil-A Appreciation Day," an event organized by former Arkansas governor Mike Huckabee. Hundreds of thousands of American families turned out to buy sandwiches and show their support for the besieged company. Sergeant Mark Johnson was reassigned to the overnight shift in the jail after the lesbians whined about how offended they were at the sight of a Chick-fil-A bag.

And did you notice the network news gave more coverage to the counter-protest than the national appreciation day event? In the eyes of the mainstream media, a few dozen gay activists playing tonsil hockey inside a Chick-fil-A is more newsworthy.

Go figure.

Perhaps the saddest encounter came from a protester who posted a video of himself berating a young cashier. "I don't know how you live with yourself and work here," he sneered. "I don't understand it. This is a horrible corporation with horrible values."[13]

He demanded a cup of "free water" and boasted about how he felt "purposeful" insulting the young lady. "Anti-gay breakfast sandwich always tastes better when it's full of hate," he said.[14]

A lesser person might have flogged that man with a waffle fry. But the Chick-fil-A cashier simply smiled, handed the bully a cup of water, and replied, "It's my pleasure to serve you."[15]

The lesson here is that those who preach tolerance are the least tolerant of all. And I suspect Councilman Kenney spoke for many when he issued a not-so-subtle threat to individuals like Mr. Cathy who support traditional marriage. "If he really, truly believes what he believes, that is his right to do so," he told Fox News. "But there is often a price to pay for that."

In other words, Councilman Kenney wants people with dissenting views to shut up or else face the consequences. What is he advocating—a public flogging?

Pastors across the fruited plain addressed the attacks on Chick-fil-A from their pulpits, but none was more eloquent or passionate than Charles Lyons, the pastor of Armitage Baptist Church in Chicago. Lyons issued an appeal to Mayor Rahm Emanuel, urging him to reconsider the verbal assault he made on people of faith.

"Mr. Mayor, please do not dismiss us," Lyons implored. "Do not disrespect us....We, too, are Logan Square. We, too, are Chicago."[16]

The pastor admonished Mayor Emanuel without so much as a shout or a hint of anger. His remarks were peppered with applause and the occasional *amen*.

Then, midway through his appeal, Pastor Lyons paused and delivered a not-so-subtle warning to city leaders. "If the thought police come to Armitage Baptist Church, we will meet them at the door respectfully, unflinchingly, willing to die on this hill, holding a copy of the Sacred Scriptures in one hand and a copy of the U.S. Constitution in the other," he said.[17]

Pay attention, people of faith. And for the record, I still don't understand why homosexuals have a problem with plump, juicy chicken breasts.

Chapter 4

NO CHRISTIAN LEFT BEHIND

MERICAN PASTOR SAEED Abedini is a prisoner of Iran. He's serving an eight-year sentence in one of the Muslim country's most notorious prisons—all because of his faith in Jesus Christ.

Abedini is a former Muslim who converted to Christianity in 2000. In the early 2000s he helped establish about one hundred house churches in thirty Iranian cities during a time when the Iranian government tolerated such activity. In 2008 he became an American citizen and had been living the past several years in Idaho with his wife, Naghmeh, and their two children.[1]

In 2009 Pastor Saeed made an agreement with the Iranian government to stop serving as the leader of a network of house churches. But he made clear to the regime that he could not stop professing his faith in Christ.

He had also received permission to build an orphanage and nine times had traveled between Iran and the United States without incident. It was on that ninth trip, however, when he was arrested and detained without public notice of the charges.

On January 27, 2013, Pastor Saeed was convicted of endangering national security through his leadership in the house churches and sentenced by the Iranian Revolutionary Court's "hanging judge" to eight years in prison.

The American Center for Law and Justice said he was actually arrested because of his Christian faith as well as his efforts to help

Iranian Christians in underground churches. He had been building an orphanage at the time of his arrest.

There was some hope that Pastor Saeed would be released when the Obama administration opened talks with the Iranians in the latter months of 2013. Instead, the White House made a deal with his captors: they got to keep enriching uranium, and Pastor Saeed was beaten. They received billions of dollars in sanctions relief, and Pastor Saeed was abused. They received "humanitarian transactions" from the United States, and Pastor Saeed was tortured.[2]

The Obama administration made a deal with the Iranian Islamists, but the American Christian was forsaken. Saeed Abedini is the Christian that President Obama left behind.

"It is unconscionable that senior American diplomats, including the secretary of state…could not bring themselves to even mention [Pastor Saeed's] name, or those of fellow Americans detained in Iran," senator Ted Cruz, the Republican lawmaker from Texas, said in a statement.[3]

"We pledged humanitarian aid for the Iranians," Jay Sekulow, of the American Center for Law and Justice, eloquently wrote in a Fox News essay. "Where is Iran's humanitarian gesture for America?"

It's been more than a year since Pastor Saeed has seen his immediate family—his wife and their two children. Birthdays without a father. Anniversaries spent alone. No one to play Santa Claus at Christmastime.

In December 2013 Naghmeh Abedini testified before Congress on behalf of her husband. She pleaded for the State Department not to leave her husband behind. Her testimony was gut-wrenching:

> I had anticipated that I would battle the Iranian government for my husband's freedom. I never anticipated that I would also have to battle my own government and that the journey would become even much more difficult than it had been. My husband is suffering because he's a Christian. He's suffering because he's an American. Yet his own government did not fight for him when his captors were across the table from them.[4]

"The president has done nothing," said Sekulow, expressing outrage that the administration had not made the Abedini case a national concern. "This is an American citizen," he said. "This is not just someone's human rights being violated. It's an American whose human rights are being violated."

When I spoke with Naghmeh in March 2013, she confirmed to me personally that she has never heard from the commander in chief. "I have not received a telephone call from President Obama," she said. "I have not received a telephone call from Secretary of State John Kerry—unfortunately."

It took the president more than eighteen months to finally call for Pastor Saeed's release publicly, which he did at the 2014 National Prayer Breakfast.[5]

The plight of Pastor Saeed and the president's handling of the matter has enraged Representative Frank Wolf, a Republican congressman from Virginia. "This White House is a disaster on this issue," Wolf said. "There is an innate bias against Christians and the faith community in the State Department."

Sekulow speculated that the reason the administration has not been more vocal is because Abedini is a former Muslim. "It's because he's a Christian, and it's because he left Islam," Sekulow said. "I think it's the fact that he left Islam and became a Christian that the administration has this policy of 'Well, what did you expect from a religion that tells you, "We will threaten your life if you leave the religion"?'"

Wolf said that may be the reality. "This administration is one of the weakest administrations to advocate for people [of faith]," he said. "Whatever his denomination, we should advocate."

The lackluster support for Abedini stands in stark contrast to how the administration handled two other high-profile incidents. In 2009 President Obama dispatched former President Clinton to North Korea, where he succeeded in winning the release of two American journalists.[6] In 2011 the White House released more than a dozen mentions of three American hikers arrested and put on trial in Iran. President Obama issued a lengthy statement condemning their capture and demanding their release. It was a passionate plea. The White House also published links to websites supporting the hikers.[7]

Additionally, CNN reported that Obama spoke with the wife of Robert Levinson, a former FBI agent who went missing in Iran seven years ago.[8]

By comparison—according to a search of the White House online archives—there have only been ten mentions of Abedini, and one of those included press secretary Jay Carney saying he had no information about the incident.

Not once has President Obama called Mrs. Abedini. Not once has he written her a letter. Not once has Secretary of State John Kerry called or written the pastor's wife. Not once. There have been no White House links to websites supporting Pastor Abedini. "Our president and our secretary of state need to speak out for Saeed," Sekulow said.

Unlike America's president, America's pastor has been outspoken about Pastor Saeed's imprisonment. Billy Graham, evangelical Christianity's elder statesman, penned a letter to the president of the Islamic Republic of Iran. Here are the contents of that dispatch:

> Dear President Rouhani,
>
> I have been watching with great concern about the case of Pastor Saeed Abedini, an American citizen who is currently a prisoner in your country. He was in Iran working to build an orphanage when he was arrested and later sentenced to eight years in prison. His situation has been receiving an increasingly high level of attention in the United States. Unfortunately this publicity has been entirely negative for Iran, with the belief that the primary reason for Pastor Abedini's imprisonment was because of his Christian faith.
>
> As you may know, as a religious leader I have often spoken (both publicly and also privately with our national leadership) about the need for greater understanding and peace among the nations of the world. As you come to the United States this week for the U.N. General Assembly in New York, it is my sincere hope that ways may be found to reduce the current

tensions between the United States and the Islamic Republic of Iran.

The announcement on Monday that your country has freed 80 political prisoners is very encouraging. I fear, however, that the current publicity surrounding the continued imprisonment of Pastor Abedini, an American citizen, may further harm the already fragile relationship that presently exists between our two nations.

On September 26, the one-year anniversary of Pastor Abedini's imprisonment, thousands will attend prayer vigils in more than 70 U.S. cities, calling on your country to release this husband, father and servant of God. I join them by respectfully asking you to release Pastor Saeed Abedini from prison. Such an action would, I believe, have a positive impact in our nation, and might well be perceived by our leadership as a significant step in reducing tensions.[9]

The days are getting longer for Naghmeh. She told me her husband has been suffering in the Iranian prison. "He's been beaten, tortured—suffering internal bleeding and suffering from medical issues," she said. "He's been there long enough."

She appealed to President Obama as one parent to another, but at the time of this writing the administration had not responded. "I would expect him to step in and demand his release," she said. "I would expect our government to take every action to want him released now. Every day in there is horrific, and he's only there because of his religious belief."

Naghmeh said it's been difficult raising their children as a single mother. "The kids don't understand," she said. "My daughter has cried out, 'Daddy, where are you? Daddy, why aren't you coming home? Daddy, I miss you.' And she'll start talking to him at night and just crying, and I hold her as she has tears coming down her face. She's only six years old.

"It's just hard seeing them in so much pain but you can't do anything about it," she said.

The Iranians told Abedini that if he renounced his faith in Jesus

Christ, he might be released. But in a letter he wrote to his wife, the American pastor said that won't happen. "Saeed is pretty stubborn," Naghmeh said. "He won't give in. I smiled to myself and said, 'They don't know who they are dealing with.' He's a pretty stubborn person when it comes to his faith."

Chapter 5

SO ABSURD IT COULD BE TRUE: THE GOSPEL ACCORDING TO BARACK OBAMA

OST AMERICANS HAVE no idea if President Obama goes to church. A Gallup poll confirms that 44 percent have no idea if he's a Methodist, Lutheran, or Hindu.[1] It's a problem that has perplexed the White House from the early days of the administration. How in the world can his handlers convince the folks in Middle America that President Obama is a regular churchgoing, pot-luck-dinner-eating guy?

My curiosity got the better of me, so I called my friend Miles O'Leary. He's a Washington bureaucrat from years gone by who was recently promoted to a new position within the president's Office of Faith-Based Initiatives. If anyone knew how the White House was handling President Obama's "Jesus problem," Miles would be the guy.

Our original plan was to meet at the National Cathedral, but an earthquake seriously damaged the building. Instead we met at a coffeehouse a few blocks away on Wisconsin Avenue. As we sipped on our pumpkin spice lattes, I decided to get right to the point.

"Miles, it seems to me that the problem is two-pronged," I said. "First, you've got millions of Americans who don't have a clue what religion the president is, and second, you've got millions of his followers who claim that he's some sort of deity."

There was the time in Daytona Beach, Florida, when thousands of the president's followers chanted, "Hail, Obama. Hail, Obama."

Public school teachers across the fruited plain instructed boys and girls to raise their hands to the sky and proclaim, "Barack Hussein Obama, *mmm-mmm-mmm.*"[2] And who can forget when actor Jamie Foxx called him "our Lord and Savior Barack Obama"?[3]

Florida A&M professor Barbara Thompson published a book titled *The Gospel According to Apostle Barack*. It likens Obama to Jesus Christ. "Apostle Barack, the name he was called in my dreams, would walk the earth to create a more equalized society for the middle class and working poor," she wrote in an excerpt published by the *Daily Caller*.[4]

And, of course, Oprah Winfrey prophesied that the man who was born in Hawaii and grew up in a Kenyan hut was indeed "the One."[5]

Miles paused for a moment, poured more cream into his coffee cup, stirred twice, and smiled as he continued stirring. "You look at it as a problem, but the White House looks at it as an opportunity," he said. "We realized that we had a chance to truly make history—to change the world. Do you remember what happened at the Democratic National Convention, when the Democrats booed God?"

Who could forget? Delegates to the 2012 DNC meeting in Charlotte had voted God out of the party platform.[6] "There's only room for one god in the Democratic National Convention," Miles said.

The Almighty was subsequently reinstated into the party, which resulted in a round of contentious jeers from the crowd full of atheists and God-haters. I was there. It was one of the most incredulous moments in American politics—a major political party giving God a Bronx cheer.

"We took an immediate flash poll of God's approval rating among Democrats, and we got a shocking wake-up call," Miles told me. "He was only polling at 10 percent—and that was mostly among Southern Blue Dog Democrats. So we decided to immediately implement a top-secret program—code name G-O-D."

GOD?

"It stands for Get Obama Deified," Miles said in a hushed voice. "We decided to create a national religion based solely on President

Obama. Our internal polling data on the deification of the president is spectacular."

I was dumbfounded. How in the world could they do something like that—something so brazen, so blasphemous, so unconstitutional?

"Todd, we've already done it," Miles said. "I was just put in charge of President Obama's new Office of Theological Repatriation. We're in the process of destabilizing other religions so that we can recruit more followers. Why do you think we've been marginalizing Christianity within the armed forces and public schools?"

"But why make the president a god?"

"Let's face it, Todd," Miles explained. "He's a young man. He's going to need to do something to earn a paycheck after he leaves the White House."

"So when did you guys decide to go forward with this hair-brained scheme?" I asked.

"Ironically it was just a few hours before that earthquake hit Washington," he said. "About two minutes after President Obama signed the executive order declaring himself to be America's Lord and Savior, the earth started shaking."

"How does one even go about creating a new religion?" I wondered.

"Well, as I said, I head up the Office of Theological Repatriation," Miles said. "Once the Christians and Jews renounce their faiths, they are assigned to a six-month session of theological conversion therapy. After they complete the appropriate coursework, the new followers are then turned over to the Office of Spiritual Indoctrination."

"What about the Muslims?" I asked.

"Um, yeah, we're not going to touch the Muslims," Miles said.

I found it unbelievable to imagine Baptists and Presbyterians and Pentecostals willing to abandon their faith for President Obama. But Miles said it was easier than one might think.

"It's all about having a good back story," he said. "That's why we've employed the best screenwriters in Hollywood to create our version of the Bible. It's called *The Gospel According to Barack.*"

Miles laid out some sample chapters for me, including Obama's version of the Golden Rule: "Do unto others before they do it to you."

And they've also started working on the origins story. Miles said the White House has pending legislation that would make December 25 "Barack Obama Day."

"We've even got a few passages of the origins scripture ready for Hallmark cards," Miles said. "'For unto you is born this day in a city of undetermined origin—a savior who is Barack the Lord.'"

Suddenly the skies outside the coffeehouse darkened. I could hear the distant rumbling of thunder and an occasional flash of lightning.

Miles said they'd also commissioned choirs to perform some new holiday anthems with lyrics such as, "Joy to the world / Barack has come / Let earth receive her king." They also created the new songs "Jingle Bell Barack" and "Michelle, Did You Know?"

"We've recently acquired the Mormon Tabernacle Choir, which we've renamed the Obama Tabernacle Choir, and they are going to be producing our signature song, a new rendition of the 'Hallelujah Chorus,'" Miles said. "Instead of 'Hallelujah,' they sing 'Barack Obama.'"

But what about the inner workings of the religion? What about the doctrine?

Miles conceded that to be a bit more problematic. He said there'd been fierce debate over who gets to sit at the right hand of Obama.

"Valerie Jarrett wants to sit at the left *and* the right hand," he said. "Michelle's not too happy about that, but we may have a solution. We're contemplating making Michelle the Holy Mother."

What about the sacraments?

"Well, we require followers of Obama to drink the Kool-Aid at least once a week," Miles said. "We've also got the folks over at the Food Network developing a wafer made in the president's likeness from organically harvested wheat."

As for confessional booths, Miles said there aren't going to be any.

"That's what we've got the NSA for," he said. "They already know your darkest secrets."

And how does one become a follower of Obama?

"We believe in predestination," Miles said. "All Americans are pre-destined to follow the president and do his bidding."

Last rites, he said, were being outsourced to the Department of Health and Human Services death panels.

I still wasn't totally convinced this wild scheme would work. How in the world could they indoctrinate so many people?

"We bought ourselves a cable television network," Miles crowed, proudly. "We're calling it MSNBC—the Messianic Savior Named Barack Channel."

Well, that explained a lot. The mainstream media has certainly bought into the messianic complex. One front-page cover heralded Obama as "The Second Coming."[7] "In Obama We Trust," declared another.[8]

Newsweek featured a headline titled "God of All Things,"[9] and editor Evan Thomas told MSNBC that Obama is, in fact, a god.[10]

"In a way, Obama is standing above the country, above the world," Thomas said. "He's sort of *God*. He's going to bring all different sides together."[11]

Spike Lee, the famed director, predicted Obama would create a new rift in time and that from this point on, history would be labeled "Before Obama" and "After Obama."[12]

And there's also the cottage industry of artists churning out Obama icons—including an Obama-themed Nativity.[13]

Miles confirmed the Office of Theological Repatriation was responsible for organizing vendors who sold Obama icons at the DNC in Charlotte. There were posters that declared Obama as "prophecy fulfilled." Prayer shawls embroidered with his name. A calendar that declared him "heaven sent." One painting showed the president with arms outstretched, a crown of thorns on his head.

But Miles said the key moment that could revolutionize this religious movement happened when a mother filmed her child praying to Obama.

"Barack Obama, thank you for doing everything and all the kind stuff," he said in his prayer. "Thank you for all the stuff that you helped us with.... You are good, Barack Obama. You are great. And when you get older, you will be able to do great things. Love, Steven."[14]

Some folks might call that worshipping an idol or blasphemy. Miles called it a "godsend."

"It's proof positive that Americans will one day bow down and worship Barack Hussein Obama," he said, adding quickly, "The *h* is silent."

"To quote Michelle Obama," he said, "this president has brought us out of the dark and into the light."[15]

Then Miles pulled out a copy of *The Promise: President Obama, Year One*, and read the words of Jonathan Alter, detailing what he said was further proof of the president's omnipotence: "A beam of morning light shown [sic] through the stained-glass windows and illuminated the president-elect's face. Several of the clergy and choir on the altar who also saw it marveled afterward about the presence of the Divine."[16]

Suddenly, outside there was a massive flash of lightning and the lights inside flickered off, plunging the coffeehouse into darkness. I quickly gathered my belongings and wished Miles the best.

"Todd, before I leave, I would be remiss if I did not offer you the chance to accept Barack Obama as your Lord and Savior," he said. "Will you relinquish your physical possessions and follow this man from Chicago?"

I smiled and politely declined. For what it's worth, I'd rather put my trust in John 3:16 Jesus than Chicago Jesus.

Chapter 6

ARE YOU NOW OR HAVE YOU EVER BEEN A CHRISTIAN?

CONSERVATIVE RELIGIOUS LEADERS across the nation accused the Obama administration of religious bigotry and moral McCarthyism after evangelical pastor Louie Giglio was pressured to back out of delivering the benediction at President Obama's 2012 inauguration.

Giglio, the pastor of Passion City Church in Georgia, said he would no longer deliver the prayer after gay rights activists became enraged over a sermon he delivered in the 1990s calling homosexuality a sin—a sermon they considered to be anti-gay.

The White House quickly distanced itself from the evangelical leader and said his participation would not have reflected their desire to have a diverse inauguration.

"We were not aware of Pastor Giglio's past comments at the time of his selection, and they don't reflect our desire to celebrate the strength and diversity of our country at this Inaugural," said Presidential Inaugural Committee spokesperson Addie Whisenant. "As we now work to select someone to deliver the benediction, we will ensure their beliefs reflect this administration's vision of inclusion and acceptance for all Americans."[1]

Well, sweet mercy! What in the world did Pastor Giglio say? Did he utter gay slurs from pulpit? Did he say something about Ellen? Did he wear white after Labor Day?

At issue were comments Giglio made in the 1990s during a sermon. They were uncovered by the liberal website Think Progress:

"We must lovingly but firmly respond to the aggressive agenda of not all, but of many in the homosexual community....Underneath this issue is a very powerful and aggressive [movement]. That movement is not a benevolent movement, it is a movement to seize by any means necessary the feeling and the mood of the day, to the point where the homosexual lifestyle becomes accepted as a norm in our society and is given full standing as any other lifestyle, as it relates to family."[2]

Hold on just a moment. I can't hear the shock and outrage because of all the crickets chirping. That's it? That's what got Louie Giglio banned from President Obama's inauguration? There wasn't even so much as a harsh word uttered against Dolce & Gabbana or men who groom their body hair!

Sources tell me Pastor Giglio came under a brutal attack by gay rights activists who demanded he be removed from the inauguration ceremony and that the pro-gay, anti-Christian minions in the administration were more than happy to oblige.

The pastor from Georgia had committed an unpardonable sin: he affirmed a long-held Christian belief that homosexuality is a sin. And the White House nearly keeled over. Maybe they had no idea someone had invited an evangelical pastor to deliver a prayer. How in the world could they have a diverse inaugural ceremony if an evangelical was part of the program?

The *New York Times* reported that people familiar with internal discussions between administration and committee officials said the White House viewed the selection as a problem for Mr. Obama and told the panel to quickly fix it.[3] That led to the following press statement from the pastor:

"Due to a message of mine that has surfaced from 15–20 years ago, it is likely that my participation, and the prayer I would offer, will be dwarfed by those seeking to make their agenda the focal point of the inauguration. Clearly, speaking on this issue has not been in the range of my priorities in the past 15 years. Instead, my aim has been to call people to ultimate significance as we make much of Jesus Christ."[4]

In other words, Giglio was given the heave-ho. The militant gay bullies could stick another feather in their caps. Unless you follow the teachings and beliefs of President Obama and his left-wing culture warriors, your voice is simply not welcome in the public marketplace.

It didn't matter that Pastor Giglio has an international reputation for exposing the injustices of modern-day slavery. It didn't matter that his Atlanta-area church helps refugees from third-world countries or provides school supplies for impoverished boys and girls. It didn't matter that he informed thousands and thousands of young Americans about the travesty of human-trafficking. It just didn't matter.

Ruth Malhotra and Jennifer Keeton have been passionate followers of Giglio's ministry, and they wrote an essay titled "The Tolerance Tyrants Strike Again." These young ladies made clear what is now quite evident.

"Despite all the sacrificial efforts one may have invested into humanitarian causes for the greater good, there is this rabid insistence that in order to do anything in the civic arena—including offer a prayer at a monumental event for our nation—you must not have, at any time in your history, spoken in a way that is disagreeable to a certain group of activists," they wrote. "We don't expect everyone to agree with us. That being said, it is frightening that a small group of activists are able to exercise such absolutist control of public discourse."[5]

Amen, sisters!

Giglio's ouster rightfully outraged Christian conservatives such as Robert Jeffress, pastor of First Baptist Church in Dallas, Texas. "It is the ultimate hypocrisy for the Obama administration to pretend it supports diversity and yet denounces anyone who dares to disagree with its radical homosexual agenda," Jeffress said. "Rev. Giglio's comments about homosexuality from more than a decade ago were not hateful but represent the historical teachings of the world's three major religions. Apparently the Obama administration's definition of tolerance is only broad enough to include its own views."

Tony Perkins, president of Family Research Council, said he was shocked at the attacks from homosexual activists. "What's becoming ever so clear to those who thought homosexual activists could be appeased is that their ultimate goal is to sanitize the public space of anyone who holds to a biblical view of morality," Perkins said. "It pulls back the curtain and shows us the true agenda here. It's not about tolerance. It's about forced acceptance."

But perhaps the most brilliant rebuke came from Albert Mohler, president of Southern Baptist Theological Seminary. He called it "the clearest evidence of the new Moral McCarthyism of our sexually 'tolerant' age."[6]

"An imbroglio is a painful and embarrassing conflict," he wrote on his website. "The imbroglio surrounding Louie Giglio is not only painful, it is revealing. We now see the new Moral McCarthyism in its undisguised and unvarnished reality. If you are a Christian, get ready for the question you will now undoubtedly face: 'Do you now or have you ever believed that homosexuality is a sin?' There is nowhere to hide."[7]

Mohler said it's important to note that Giglio has not been known for taking any stand in recent years on the issue of homosexuality. "If a preacher has ever taken a stand on biblical conviction, he risks being exposed decades after the fact," Mohler wrote. "Anyone who teaches at any time, to any degree, that homosexual behavior is a sin is now to be cast out."[8]

"The Presidential Inaugural Committee and the White House have now declared historic, biblical Christianity to be out of bounds, casting it off the inaugural program as an embarrassment," wrote Mohler. "By its newly articulated standard, any preacher who holds to the faith of the church for the last 2,000 years is *persona non grata*."[9]

Bryan Fischer, who hosts a popular national show on American Family Radio, said Giglio was banished in a "naked display of bigotry."

"It's clear from the statement from the inaugural committee that

Giglio was bounced from the program. It clearly wasn't his idea," Fischer told Fox News. "The banishment of Giglio is a naked display of bigotry and hatred directed at the last safe target in America for angry intolerance: Americans who believe what the Scriptures teach about human sexuality. Truth about homosexuality has now become hate speech, and speaking the truth about homosexuality has now become a hate crime."

Fischer said the bottom line is that "bullies and bigots have won a major victory."

"The inauguration committee says their 'vision' is one of 'inclusion and acceptance for all Americans,'" he said. "Why doesn't somebody ask Pastor Giglio just how 'included' and 'accepted' he feels right now?"

Pastor Giglio was a portrait of grace in the aftermath of this ugly, ugly incident. He vowed to continue to pray for President Obama.

"Our nation is deeply divided and hurting, and more than ever we need God's grace and mercy in our time of need," the pastor wrote in a letter to his congregation.[10]

And still the Obama administration deemed this man—Louie Giglio—to be unworthy of invoking the Lord's name on Inauguration Day. A man who feeds the poor. A man who helps free those enslaved. A man who lives out his faith in Jesus.

In 1954, during the final moments of the McCarthy hearings, attorney Joseph Welch made comments that I believe are appropriate to the events at hand. I paraphrase them here: Until this moment, President Obama, I think I never really gauged your cruelty or recklessness. Let us not assassinate this man further, Mr. President. You have done enough. Have you no sense of decency?[11]

Chapter 7

FROM THE ANNALS OF GOD-BLESSED LIVING: MOM'S SWEET POTATO PIE

A BUZZ RIPPLED ACROSS the pews at our First Baptist Church. The pastor announced that the following Sunday, President and Mrs. Carter would be coming to town. They not only would be attending the morning worship service, but the pastor announced Mr. Jimmy and Miss Rosalynn also would join the congregation for the annual dinner-on-the-grounds. My mother could hardly contain herself.

Imagine preparing a meal for the former president of the United States! But my father was not all that impressed. President Carter was a Democrat, he reminded Mother. When it came to home cooking, though, Kathy Starnes was bipartisan. She firmly believed world peace could be achieved through a dinner table piled high with hams, country fried steak, buttermilk biscuits, butter beans, sweet potato pie, and a few gallons of sweet tea.

Mom left church that afternoon with a newfound sense of purpose—sort of like a Paula Deen on crack. She was determined to prepare a dish that would change the course of history, a dish that future generations would define as the turning point in American politics. The dish she selected? Potato salad.

Mom ordered dad to the supermarket with a list of ingredients. Only the finest would do—potatoes, onions, celery, mayonnaise, a variety of spices, plus her secret ingredient: a dash of mustard.

She started off the week making practice batches, working night and day, much to the chagrin of my father, who did not care for potato salad. But by Thursday Mom was getting exasperated. The potato salad was either too lumpy or too mushy. She tossed aside her apron and huffed out of the kitchen. "I've only got seven days to get this right," she complained.

My dad wasn't very helpful.

"I don't see what the big deal is," he replied. "It only took God six days to make the world."

Fortunately she didn't have a cast iron skillet handy.

Mother called her prayer circle for a bit of divine intervention, and it must have worked. On Sunday morning she produced a potato salad worthy of a former-peanut-farmer-turned-president.

The preacher that day was particularly longwinded. He took us to the lake of fire and to the pearly gates, tossing in some hell, fire, and brimstone for good measure. And after singing all five verses of the invitation hymn, the congregation had worked up quite an appetite.

Mr. Jimmy and Miss Rosalynn dutifully got in line and began loading up their plates—and, sure enough, both managed to find room for some of my mother's potato salad. A while later, Miss Rosalynn came over to meet my mom and, with a flourish of grace, pronounced the potato salad absolutely delicious.

Well, praise the Lord! My father was relieved, I was astonished, and my mother was on cloud nine. First Lady Rosalynn Carter loved her potato salad. It was even more remarkable because mom was a registered Republican!

It seemed like such an insignificant moment in life, but to my mother that compliment meant the world. Many years later and many miles away from Georgia, I would come to understand why.

The telephone call came shortly before I delivered the evening newscast. The voice on the other end sounded distant and void of emotion. He identified himself as a police officer.

"It is my duty to inform you..."

I asked him to stop, somehow hoping if he did not recite his message it wouldn't be true. But it was. My mother was gone. After sixty-one years, her heart simply ran out of seasons.

I've thought a lot about my mother's life. She could've done whatever she wanted. She was a gifted seamstress and beautiful singer. But she chose to make her life at home.

She was a housewife, and the kitchen was her kingdom. She never achieved fame or fortune. Instead, she found joy in cooking a good meal and found satisfaction in the full bellies and empty plates at her table.

During her funeral, the preacher asked for people to share something special about my mom. The piano player went first. She said it might seem odd, but she would always remember my mom's sweet potato pie. Then somebody else chimed in about her cornbread dressing. There were a few nods and a few amens. Then Aunt Lynn got teary-eyed when she talked about Momma's ambrosia.

And then I remembered that day a long time ago at First Baptist Church. I remembered my mother beaming with pride at her presidential potato salad.

My mother used her culinary gifts to serve up heaping helpings of love, piled high with sugary sweetness and a dollop of buttery goodness on top. It was her legacy.

I was reminded of that a few days ago as I was walking near a bakery. I was lost in my thoughts, truly dreading Mother's Day without her—until, that is, a passing aroma caught my attention. *"That smells like cinnamon,"* I thought, as a smile crossed my face. The kind Mom used to put in her sweet potato pies.

The Bible reminds us that God's mercies are new every morning—and sometimes they smell just like sweet potato pie.

Chapter 8

GAY RIGHTS VS. RELIGIOUS RIGHTS

BELIEVE WE ARE just a few years away from American pastors being brought up on charges of hate speech against homosexuals. I believe we will see attempts made to shut down churches and remove Bibles from public libraries—all because of what the Scriptures teach about homosexuality.

A study released by the First Amendment Center reveals that a majority of Americans believe gay equality trumps religious objections: "Fifty-two percent of Americans believe that businesses providing wedding services to the public can be required by the government to provide services to same-sex couples, even if the business owner has religious objections to same-sex marriage."[1]

"When two cherished rights clash—the right to be free from discrimination and the right to follow the dictates of religious conscience—society must make painful choices that inevitably uphold one at the expense of the other," wrote Charles Haynes, director of the Religious Freedom Education Project. "According to the latest numbers, most citizens now believe that our commitment to non-discrimination must trump religious objections to homosexuality in the public square of America."[2]

Christian Americans should be deeply disturbed by that study.

US Senator Ted Cruz of Texas told the Christian Broadcasting Network's David Brody that he foresees a tragic assault on religious liberty. "If you look at other nations that have gone down the road toward gay marriage, that's the next step where it gets enforced. It gets enforced against Christian pastors who decline to perform gay marriages, who speak out and preach biblical truths on marriage," Cruz said. "There is no doubt that the advocates who are driving this effort in the United States want to see us end up in the same place."[3]

My philosophy on homosexuality is pretty straightforward (pardon the pun): How you butter your biscuit is your own business, as they say in Mississippi. It's truly none of my business what happens in the private life of a gay person. I do not expect them to affirm my religious beliefs or my political beliefs. Live and let live, I say.

But the militant gay rights community believes otherwise. They not only expect you to accept their lifestyle, but they also want you to affirm it. They want your children exposed to it in their public school classrooms. They want private business owners to endorse their court-sanctioned "marriages." And woe be to any person who dares object.

Phil Robertson of *Duck Dynasty* fame is perhaps the most prominent national figure to come under attack for his religious beliefs on this. But many average Americans without the platform of a reality television show are facing grave injustices because of their stance on traditional marriage.

Christians are losing their jobs, businesses are being targeted with lawsuits and discrimination investigations, and students are being indoctrinated. You won't see these stories on the evening news. You won't even read about them in the newspaper. But the attacks are happening. The anti-bullying crowd is bullying.

You'll read about some of the more egregious examples over the next few pages, but consider this as an appetizer:

- Hands On Originals, a Christian-owned T-shirt company in Kentucky, was sued by gays after it refused to make gay pride shirts. The suit alleges discrimination based on sexual orientation.[4]

- Frank Turek, an employee of Cisco, was fired for his religious view that marriage should be between a woman and a man. Townhall reported that he never expressed his view at work, but his boss found a book he authored on the subject online.[5]

- A Cargill Foods employee was fired because he had a sign on his private vehicle supporting traditional marriage. The company said other employees were offended.[6]

- A North Carolina teenager was suspended after he wore a shirt with a religious message on a school-sponsored "Day of Truth" event. The school said the child was promoting religion. But it's OK for the school to promote homosexuality?[7]

- A Catholic student was kicked out of a class in Howell, Michigan, for speaking out against homosexuality. The student said the gay lifestyle was offensive.[8]

- A family-owned bakery in Indianapolis was subjected to a city investigation after it declined to make cupcakes for National Coming Out Day. The owner of Just Cookies explained to local media they have "two young, impressionable daughters and we thought maybe it was best not to do that."[9]

- The artistic director of California Musical Theater resigned under significant pressure after he gave money to support a measure that outlawed same-sex marriage in California. Scott Eckern, who is Mormon, was outed by activist bullies. As one activist told the *New York Times*, "I do believe there comes a time when you cannot sit back and accept what I think is the most dangerous form of bigotry."[10] Spoken like a true bigot.

- The *Washington Blade* published the names and addresses of 110,000 Maryland residents who signed a petition to put the state's new marriage equality law onto the November ballot.[11] I suspect the names were not published so readers could send them Christmas cards.

- Two preachers were brutally beaten, punched at, and kicked by a crowd at a gay pride festival.[12]

Now let's take an in-depth look at some of the more egregious instances of Christians coming under assault for their religious beliefs.

Judge: Bakers Must Make Gay Wedding Cakes

A judge in Colorado said that a baker who refused to make a cake for a same-sex wedding ceremony must serve gay couples despite his religious beliefs, a ruling that a civil rights group hailed as a victory for gay rights.[13]

Administrative Law Judge Robert N. Spencer ruled that Jack Phillips, the owner of the Masterpiece Cakeshop in suburban Denver, would be fined if he continued to turn down orders from gay couples who wanted to buy wedding cakes. "The undisputed facts show that Respondents [Phillips] discriminated against Complainants because of their sexual orientation by refusing to sell them a wedding cake for their same-sex marriage," Spencer wrote.[14]

David Mullins and Charlie Craig visited the Masterpiece Cakeshop to order a cake for their wedding reception. The couple had planned to marry in Massachusetts and hold a reception in Colorado.

Phillips told the men that he could not bake their cake because of his religious beliefs opposing same-sex marriage. He offered to make them any other baked item, but not a wedding cake. The couple immediately left the shop and later filed a complaint with the Colorado Civil Rights Division.

"Being denied service by Masterpiece Cakeshop was offensive and dehumanizing especially in the midst of arranging what should be a joyful family celebration," Mullins said in a statement. "No one should fear being turned away from a public business because of who they are."[15]

Judge Spencer said Phillips did not demonstrate that his free-speech rights had been violated and that there's no evidence that forcing him to make a cake for a same-sex ceremony would hurt his business. "On the contrary, to the extent that the law prohibits Respondents' [Phillips] from discriminating on the basis of sexual orientation, compliance with the law would likely increase their business by not alienating the gay community," he wrote.[16]

The American Civil Liberties Union of Colorado hailed the ruling and said it served as a warning. "While we all agree that religious freedom is important, no one's religious beliefs make it acceptable to break the law by discriminating against prospective customers," ACLU staff attorney Amanda C. Goad said in a statement. "No one is asking Masterpiece's owner to change his beliefs, but treating gay people differently because of who they are is discrimination plain and simple."[17]

Phillips was represented by the Alliance Defending Freedom, a legal firm specializing in religious liberty cases. Attorney Nicolle Martin condemned the judge's ruling. "America was founded on the fundamental freedom of every citizen to live and work according to their beliefs," Martin said in a prepared statement. "Forcing Americans to promote ideas against their will undermines our constitutionally protected freedom of expression and our right to live free."[18] Martin said this was simply a case of a baker who declined to use his personal creative abilities to promote and endorse a same-sex ceremony. "If the government can take away our First Amendment freedoms, there is nothing it can't take away," she said.[19]

Martin added that Phillips is a devoted Christian who has an unwavering faith. She said he is a person of such deep faith that he won't even bake Halloween-themed treats for his bakery—at all. "He's just trying to live within a certain set of biblical principles because he believes that he answers to God for everything that he does," Martin told me.

Militant Gays Force Christian Bakery to Close

A family-owned Christian bakery, under investigation for refusing to bake a wedding cake for a lesbian couple, was forced to close its doors after a vicious boycott by militant gay activists.

Sweet Cakes by Melissa posted a message on its Facebook page alerting customers that their Gresham, Oregon, retail store would be shut down after months of harassment from pro-gay marriage forces. "Better is a poor man who walks in integrity than a rich man who is crooked in his ways," read a posting from Proverbs on the bakery's Facebook page.

"It's a sad day for Christian business owners, and it's a sad day for the First Amendment," owner Aaron Klein told me. "The LGBT attacks are the reason we are shutting down the shop. They have killed our business through mob tactics."

Last January Aaron and Melissa Klein made national headlines when they refused to bake a wedding cake for a lesbian couple. Klein tells me he has nothing against the LGBT community but that because of their religious faith, the family simply cannot take part in same-sex wedding events. "I believe marriage is between a man and a woman," he said. "I don't want to help somebody celebrate a commitment to a lifetime of sin."

The lesbian couple filed a discrimination suit with the Oregon Bureau of Labor and Industries and told their story to local newspapers and television stations. Within days pro-gay groups launched protests and boycotts. Klein told me he received messages threatening to kill his family. They hoped his children would die.

The LGBT protestors then turned on other wedding vendors around the community. They threatened to boycott any florists, wedding planners, or other vendors who did business with Sweet Cakes by Melissa.

"That tipped the scales," Aaron said. "The LGBT activists

inundated them with phone calls and threatened them. They would tell our vendors, 'If you don't stop doing business with Sweet Cakes by Melissa, we will shut you down.'"

To make matters worse, Oregon's Bureau of Labor and Industries announced it had launched a formal discrimination investigation against the Christian family.

Commissioner Brad Avakian told the *Oregonian* that he was committed to a fair and thorough investigation to determine whether the bakery discriminated against the lesbian couple. "Everybody is entitled to their own beliefs, but that doesn't mean that folks have the right to discriminate," he told the newspaper. "The goal is to rehabilitate. For those who do violate the law, we want them to learn from that experience and have a good, successful business in Oregon."[20]

In other words, Christians who live and work in Oregon must follow man's law instead of God's law. But in a show of benevolence, the state is willing to rehabilitate and reeducate Christian business owners like the Kleins.

Aaron Klein said the closing of their retail store was a small price to pay for standing up for their religious beliefs. "As a man of faith, I am in good spirits," he said. "I'm happy to be serving the Lord and standing up for what's right."

But he said what's happened to Sweet Cakes by Melissa should be a warning to other Christians across the nation. "This is a fight that's been coming for a while," he said. "Be prepared to take a stand. Hopefully, the church will wake up and understand that we are under attack right now."

The Kleins told television station KPTV their philosophy remains unchanged by recent events. "The Bible tells us to flee from sin," Aaron said. "I don't think that making a cake for it helps."

Melissa added: "I guess in my mind I thought we lived in a lot nicer of a world where everybody...tolerated everybody."[21]

The plight of the Klein family exposes the true nature of the left. Those who preach tolerance and diversity are the least tolerant and the least diverse of all.

Court: Photographers Must Film Gay Weddings

The New Mexico Supreme Court ruled that two Christian photographers who declined to photograph a same-sex union violated
the state's Human Rights Act. One justice said the photographers
were "compelled by law to compromise the very religious beliefs that
inspire their lives."[22]

In 2006 Vanessa Willock asked Elaine and Jonathan Huguenin,
owners of Elane Photography, to photograph a same-sex "commitment ceremony" in the town of Taos. Huguenin and her husband
declined the job because their Christian beliefs were in conflict with
the message communicated by the ceremony.

Willock found another photographer at a cheaper price but
nevertheless filed a complaint with the New Mexico Human Rights
Commission accusing Elane Photography of discrimination based
on sexual orientation. The photographer was later found guilty and
ordered to pay thousands of dollars in fines.

"The Huguenins today can no more turn away customers on the
basis of their sexual orientation—photographing a same-sex marriage ceremony—than they could refuse to photograph African-
Americans or Muslims," Justice Richard Bosson wrote in the court's
unanimous decision.[23]

"Though the rule of law requires it, the result is sobering," he
wrote. "It will no doubt leave a tangible mark on the Huguenins and
others of similar views."[24] Bosson said the case provokes reflection
on what the nation is about. "At its heart, this case teaches that at
some point in our lives all of us must compromise, if only a little, to
accommodate the contrasting values of others," he wrote.[25] He said
the Constitution protects the rights of the Christian photographers
to pray to the God of their choice and to follow religious teachings,
but he offered a sobering warning.

"There is a price, one that we all have to pay somewhere in our
civic life," the justice wrote. "The Huguenins have to channel their
conduct, not their beliefs, so as to leave space for other Americans
who believe something different. That compromise is part of the glue

that holds us together as a nation, the tolerance that lubricates the varied moving parts of us as a people."[26]

Alliance Defending Freedom represented the photographers, and attorney Jordan Lorence said the ruling, in effect, means gay rights now trump religious rights. "Government-coerced expression is a feature of dictatorships that has no place in a free country," Lorence said. "This decision is a blow to our client and every American's right to live free."[27]

Lorence said the New Mexico Supreme Court undermined the constitutionally protected freedoms of expression and conscience. "If Elane [Photography] does not have her rights of conscience protected, then basically nobody does," he said. "What you have here is the government punishing someone who says, 'I, in good conscience, cannot communicate the messages of this wedding.'"

Ken Klukowski of the Family Research Council called the ruling profoundly disturbing. "This decision may bring to Americans' attention the serious threat to religious liberty posed by overbearing government agencies when it comes to redefining marriage," he said. "Rather than live and let live, this is forcing religious Americans to violate the basic teachings of their faith or lose their jobs."

Professor Orders Students to Support Gay Rights

A Tennessee community college professor ordered her students to wear ribbons supporting gay rights and said those who believed in the traditional definition of marriage are just "uneducated bigots" who "attack homosexuals with hate," according to a legal firm representing several of the students in the class.

Students in a general psychology class at Columbia State Community College were directed by their professor to wear "Rainbow Coalition" ribbons for an entire day and express their support for the gay community, said Travis Barham, an attorney with Alliance Defending Freedom. "Dr. Brunton essentially turned her general psychology class into a semester-long clinic on the demands of the homosexual movement," Barham told me.

Alliance Defending Freedom said the professor told students to write a paper about how they were allegedly "discriminated against" because of their support for homosexual conduct. Several students objected to the assignment because their religious convictions prohibit them from supporting conduct their faith teaches them is immoral and unnatural.

Barham said the professor made it clear they had to follow the rules of the assignment to receive credit and allegedly told the students their own beliefs and viewpoints were irrelevant—even when they wrote their papers. The students were also barred from defending or explaining any other views regarding homosexual conduct, dismissing such arguments as "throwing Bible verses at her," the attorney said.

"When students objected to how she was pushing her personal views on the class, she explained that it is her job 'to educate the ignorant and uneducated elements of society' that oppose this movement's demands and to correct their 'hateful and close-minded' views," Barham said.

Barham said the assignment violated the constitutional rights of students by forcing them to advance a particular political agenda. "The Constitution does not allow any government official to force another person to adopt or advocate a particular moral or political view. But this professor did just that with this assignment and thus clearly violated freedoms protected by the First Amendment."

Gays Target Superman Writer

Orson Scott Card, the well-known science-fiction author of *Ender's Game*, is part of a team of writers and artists assembled by DC Comics to create an anthology series of comics called Adventures of Superman. Card, who is Mormon, is also an opponent of same-sex marriage. He once called gay marriage the end of democracy in America and wrote that "the left is at war with the family," and suggested gays could change.[28]

"Same-sex attraction is not a straitjacket," he wrote in an op-ed.

"People's desires change over time; gay people still have choices; a reproductive dysfunction like same-sex attraction is not a death sentence for your DNA or for your desire to have a family in which children grow up with male and female parents to model appropriate gender roles."[29]

Accordingly Card's participation in the Superman project has sparked outrage across the nation's gay community. Thousands signed a petition calling for DC Comics to fire Card, saying that if they didn't, the comic book publisher could face a boycott.

"He's written publicly that he believes marriage equality would lead to the end of civilization," the petition states. "We need to let DC Comics know they can't support Orson Scott Card or his work to keep LGBT people as second-class citizens. They know they're accountable to their fans, so if enough of us speak out now, they'll hear us loud and clear."[30]

A DC Comics spokesperson released a statement to Fox News defending Card. "As content creators we steadfastly support freedom of expression; however, the personal views of individuals associated with DC Comics are just that—personal views—and not those of the company itself," the statement read.

The comic-maker's defense of Card is not likely to quell the anger building in the gay community. The website Queerty addressed the controversy in a column titled "Why Did DC Comics Hire Rabid Homophobe Orson Scott Card to Write 'Superman'?"[31] Jono Jarrett of the Geeks Out fan group called the inclusion of Card "deeply disappointing."[32]

"Superman stands for truth, justice and the American way," Jarrett told the *Guardian*. "Orson Scott Card does not stand for any ideas of truth, justice, or the American way that I can subscribe to."[33]

Actor Michael Hartney wrote online that Card is an embarrassment to the company. "If this was a Holocaust denier or a white supremacist, there would be no question," he wrote on Tumblr. "Hiring that writer would be an embarrassment to your company."[34]

Card is also a board member of the National Organization for Marriage, a group that promotes the traditional version of marriage.

The organization's president, Brian Brown, told me he was simply stunned that gay rights activists are trying to destroy a man's career.

"This is completely un-American, and it needs to be stopped," Brown said. "Simply because we stand up for traditional marriage, some people feel like it's OK to target us for intimidation and punishment."

Brown called the attacks on Card frightening and said it's another example of gay rights activists trying to punish those who believe marriage should be a union between a man and woman. "Marriage is the union of a man and a woman," Brown said. "That is not hateful. That is not bigoted."

Teacher Punished for Refusing to Attend Gay Celebration

An assistant professor of theatre and dance at a Texas university sued the school for religious discrimination, alleging she was punished for refusing to attend a series of gay-themed theatrical productions.

Linda Ozmun filed suit against Lamar University for discrimination, creating a hostile work environment, retaliation, and improper denial of promotions or advancement, according to the lawsuit filed in federal court.[35]

Ozmun was in her fourth year of a tenure-track position when the incidents occurred. The Department of Theatre and Dance had scheduled a 2010 performance by Tim Miller, described in court papers as an "openly homosexual man who advocates for normalizing homosexuality and for homosexual marriage."[36]

Miller's one-man show is about "his homosexual lifestyle using obscene language and sexual gestures."[37]

Court papers indicate the show was cancelled after complaints from the community. In response to the cancellation, several students organized a show billed as a "celebration of homosexuality."[38]

Ozmun said she declined to attend the student event because of her religious beliefs and was later questioned by the head of her department.[39] In March 2011 she received her annual review and was given a grade of "unacceptable" for refusing to attend the celebration of homosexuality. She filed a grievance, which was returned and noted "unheard."[40]

In the fall of 2011 Miller was invited to return to the university to perform his show *Glory Box*. He was also conducting a workshop with students to "help them find their voice."[41] Ozmun asked to be excused from what she called an "offensive production,"[42] but the university refused.

Ozmun alleges in her lawsuit that not only was she told to attend, but she was also threatened with disciplinary action if she failed to attend. Ozmun stood her ground and did not attend and alleges she was punished as a result of her religious beliefs.

High School Teacher Investigated for Opposing Homosexuality

A New Jersey high school teacher was investigated after she allegedly posted a message on her private Facebook page that she opposed homosexuality because of her Christian faith.

The Union Township School District said it was probing to determine whether Viki Knox violated school policies when she allegedly posted remarks saying homosexuality is a sin that "breeds like cancer" and describing it as "perverted."[43]

Knox also complained on her private Facebook page that Union High School featured a display recognizing October as Lesbian, Gay, Bisexual and Transgender History month. The display reportedly featured photos of Harvey Milk, Neil Patrick Harris, and Virginia Woolf.

"The district is taking the matter very seriously," school superintendent Patrick Martin said. "We are running a thorough investigation. The board of education will act appropriately based on the outcome of the investigation."

"They can persecute her, but they can't prosecute her," Viki's husband, Gene Knox, told WCBS-TV, stating that "everybody's entitled to an opinion."[44]

But a spokesman for Garden State Equality, a group that advocates gay rights, said that's not true. "She should not be teaching in the classroom," said Steven Goldstein, chair of the gay rights group. He said her "vicious, anti-gay remarks on Facebook crossed the line."

Goldestein's group launched a statewide campaign to have the Christian teacher fired, sending hundreds of phone calls and e-mails to the school district. "I find what she wrote on Facebook endangers the learning atmosphere for students beyond repair and violates the school district's own policy of a safe and comfortable environment for all," Goldstein said. "She's no longer in a position to teach in the classroom because she will make many students fearful of her hatred."

Ada Davis, an attorney with Alliance Defending Freedom, said she was very alarmed at how the school system is treating the Christian teacher. Alliance Defending Freedom recently represented a Florida school teacher accused of posting similar anti-gay Facebook messages. "The problem is they don't want anyone who believes homosexuality is a sin to be a teacher," Davis said. "Teachers obviously should not be punished for exercising these kinds of constitutionally protected rights. She has a right to communicate her religious beliefs."

Worker Placed on Leave for Supporting Traditional Marriage

Conservatives and even some liberals across the nation were outraged after Gallaudet University suspended the school's chief diversity officer after she signed a petition in her church to put a gay marriage referendum on the ballot in Maryland.[45]

Angela McCaskill, a twenty-three-year veteran of the university, was placed on paid leave as the university investigated her support for traditional marriage. "It recently came to my attention that Dr. McCaskill has participated in a legislative initiative that some feel is inappropriate for an individual serving as Chief Diversity Officer; however, other individuals feel differently," wrote Gallaudet president T. Alan Hurwitz in an e-mail sent to the campus community.[46]

McCaskill was one of two hundred thousand residents who signed a petition to put Maryland's Question 6 on the ballot. The measure was a referendum on same-sex marriage. The *Washington Blade* published the names and addresses of every person who signed the petition. An anonymous faculty member spotted McCaskill's name in the newspaper and immediately notified authorities.

Hurwitz said McCaskill, who earned the school's first PhD as a deaf African-American woman, was immediately placed on leave. McCaskill's pastor denounced the university's decision and called it "beyond the boundaries of civility."[47]

"Unfortunately, Dr. McCaskill and her family have been subjected to threats and intimidation as a result of the media coverage of the actions taken by President Hurwitz on behalf of Gallaudet University," said Lee Washington, pastor of Reid Temple. "As her church family, we stand firmly by her side and welcome all persons of good faith, regardless of their ideological views, to denounce these actions of cowardice and bullying."[48]

McCaskill was eventually reinstated, but, as Washington said, what happened to her should serve as a warning to all Americans who support traditional marriage. "It is a clarion call for Marylanders who value religious liberties and individual rights to vote against Question 6," Washington wrote in a statement on the church's website.[49]

Tony Perkins, president of Family Research Council, said the university's president should be fired "for violating our most basic civil rights."[50]

"Gallaudet University's action underscores that far more is at stake in redefining marriage than two people walking down the aisle," Perkins said. "Indeed, the very livelihood of business owners and employees is at stake."[51]

The *Washington Post* weighed in on the matter in an editorial titled "Gallaudet's Mistake."

"Firing, or threatening to fire, a diversity officer for off-campus political activity strikes us as inconsistent with 'open sharing of thoughts and ideas,'" the newspaper wrote.[52]

DOJ: Affirm Gays, or Else

The Department of Justice was accused of religious intolerance and viewpoint discrimination after workers were sent an e-mail directing them to verbally affirm homosexuality, according to a law firm specializing in religious liberty and now representing a DOJ whistleblower.

Liberty Counsel, a Christian legal advocacy firm, said DOJ employees were e-mailed a brochure called "LGBT Inclusion at Work: The 7 Habits of Highly Effective Managers." The brochure was created as a resource by DOJ Pride, an association of lesbian, gay, bisexual, and transgender employees of the DOJ.

Among the directives in the brochure is for workers to vocally affirm homosexuality. "Don't judge or remain silent," the brochure read. "Silence will be interpreted as disapproval."

They were also told to post "DOJ Pride" stickers in their office to indicate that it is a "safe place."[53]

One gay DOJ employee is quoted in the directive saying, "Silence seems like disapproval. There's still an atmosphere of LGBT issues not being appropriate for the workplace (particularly for transgender people), or that people who bring it up are trying to rock the boat."[54]

Mat Staver, founder of Liberty Counsel, said every American should be outraged by the DOJ directive. "This administration is pushing the most radical, immoral agenda on the American people," Staver said. "Christians are not merely required to shut up, but now they are being coerced to embrace immorality that goes against their sincerely held religious beliefs."

Liberty Counsel is representing an unidentified female DOJ worker in Washington DC who received the brochure. Staver said the woman is terrified she might lose her job unless she publicly affirms homosexuality—and she's not the only one.

"Christians are frightened and terrified of losing their jobs," Staver told Fox News. "You just can't keep your head down and do your job. Now you have to become an advocate for the LGBT agenda—and if you don't, the DOJ will consider that to be intolerant."

Staver said the idea that Christians who might oppose homosexuality have to put up a pro-gay symbol in their office smacks of thought police. "Under this directive, one cannot be a Christian and a manager at the Department of Justice," he said. "How does one who believes in the teachings of Jesus Christ and the Bible display 'gay pride' stickers?"

Liberty Counsel vice president Matt Barber told Fox News that the DOJ has created an extremely hostile work environment for Christians. "This is *1984* just a few decades late," Barber said. "This is so Orwellian. President Obama said he intended to fundamentally transform America. That's exactly what they are doing, and they are doing it within the Department of Justice."

Barber said some female DOJ workers have also expressed concerns about transgender workers using their bathroom facilities. "They [DOJ leaders] have said if you are uncomfortable with a man in a skirt using the facilities, then tough—you need to get over it," he told Fox News.

The brochure quoted a male employee who dresses like a woman: "I want people to understand that I'm real. I want to be recognized as the gender I really am....Just imagine if people were constantly debating YOUR bathroom privileges. Imagine how humiliating that would be."[55]

Workers were also told to use "inclusive" words such as *partner* or *significant other*, rather than traditional terms such as *husband* or *wife*. They were also told to use a transgender person's chosen name and the pronoun that is consistent with the person's self-identified gender.

DOJ employees were told to stop using phrases such as *gay lifestyle* or *sexual preference* because those words are "considered by many as offensive."

Barber said it is a form of sexual harassment. "If you feel sexually harassed and complain about it, then you are the one who could get in trouble because you've violated the transgender person's rights," he said.

So there you have it, ladies. If you feel uncomfortable with a guy sashaying around the powder room in pantyhose, you're the one with the problem.

Gays Target Catholic University Chaplain

Religious liberty groups mobilized to defend the chaplain of George Washington University's Newman Center after gay students launched an effort to have the priest fired for preaching against homosexuality and abortion.

"It's discrimination against Catholics," said Patrick Reilly, president of the Cardinal Newman Society. "Secular colleges are fast becoming a very unsafe place for Catholics who hold true to their faith. This is a very, very sad situation."

Two gay students at George Washington told the *GW Hatchet* student newspaper they wanted Father Greg Shaffer removed from campus over his anti-gay and anti-abortion views. Damian Legacy and Blake Bergen said they wanted the university's Office for Diversity and Inclusion to investigate the priest and called for the student government association to defund the Newman Center. They were particularly offended by a blog post the priest wrote calling gay relationships "unnatural and immoral," the newspaper reported.[56]

"To have my faith leader view me that way, just because of one piece of the way that God made me, and to think that one part is responsible for the destruction of my human dignity, it just didn't, I can't even begin to describe the mental conflict that it creates," Legacy told the newspaper.[57]

The two students also cited academic studies that linked the inability to sleep and loss of appetite with being around homophobic behavior.[58]

Reilly said he found the incident "absolutely disturbing." "Chastity outside of marriage has been the Catholic Church teaching for more than 2,000 years," he said. "The only discrimination occurring there is trying to silence a priest for trying to teach the Catholic faith."

Peter Sprigg of the Family Research Council said that while the incident is extremely shocking, it should come as no surprise. "This is a shot across the bow to anyone who would dare speak out and dare to express a biblical view on homosexuality," Sprigg said. "This is an indication of what we...have been warning, regarding the threat to religious liberty that is posed by the homosexual movement."

Sprigg said the goal of gay activists is to "intimidate people into silence." "The world they seek to create is one in which no one ever says anything wrong about people engaging in homosexual conduct," he said. "The attitude of some of these homosexual activists seems to be that religious liberty has to be thrown out the window for the sake of preventing any kind of situation that might make homosexuals feel uncomfortable."

Reilly said he never thought he'd see the day when Catholic priests would come under such assault. "Catholic priests have an obligation to teach the Catholic faith," he said. "Those who go to a Catholic center ought to expect them to do that."

But now, Reilly said, "Simply holding to the moral teachings of the faith are considered to be discrimination."

I'm just thinking out loud here, but if the gay students feel uncomfortable with the teachings at the Cardinal Newman Center, perhaps they might want to go somewhere else.

Church Faced Eviction for Position on Homosexuality

The head of Miami-Dade County Public Schools wanted to evict a Southern Baptist church that rents space in one of their buildings because of the congregation's opposition to homosexuality.

Superintendent Alberto Carvalho released a statement to a local television station alleging that Impact Miami's opposition to homosexuality "appears to be contrary to school board policy as well as the basic principles of humanity."

He told Local10.com that he wanted the church thrown out of the public school as a "rejection of prejudice and intolerance."[59]

When President Obama announced he had evolved on the issue of gay marriage, pastor Jack Hakimian preached two sermons explaining the biblical position on homosexuality. One of the sermons was titled "Gays and Sex Addicts Can Change and Should Change."

"The school board chair, as well as the superintendent, have both reviewed the allegations and found this disturbing and appalling," school spokesman John Schuster told Local10.com.[60]

Pastor Hakimian said he and his congregation have been unfairly labeled as bigots. He said they faced eviction from their space simply because he preached that homosexuality is a sin.

"It's about a message that homosexuality is a sin that God wants to redeem as all other sins," he told Fox News.

The church was paying nearly $1,500 a month to rent the high school facility, and Hakimian said, "As taxpayers we have the right to assemble in public spaces."

"I never thought I would be penalized for teaching on Christian marriage and sexual ethics from the Bible—the very Bible that presidents swear on," he said.

Impact Miami is affiliated with the Southern Baptist Convention, the nation's largest Protestant denomination. SBC President Fred Luter told me the controversy is a "sign of the times."

"We're living in a day and time when people are calling wrong right and they're calling right wrong," Luter said. "Any time a man of God stands up for the Word of God, I think we should expect opposition—simply because of the fact that God's ways are not man's ways."

The incident enraged religious liberty groups, several of whom volunteered their services to defend the pastor and the church should they be thrown out of their meeting space. "He has the right to be able to speak on Sunday from the Scriptures and speak about his viewpoint on human sexuality," said Mat Staver, president of Liberty Counsel. "This is not someone who is advocating violence or some whacko that is extreme that would be a threat to society. This is a pastor who is speaking on issues from their own moral, political, and biblical perspective."

Staver told Fox News he had a chance to review the pastor's sermons and noted that the messages were in line with that millions of

Americans believe. "It is not contrary to humanity," he said, refuting the school superintendent's allegations. "It is absolutely outrageous that you would have a superintendent who would [think] along these lines."

Staver called the attack on the Miami church a serious threat. "It's serious for all of us," he said. "If we lose the right to free speech in this area, we lose it in every other area."

Staver said Liberty Counsel and other religious liberty groups have feared homosexual advocates might use anti-bullying laws to go after ministers. "This is coming right into the very pulpits of churches, and pastors will ultimately have their messages censored and they'll be discriminated against because of the positions they take on human sexuality—and specifically homosexuality," Staver said. "This is Exhibit A of that threat."

Joel Oster, senior counsel with Alliance Defending Freedom, said the US Constitution is clear on matters regarding free speech. "A school cannot be listening to sermons and then discriminate against the church based on the content of the sermons," Oster said. "This church does have a constitutional right to use these facilities. Public schools cannot discriminate against religious use of their facilities based upon viewpoints—and that's exactly what's going on here."

The church was eventually able to maintain its lease with the school district, but this sordid affair proves that churches and pastors are not exempt from threats, intimidation, and abuse as a result of their biblical beliefs.

Church Camp Punished for Refusing to Host Gay Wedding

A New Jersey judge ruled that a Christian organization engaged in wrongdoing and violated the state's discrimination laws when it prevented a gay couple from holding a civil union ceremony on its property.

Administrative Law Judge Solomon Metzger made the ruling in a case involving the Ocean Grove Camp Meeting Association. In 2007 the group stopped a lesbian couple from using its boardwalk pavilion.

"Respondent opposes same-sex unions as a matter of religious belief, and in 2007 found itself on the wrong side of recent changes in the law," Judge Metzger wrote in his ruling. "The respondent violated the LAD [Law Against Discrimination] when it refused to conduct a civil union ceremony."[61]

Jim Campbell, an attorney with Alliance Defending Freedom, said the Ocean Grove Camp Meeting Association has been operating on the Jersey shore for more than one hundred twenty-five years and has its history rooted in the Methodist Church. "According to their Book of Discipline, they cannot host same-sex unions on their property," Campbell told me. "He is saying they engaged in wrongdoing under the law simply for refusing to use the property in a way that would violate their religious beliefs."

But that's only part of the judge's concern. In 1989 Ocean Grove applied for a Green Acres real-estate tax exemption for a section of land that included the pavilion and the boardwalk. One condition of the exemption is that the property had to be "open for public use on an equal basis."[62]

When the camp first applied for the tax exemption, civil unions were not yet legal in New Jersey. That changed in 2006 when the New Jersey Supreme Court granted same-sex couples equal rights under the state constitution.

The judge's decision suggests he doesn't see a conflict with religious liberty in the case, Campbell said. Metzger rejected the church's contention that the pavilion was an extension of its wedding ministry. But Campbell said the ruling could have troublesome implications for religious groups across the state—including the possibility that churches may be forced to host same-sex unions in their houses of worship.

"That's the danger of this ruling," Campbell said. "It could be applied to other religious entities, and it could be applied to other places of worship."

He said he hopes New Jersey's director of civil rights will reconsider the ruling and find that religious groups have a right to use their private property in a way that's consistent with their beliefs. If not, he said anyone could use the ruling to demand that churches host events and other ceremonies that would conflict with their faith.

"We've seen a clash over the past five to ten years that's building and building, where the homosexual legal agenda comes in conflict with religious liberty," he said. "There's always been the concern that courts would incorrectly interpret constitutional freedoms, and that's what we are seeing in this case."

Owners of B&B Guilty of Discrimination

A retired Canadian couple who refused to give a lesbian couple a room at their bed and breakfast was found guilty of discrimination based on sexual orientation and ordered to pay thousands of dollars in fines.

Les and Susan Molnar argued they had a constitutionally protected right to freedom of religion and that the cancellation of the gay couple's reservation was justified. The Molnars said the Riverbend Bed and Breakfast, which has since closed, was also their home, where they hosted Bible studies.

However, the British Columbia Human Rights Tribunal ruled in favor of Shaun Eadie and Brian Thomas. They said the bed and breakfast was separate from the Molnars' personal living space and was operated like a hotel.

"Having entered into the commercial sphere, the Molnars, like other business people, were required to comply with the laws of the province that prohibits discrimination based on sexual orientation," tribunal member Enid Marion told the *Vancouver Sun*.[63]

Thomas told the *Edge* he was delighted in the ruling. "Sometimes you have to stick your neck out, and we stuck our necks out and we feel good and vindicated that we did for the benefit of the people coming behind us," he told the publication.[64]

The Molnars were required to pay more than $4,500 in fines. "We, in clear conscience, did what we did," Lee Molnar told *One News Now*. "From the beginning, we had no ill will towards anybody. And now that the case is finished, we respect the decision of the tribunal and we still have no ill will against anybody."[65]

The website Queerty.com hailed the ruling. "Did they really think they could run a bed and breakfast and turn away queer couples?" the website pondered. "We're, like, the backbone of the B&B industry."[66]

The Molnars paid a hefty price for deciding to remain faithful to their Christian faith. They said they were victims of harassment and worried about future complaints. As a result, they closed the bed and breakfast just a few months after the couple had tried to rent a room.

"It hasn't been easy, but we're still thanking the Lord for the blessings," Lee said. "We believe that our Lord set certain absolute standards, and that's what we attempt to do," he told *One News Now*. "We're not perfect, like anybody else, but we do attempt to live by the Bible and what the Bible says."[67]

Professor Investigating for Opposing Homosexuality

A tenured California college professor was the focus of a four-month investigation after he wrote a letter to the local newspaper critical of the school's plans for a new degree in LGBT studies.

The letter appeared in the *Alameda Journal* after the College of Alameda announced it was creating a new degree program in lesbian, gay, bisexual, and transgender studies. The faculty member raised questions about budget priorities and the appearance of nepotism related to the new degree.[68]

Shortly afterward, the professor was confronted by an irate co-worker who filed a formal complaint of sexual harassment stemming from what the letter said. The investigation took four months.

The professor did not face disciplinary action but was warned not to discuss the investigation with anyone but his legal counsel. "This is an egregious violation of his rights under the First Amendment and shows the growing intolerance and one-sided tyranny of community colleges like Alameda," said Brad Dacus, president of Pacific Justice Institute and the professor's legal counsel.

"This action by the community college against this professor, simply for critiquing a new, controversial class on LGBT, is a serious violation of the free speech rights of this professor," he said.

Dacus said they are not releasing the name of the professor for fear he might suffer additional reprisals in the community.

"They treated him like he was some sort of criminal simply because he questioned the merits of the community college spending their limited resources on a class that was purely for the purposes of exploring and discussing controversial sexual lifestyles," Dacus said.

The college has a history of restricting free speech. Several years ago it stood as the defendant in a federal lawsuit after two students were suspended and threatened with expulsion for praying on campus. That case was later settled.[69]

Dacus said it's not unusual for opinions to be stifled in that part of California, which is near San Francisco.

"That community likes to pride itself on being tolerant," he said. "But one-way tolerance is not tolerance at all. It's tyranny."

Teacher Suspended for Supporting Traditional Marriage

A former Teacher of the Year in Mount Dora, Florida, was suspended and his job threatened after he voiced his objection to gay marriage on his private Facebook page.[70]

Jerry Buell, a veteran American history teacher at Mount Dora High School, was removed from his teaching duties as school officials in Lake County investigated allegations that what he posted was biased against the gay community.

"We took the allegations seriously," said Chris Patton, a communications officer with Lake County Schools. "All teachers are bound by a code of special ethics [and] this is a code ethics violation investigation."

Patton said the school system received a complaint about something Buell had written on his Facebook page when New York legalized same-sex unions. Soon after he was temporarily suspended from the classroom and reassigned.

Patton said Buell has taught in the school system for twenty-two years and has a spotless record. The previous year he was selected as the high school's Teacher of the Year. But suddenly his job was on the line because of what some have called anti-gay and homophobic comments.

Buell told me he was stunned by the accusations. "It was my own personal comment on my own personal time on my own personal computer in my own personal house, exercising what I believed as a social studies teacher to be my First Amendment rights," he said.

The school system declined to comment on the specific Facebook messages that led to their investigation, but Buell provided me with a copy of the two Facebook messages that he said landed him in trouble. The first was posted as he was eating dinner and watching the evening news.

"I'm watching the news, eating dinner when the story about New York okaying same-sex unions came on and I almost threw up," he had written. "And now they showed two guys kissing after their announcement. If they want to call it a union, go ahead. But don't insult a man and woman's marriage by throwing it in the same cesspool of whatever. God will not be mocked. When did this sin become acceptable?"

Three minutes later Buell posted another comment: "By the way, if one doesn't like the most recently posted opinion based on biblical principles and God's laws, then go ahead and unfriend me. I'll miss you like I miss my kidney stone from 1994. And I will never accept it because God will never accept it. Romans chapter one."

According to the school system, what Buell wrote on his private account was disturbing. They were especially concerned gay students at the school might be frightened or intimidated walking into his classroom.

Patton also disputed the notion that Buell's Facebook account is private. "He has [more than] seven hundred friends," he said. "How private is that—really? Social media can be troubling if you don't respect it and know that just because you think you are in a private realm—it's not private."

Buell's attorney strongly disagreed and accused the school system of violating Buell's First Amendment rights. "The school district is being anti-straight, anti-First Amendment and anti-personal liberty," said Horatio Mihet, an attorney with Liberty Counsel. "The idea that public servants have to wholeheartedly endorse homosexual marriage is repugnant to the First Amendment of the US Constitution," Mihet said. "All [Buell] did was speak out on an issue of national importance, and because his comments did not fit a particular mold, he is now being investigated and could possibly lose his job. What have we come to?"

Buell said he does not know the individual who filed the complaint but that the entire incident caused his family "heartache." "To try and say you could lose your job over speaking about something in the venue that I did in the manner that I did is not just a knee-jerk reaction," he said. "It's a violent reaction to one person making a complaint."

But Patton said the school system has an obligation to take the comments seriously. He said Buell will not be allowed back in the classroom "until we do all the interviews and do a thorough job of looking at everything—past or previous writings."

To accomplish that, Patton said people have been sending the school system screenshots of Buell's Facebook page. "Just because you think it's private, other people are viewing it," Patton said, noting that the teacher's Facebook page also contained numerous Bible passages.

Mihet, as Buell's lawyer, was livid. "These are not fringe ideas that Mr. Buell espoused on his personal Facebook page," he said. "They are mainstream textbook opposition to homosexual unions—and now he's been deemed unfit to teach children because he opposes gay marriage? My goodness."

Buell believes the school system is trying to send a message to Christian teachers. "There is an intimidation factor if you are a Christian or if you make a statement against it [gay marriage] you are a bigot, a homophobe, you're a creep, you're intolerant," he said. "We should have the right to express our opinions and talk about things." Clayton Cloer, senior pastor of First Baptist Church of

Central Florida, said he's not terribly surprised by what happened to the school teacher. "The environment for a believer has become more restrictive and more persecuted in recent years," he said. "This is a day where religious freedom is beginning to be dramatically questioned in this country."

Cloer said he's heard a growing number of concerns about religious liberty from his congregation. "They have to be careful what they say about the name of Jesus, about the Bible, about the gospel, about moral views. Whereas the environment for those who don't share those views—they're not at all restrained or restricted from persecuting those who share those views."

The question facing the nation, Pastor Cloer said, is, "Can we really speak up and say what we believe and be free to do it without repercussions?"

The cold hard truth is you can either have gay rights or religious rights. As the stories in this chapter have proved, you can't have both. And I'm afraid Christians aren't going to like which side of the biscuit gets buttered.

Chapter 9

MACY'S KINKY
THANKSGIVING DAY PARADE

T HE TURKEY WAS on the smoker, a fresh pot of Community Coffee was percolating on the stove, and a hickory log was crackling in the fireplace. According to Google Maps, I was in Tennessee. But in my mind I was in heaven.

There's nothing quite like spending Thanksgiving in the Deep South. The day before I had bolted from my office at the Fox News Corner of the World and made a beeline to LaGuardia Airport, where I boarded the first Delta jetliner I could find heading due south of the Mason-Dixon Line.

Uncle Jerry picked me up at Memphis International Airport in his brand-new convertible. Aunt Lynn said it was one of those midlife crisis automobile purchases. "But he bought it about twenty years too late," she said.

So I piled my luggage into the back seat and sped off to cousin Clint the Firefighter's house, where I would be embedded for the next few days visiting with his lovely wife and their three boys.

And that's how it came about that I was nestled in an overstuffed easy chair with Biscuit the dog sleeping on my feet, a cat diagnosed with Attention Deficit Disorder chewing my sweater, and two little boys peppering me with questions about the origins of the universe.

I needed a distraction—and that's when I remembered the Macy's Thanksgiving Day Parade. I fumbled with the remote control and turned to NBC just as the announcers told us the cast of *Duck*

Dynasty would be waddling their way down Sixth Avenue in the Big Apple.

The eyes of the four-year-old and the six-year-old were glued to the flat screen as they searched for ducks, beards, and camouflage. Instead, they were exposed to drag queens prancing about Herald Square in bright-red stiletto boots and boxer shorts. I suspect the Starnes family wasn't the only household across the fruited plain wondering why in the name of R. H. Macy grown men were dressed like women.

Biscuit started growling at the television.

The drag queens were cast members of the hit Broadway musical *Kinky Boots*. They were decked out in all the trappings of a cross-dresser, along with thigh-high red stiletto boots, and they were performing a song from the Tony Award-winning show at the start of the parade.

The musical tells the story of a drag queen who saves a shoe business with "fun fetish footwear." It was quite the shock for American families who were expecting a more family-friendly parade.

"You've completely removed the family part of Thanksgiving," wrote one critic on the department store's website. "Absolutely disgusting."[1] "In the words of my ten-year-old, 'well, that was inappropriate,'" one mom wrote.[2]

"I'm sending Macy's an e-mail to tell them to keep their agenda out of the parade," another parent wrote. "We will no longer watch the parade and that's sad because it's been a tradition in my family for years."[3]

"There is a time and place to push an agenda and the Thanksgiving parade isn't it," one dad wrote. "This will no longer be a part of our family tradition. I shouldn't have to monitor the stinking parade. My boys are asking me, 'Are those boys?'"[4]

The *Huffington Post* said the performance was "relatively tame" and lashed out at moms and dads who objected. "Homophobia reared its ugly head," the website declared.[5] In other words, the stubble-faced men wearing girdles and lumberjack shirts doing jazz hands in the middle of Sixth Avenue aren't the problem—mommy and daddy are.

And contrary to the mainstream media's assertion that *Kinky Boots'* inclusion in the parade was just a bit of good-natured fun, many parents were doubtful. "I'm sad that our kids have to see stuff like this—none of which is done in fun," one dad wrote on my Facebook page. "It's done in all seriousness with an expectation of acceptance."[6]

And it turns out that dad was absolutely correct. Harvey Fierstein, the co-creator of the show, told the *New York Post* there was a point to the Thanksgiving Day performance. "You have to start a dialogue," he said. "And you can't have a dialogue unless someone says something first. It takes actual work to open up [people's] minds."[7]

That might explain why the folks at Macy's invited a group of young people to perform a Lady Gaga-inspired dance routine. Miss Gaga is a world-famous American singer and songwriter. She is perhaps best known for warbling a ditty about alternative lifestyles called "Born This Way." Miss Gaga also generated headlines for wearing a dress made entirely from raw meat at the MTV Video Music Awards. Uncle Jerry suggested they should've rolled her around in batter and dropped her in a deep fryer.

Macy's also invited Richard Simmons to entertain the children. That would be *the* Richard Simmons, the flamboyant exercise guru who wears candy-striped Dolfin shorts and tank tops. Anyway, Mr. Simmons was perched atop a turtle shaking and shimmying in a *Beetlejuice*-inspired costume. It wasn't exactly clear what he was doing to the turtle, but thank goodness it had a hard shell.

Poor Biscuit took one look at Richard Simmons, started yelping, and bolted from the den.

Maybe the cast of *Glee* was in charge of selecting the musical performances. Who knows? But is it really appropriate to force parents to explain to their youngsters why grown men are wearing lace undies?

Theresa Walsh Giarrusso is the author of the *Atlanta Journal-Constitution*'s "Momania: A Blog for Busy Moms." She asked readers to weigh in on how they handled the *Kinky Boots* performance. "At my house, the girls got quiet when it came on," she wrote. "I think

Rose commented about one of the 'women.' She knew 'she' looked different. And I said, 'Rose, that's a man. They're dressing as women.'"[8]

Giarrusso said the resulting discussion was good, "but it was NOT one I was expecting to have on Thanksgiving morning watching a parade," she said.[9]

Fierstein released a statement to Playbill.com praising Macy's for defending *Kinky Boots'* inclusion in the parade. "I'm so proud that the cast of *Kinky Boots* brought their message of tolerance and acceptance to America's parade," Fierstein wrote. "Ten years ago, I was humbled to ride a float dressed as Mrs. Claus, and it was the thrill of a lifetime. Congratulations to Macy's on leading the world, not only with your salesmanship, but also your humanity."[10]

Well, that's that, folks. Wearing ladies' unmentionables makes you more tolerant.

Pushing the Suggestive Limit

When you think about it, though, the 2013 Macy's parade provided about as much tolerance and diversity as the 2013 MTV Video Music Awards. I wrote to MTV after the program aired and suggested they rename the VMAs to the STDs. They never replied to my letter.

Anyway, MTV set a new low for filth and debauchery, which is a pretty spectacular feat for the network that brought us such family-friendly hits as *Buckwild* and *Jersey Shore*. The 2013 version of the awards show was a great big freak show celebrating all that is wrong with American culture—and it was filmed in my Brooklyn neighborhood.

Our local diner looked like the bar scene from *Star Wars*. The Centers for Disease Control and Prevention advised all of us locals to lock our doors and boil our water. The NYPD rolled patrol cars through the streets and warned us over a public address system that there was an 80 percent chance of a communicable-disease outbreak during the VMAs.

Most God-fearing Brooklynites (and there aren't that many)

stayed inside. Even the atheists didn't want to risk discovering there really is a hereafter.

The show was a disaster—and it was targeted directly at young American schoolchildren, just like that Macy's Thanksgiving Day Parade.

"MTV has once again succeeded in marketing sexually charged messages to young children using former child stars and condom commercials, while falsely rating this program as appropriate for kids as young as fourteen," said Dan Isett, of the Parents Television Council. "This is unacceptable."[11]

It seemed as though every other commercial during the VMAs featured a naked man and woman peddling condoms. The show itself was a cavalcade of behavior that would have made even the mayors of Sodom and Gomorrah blush.

Lady Gaga opened the program dressed in what appeared to be a nun's costume. But she quickly shed her clothing and unveiled a getup that included two strategically placed sea shells. She then paraded around the stage with a bouquet of flowers protruding from her private parts.

Miss Gaga is no lady.

But her sexcapades paled in comparison to those of Miley Cyrus, who delivered a performance that would make even street corner harlots blush. The former Disney darling tore off her clothes and danced around in nude-colored panties while doing unmentionable things with giant dancing teddy bears.

It was indeed possible that boys and girls across the nation were collectively asking their parents, "Mommy, what is Miley Cyrus doing to that teddy bear?"

The answer, dear readers, involves something called "twerking." It's a sexually provocative form of dancing that involves lots of jiggling. Comparatively speaking, twerking makes grinding look like square dancing. (And for our Baptist friends who can't tell the Harlem Shake from the Stanky Leg, just ask a Lutheran. They've got the low-down on such worldly pursuits.)

Poor, poor Miley. I'm sure her momma and daddy were so proud.

When she wasn't simulating relations with a stuffed animal, Miss Cyrus was incessantly scratching her nether-regions. I'm sure the drug store has an ample supply of creams and ointments to remedy her ailment.

Bless her heart.

The folks at the Parents Television Council were none too happy with Miley's dirty dancing. "MTV continues to sexually exploit young women by promoting acts that incorporate 'twerking' in a nude-colored bikini," Isett said. "How is this image of former child star Miley Cyrus appropriate for fourteen-year-olds? How is it appropriate for children to watch Lady Gaga strip down to a bikini in the opening act?"[12]

The Parents Television Council has a right to be offended—as do the many parents who allowed their children to watch a show that was supposed to be friendly to younger views. But it's no surprise MTV prefers to peddle what amounts to be pornography to the nation's next generation. And it's no wonder families are turning off MTV and turning on shows such as *Duck Dynasty*—a program that proves America thirsts for shows that are family-friendly.

Honestly, it's probably a good thing the *Duck Dynasty* gang was not invited to emcee the VMAs. Uncle Si would've taken one look at Lady Gaga's flower thong and grabbed a weed whacker.

My apologies for taking you on the MTV tangent—I had to check on the smoked turkey. Now, where was I? Oh, yes. The parade. Ahem.

There may very well be a time and a place for grown men to dance around in boxer shorts and stiletto heels and frilly pantaloons, but I believe most rational folks, straight and gay, will agree the Macy's Thanksgiving Day Parade is not that time.

I'm just relieved they didn't ask Miley to twerk on Sponge Bob. Perhaps that was the year's true miracle on 34th Street.

Chapter 10

THE DAY THE GAYS TRIED TO COOK *DUCK DYNASTY*'S GOOSE

UCK DYNASTY MAKES America happy, happy, happy. And that's a fact, Jack. I was a *Duck Dynasty* fan before being a *Duck Dynasty* fan was cool. And for the sake of full disclosure, I drink my sweet tea from a green Tupperware glass just as Uncle Si does.

There is something wholesome and heartwarming about the story of the Robertson family from Monroe, Louisiana. It harkens back to the days of black-and-white television, when father knew best, when afternoons were spent down at the fishing hole, and when Mary Ellen said good night to John Boy. It was a time when right and wrong were black and white.

It's no surprise to me *Duck Dynasty* became the most-watched nonfiction cable television show in history.[1] American moms and dads have been clamoring for quite some time for family-friendly television programming—and Phil and Miss Kay and Uncle Si deliver the goods.

The Robertsons showed America you can make it in show business without cursing, backstabbing people, or getting naked. Each episode was sort of like a modern-day parable, wrapped up with the family gathered around the supper table, holding hands as they say grace.

In a sentence, the Robertsons are a throwback to a time that Hollywood used to celebrate. Their story is one of faith, family, hard work, and ducks, all wrapped up in camouflage and beards. Sweet mercy, the beards. They are biblical in proportion.

One of my favorite *Duck Dynasty* stories happened in, of all places, New York City. Jase Robertson was actually kicked out of Trump International Hotel after a staff member thought he was homeless. Apparently one Trump International Hotel staff member was not accustomed to seeing a fully bearded guest wearing camouflage pants.

"I asked where the bathroom was and he said, 'Right this way, sir,'" Jase told the hosts of the television show *Live With Kelly and Michael.* "He walked me outside, pointed down the road, and said, 'Good luck.'"[2]

The hosts appeared stunned by the story, but Robertson smiled and said he took it in stride. "I think it was a facial profiling deal," he said.[3]

Ironically, it's not the first time the men of the Louisiana family have been mistaken for homeless people. "One time, we were in New York City and people put money in Willie's coffee cup," Al Robertson, Jase's brother, told me. "Dad was speaking at a church once, and one of the members showed him where the homeless shelter was."

The Robertsons said they were "absolutely not offended" by the incident at the Trump hotel and said they love staying there. "We were laughing—wait until the Donald hears about this," Al said.

And for what it's worth, they hope the staff member doesn't get in trouble. "He was just as nice as he could be, escorting Jase to the park," Al said. "And honestly, if I was in his shoes, I'd have done the same thing."

But while the nation got a chuckle out of the hotel incident, nobody was laughing last December. It was the moment *Duck Dynasty* was sacrificed on the altar of political correctness.

You know the story. The television network A&E indefinitely suspended Phil Robertson,[4] the patriarch of the *Duck Dynasty* family, for following the teachings of the Holy Bible. Nothing says tolerance and diversity by silencing the Christians and shoving them in a closet.

Between you and me, I thought *Duck Dynasty* should have indefinitely suspended A&E. Phil ran afoul of intolerant left-wing bullies after making comments about homosexuality to *GQ* magazine. I'm not quite sure why *GQ* was interested in a guy who spends his days in the Louisiana swampland. They seem to be more in tune with men who prefer body waxing and manicures.

Anyway, when the writer asked Phil what he considered to be sinful behavior, he replied, "Start with homosexual behavior and just morph out from there. Bestiality, sleeping around with this woman and that woman and that woman and those men."[5]

Then he paraphrased Paul's first letter to the Corinthians: "Don't be deceived. Neither the adulterers, the idolaters, the male prostitutes, the homosexual offenders, the greedy, the drunkards, the slanderers, the swindlers—they won't inherit the kingdom of God. Don't deceive yourself. It's not right."[6]

That comment went over about as well as a Chick-fil-A sandwich at a gay man's cocktail party. "Phil and his family claim to be Christian, but Phil's lies about an entire community fly in the face of what true Christians believe," said GLAAD representative Wilson Cruz. "He clearly knows nothing about gay people or the majority of Louisianans—and Americans—who support legal recognition for loving and committed gay and lesbian couples."[7]

Before you could shout tolerance and diversity, gay rights organizations were demanding Phil be tarred and feathered. And A&E was more than happy to oblige. "The network has placed Phil under hiatus from filming indefinitely," A&E declared. "His personal views in no way reflect those of A&E Networks, who have always been strong supporters and champions of the LGBT community."[8]

Let's not mince words. If Phil had been twerking with a duck, Hollywood would have rewarded him with an Emmy. But because he espoused beliefs held by most Christians, he was silenced.

Perhaps the militant gay right could provide the nation with a list of what they believe is politically correct speech. Maybe they could tell us what Americans can say, think, and do. Should the US

Constitution be amended to prevent Americans from holding personal beliefs others might not agree with?

Sadly, Hollywood's values are not *Duck Dynasty's* values. And that's why I'm not surprised A&E dropped the hammer on Phil. Oh, sure, they reinstated him. How could they not, given the way Phil's superfans flocked to the streets in protest of his suspension? But it's the principle of the thing.

It's not about capitalism. It's about driving an agenda and shoving it down the throats of the American public. And Hollywood is beholden to an agenda that is anti-Christian and anti-family.

In fact, it might surprise you to hear that when A&E originally approached the family about doing a reality show, Jase was one of the few members of the family who thought it wouldn't work.

"I was one of the ones who said the reality show would never work," he told me. "We were in the hunting world. I had this perception of reality shows that you had to have all this friction and fits of rage and four-letter words."

Think *Jersey Shore* and the Kardashians.

"We're pretty calm compared to that," Jase said. "We've got some crazy characters in our family, but I didn't think people would want to see that."

I suspect the elites at A&E thought the same thing. I sometimes wonder if they really thought *Duck Dynasty* would give their highbrow audience a chance to laugh at the rednecks. But the joke turned out to be on A&E.

"People just identify with our principles and values," Jase said. "We're all about faith, family, and facial hair."

Sure, the Robertsons are a little rough around the edges, but that's their culture. That's who they are. And that's why American families are flocking to their show.

"The bottom line is we are trying to do what's right," Jase said. "We don't just say we believe in God—we have active relationships with God."

But these days it's open season on Christians, and Hollywood has both barrels aimed at folks like the Robertsons and anyone else who loves God and the traditional definition of marriage. Maybe President Obama could hold a *Duck Dynasty* summit in the Rose Garden duck blind.

I'll tell you the truth: when I read the *GQ* story, I found it both entertaining and thought-provoking. For me, the most poignant moment came near the end of the story, when Phil inquired about the *GQ* reporter's plans for the afterlife.

"So you and your woman: are y'all Bible people?" he asked.

"Not really, I'm sorry to say," the reporter replied.

"If you simply put your faith in Jesus coming down in flesh, through a human being, God becoming flesh living on the earth, dying on the cross for the sins of the world, being buried, and being raised from the dead—yours and mine and everybody else's problems will be solved," Phil said. "And the next time we see you, we will say: 'You are now a brother. Our brother.' So then we look at you totally different then. See what I'm saying?"[9]

Phil Robertson was, in the words of the great hymn writer, a wretch—once lost, now found. He was a sinner saved by grace. And his life's mission is to help others find the path to that oh-so-amazing grace.

It's a message that I find compelling. It's a message Hollywood wants to silence.

Chapter 11

SO ABSURD IT COULD BE TRUE: THE GREAT INTERSPECIES MARRIAGE ACT OF 2025

(AP) THE FUTURE—A divided Supreme Court finally legalized interspecies marriage, striking down a key section of a federal law that denied veterinary benefits to humans and pets, and marking what activists are calling the greatest civil rights ruling of the twenty-first century.

"Birds of a feather should not have to flock together," Justice Anthony Kennedy wrote in the 5-4 decision. "If a cockatoo wishes to marry a squirrel, she should have that right. The United States Constitution allows for humans to betroth themselves to whatever or whoever they so desire—whether they have feet or fin."

The president hailed the ruling on *Fluffy v. Old MacDonald, State of Kansas et al* and said on Twitter the decision is "a historic step forward for species equality."

"We are a species who declared that we are all created equal—and the love we commit to one another must be equal as well," the president said.

The landmark ruling means that more than one hundred thousand human and animal couples who are legally married will be able to take advantage of tax breaks, pension rights, and other benefits that are available to other married couples.

"No legitimate purpose overcomes the purpose and effect to disparage and to injure those whom the state, by its marriage laws, sought to protect in species-hood and dignity," Kennedy wrote. "By seeking to displace this protection and treating those species as living in marriages less respected than others, the federal statue is in violation of the Fifth Amendment."

Pet stores in California, New York, and Illinois have already announced plans to begin issuing marriage licenses. The first couples to tie the knot will receive a lifelong supply of Kibbles & Bits or Meow Mix.

The case involves a cat named Fluffy who sought to have relations with a chicken on Old MacDonald's farm. Farmer MacDonald said such a relationship would violate his religious beliefs.

An attorney for Fluffy said his client was delighted with the Supreme Court ruling. "She meowed twice and began purring," the attorney said. "And then she coughed up a fur ball."

The court decision came just weeks after the president stunned the nation and announced on national television that he had finally evolved on the issue of interspecies relationships.

"I've just concluded that for me personally it is important for me to go ahead and affirm that I think interspecies couples should be able to get married," the president told Animal Planet in an exclusive interview.

The president said he made his decision during a whirlwind listening tour of the nation's animal shelters, dog pounds, and stockyards. "I think of those K-9 troops who are out there fighting on my behalf and I must say—that it should not matter who you love," the president said. "Every single American—canine, feline, or gerbil—every single American deserves to be treated equally in the eyes of the law and in the eyes of our society."

The Supreme Court ruling was met with outrage from the handful of Christians still living in the United States. "God made Adam and Eve, not Marmaduke and Steve," said the Rev. William Povich, president of the Keep Your Paws Off Religion Coalition. "Marriage is a sacred cow. Why can't we just let sleeping dogs lie?"

The White House tried to put religious groups at ease by suggesting marriage between species is not only constitutional, but also biblical.

"Don't have a cow," the White House press secretary told reporters. "Or do have a cow. That's what so great about this nation. We are free to love whoever we choose to love. Marriage is a sacred union, whether it's a man and a woman or a man and a man or a woman and a woman or a transgender and a transgender (which could technically be all of the above) or a man and a goat. God's in the mix."

The Almighty did not immediately respond to the White House statement, but in an unrelated incident, San Francisco was suddenly turned into a pillar of salt and the Vegas strip was burned to the ground during a freak lightning storm.

The move to legitimize interspecies couples had its genesis in Hollywood. Moments after the Supreme Court ruling, a gaggle of designer purse dogs held an impromptu parade on Rodeo Drive. ABC television announced a new reality competition tentatively titled *Dancing With the Pets*. And CBS announced next season's *Big Brother* cast will include a feral cat, a gerbil, and two pot-bellied pigs. "We're eager beavers," an unnamed CBS television executive said.

Proponents pointed to a long-held Tinseltown secret: many of the biggest stars of stage and screen were having covert affairs with their furry co-stars. "Timmy and Lassie, Tony the Tiger and Cap'n Crunch, Tom and Jerry were just some of those rumored to be lovers," said Basil Rathbone, author of the *New York Times* bestseller *Hollywood's Litter Box: The Inside Scoop*. "And you can't deny the chemistry between Mr. Ed and Wilbur," Rathbone said. "It was glorious—glorious!"

Bob Barker, the longtime host of *The Price Is Right*, issued a statement of support, urging animals everywhere to "have your human spayed or neutered."

But not everyone in Hollywood supports the Supreme Court decision. "I say, I say, looky here," said legendary cartoon character Foghorn Leghorn. "What's the big idea?"

"Sufferin' succotash!" added Sylvester J. Pussycat.

And Old MacDonald, the defendant in the case, expressed dismay at the erosion of traditional values. "E-I-E-I—Oh, sweet mercy," he said, predicting that the law of the land is on shaky ground. "You can lead a horse to water, but you can't make it go skinny dipping."

Marriage experts, meanwhile, are divided over the big elephant in the room: whether interspecies relationships will work. "I can't help but imagine they will fight like cats and dogs," said well-known marriage counselor Tess Robertson. "I also believe monogamy will be an issue. You know what they say—when the cat's away, the mice will play."

In a related matter, PetSmart has launched a special interspecies bridal registry. Any couple spending more than one hundred dollars will receive his and hers flea and tick collars.

Chapter 12

WHY DOES THE NFL
HATE TIM TEBOW?

T HE SCRIPPS HOWARD News Service didn't mince words. "Should Tim Tebow be so flamboyant about his faith?" read the Sunday headline.[1]

Columnist Joel Mathis spoke on behalf of the Almighty and declared that Jesus wants the then-Denver Broncos quarterback to take it down a notch. "But most of us have learned to live with boundaries—to avoid thrusting our religion into arenas where it is unexpected or unwelcome," Mathis wrote. "If you make a big sale at work, for example, you're unlikely to bend on knee in front of co-workers and customers to start giving thanks to God."[2]

That column is but one example of the way Tebow's success on the gridiron seemed to fuel his critics who believed his faith in Jesus Christ had no business on the football field. It didn't matter how many touchdown passes he threw or how many games he won; Tebow was a lightning rod for anti-Christian bigots.

It's become something of a sport to attack Christians in this nation, and at one time it seemed Tebow had become the favorite tackle target. "Why bother bringing these people into your world if you don't have to?" CBS columnist Dan Bernstein wrote. "It's not even really about Tebow, who seems to be little more than an affable simpleton. It's the creepy true-believers lapping up every last morsel of Tebow's cheap, bumper-sticker televangelism, and conflating all of it with football."[3]

And that brings us to the National Football League and the attacks on Tebow. There aren't many superstars for evangelical kids to admire, but Tebow is one of those guys. He's a Christian who "walks the walk." He's passionate about his relationship with Jesus Christ. He prays. He studies his Bible. And for that, he's been subjected to ridicule.

Stephen Tulloch, a linebacker for the Detroit Lions, personified the anti-Christian attacks when he mocked Tebow after sacking the former quarterback. As Tebow picked himself up off the grid-iron, Tulloch started "Tebowing"—a prayer on bended knee. "I told a friend of mine that I might have a couple sacks this game and if I get him, I [am] going to Tebow it," Tulloch told the *Denver Post*.[4]

There was no outrage—no editorials of condemnation. There were no calls for religious tolerance. Nothing but silence from the chattering class.

Imagine for just a moment if Tebow had been a Muslim. Imagine Tulloch sacking the quarterback and then pulling out a prayer rug and offering a mocking prayer toward Mecca. Imagine that.

But the attacks on Tebow started long before he started playing professional football. NBC Sports reported on an incident that occurred at a Scouting Combine. Tebow suggested the group pray. Another player told him to "shut the [profanity] up."[5]

Former Broncos quarterback Jake Plummer told the *Daily Mail*, "I wish he'd just shut up after a game and go hug his teammates."[6]

Particularly disappointing is the criticism levied against Tebow by his fellow Christians. "It seems Tebow might help himself and the kingdom by getting off his knees, taking the verses off of his face, and being faithful to Christ without the public acts like all the other Christians in the NFL have done for decades," wrote Anthony Bradley in *WORLD Magazine*.[7]

"Put down the boldness in regards to the words and keep living the way you're living," opined Kurt Warner.[8]

So, Warner wants Tebow to water down his boldness? How, exactly, does one do that, Mr. Warner?

In other words, Christians are supposed to keep their mouths shut in public. Maybe we should refrain from sitting at the lunch counter or sit in the back of the bus. And while we're at it, maybe we should use separate drinking fountains.

The saddest part of this episode is that Tim Tebow has been an anomaly in a professional sports industry searching for a moral compass. The industry takes great pride in putting bad boys on superstar pedestals.

At the end of the day, though, what kind of professional athlete would you want your little boy idolizing? A dog killer? A guy who beats up his girlfriend? Someone who is communicable? Or a man who loves Jesus, helps orphans, and builds hospitals for the needy?

I'll take Tim Tebow in my huddle any day.

Chapter 13

FROM THE ANNALS OF GOD-BLESSED LIVING: THE SEVEN DEADLY SINS MINUS FIVE

I'M A SOUTHERN Baptist. My people don't believe in drinking, carousing, or cussing—unless you happen to be attending a quarterly Wednesday night church business meeting.

We also have a problem with dancing and denominations that don't dunk. I'm not sure why Baptists don't dance. Grandpa Starnes once told me the ban went all the way back to biblical times, when King David did the Watusi buck naked in the streets of Jerusalem.

From that point on it was sort of an unspoken rule among my people that we would not move in a rhythmic fashion. The denomination's official bylaws were amended in 1925 through a document called "The Charleston Accord," so named after the dance craze of the period.

According to Article 72, Section 4, Subsection B of the "Baptist Faith and Message," Southern Baptists are to "refrain from gyrating one's nether-regions, knowing full well such behavior emanates from the bowels of the Lake of Fire and would not meet with the approval of your mother. Baptists in good standing shall not boogie, jitter, or jive. In the event the Holy Spirit prompts an individual to stand and/or sway, said member must take the matter before the Committee on Committees prior to a full church vote. Should the member fail to achieve two-thirds of the affirmative vote, the chairman of the deacons must immediately quench the Spirit."

During the Jesus Movement of the 1970s, many Baptist churches began performing musicals. That led to an additional amendment "allowing young people to move about in a coordinated rhythmic way, provided that neither male nor female came within eighteen inches of one another." Music ministers were required to refer to such movements as "choreography."

The embargo was still in effect when I became a seventh-grader in the early 1980s. One particular Sunday school lesson stands out in my memory. We had just finished creating religious relics out of Popsicle sticks, yarn, and glue. Our elderly teacher, a sweet, gray-haired grandmother, summoned us. We gathered around a table as she served us Hydrox cookies and cherry Kool-Aid. (On a side note, the Episcopalian kids always got Oreos, but the Baptist kids got stuck with Hydrox. I never did understand that.)

As we feasted on our delicious snack, the teacher's demeanor changed. Her lips pursed, her eyes squinted, and a scowl enveloped her face.

"The Lord is displeased with you," she said in a measured voice. "Displeased about what you did last night."

The entire class turned white as bedsheets, and the Dixie cups filled with Kool-Aid trembled in our little junior-high-school hands. We didn't have poker faces, seeing as how we were Baptists, so it was pretty clear we were about to get in trouble for something—we just weren't quite sure what it was.

My best friend, Billy Palmer, was the only one with enough courage to raise his hand and ask what sort of mortal sin we had committed.

"You have shamed your mothers," our teacher declared as she pointed a long, crooked, wrinkly finger in our direction. "You danced with the devil."

"But all we did was play Twister," Billy protested.

"Silence, heathen child!" she shouted. "A dancing foot and a praying knee don't go on the same leg."

We were told in no uncertain terms that dancing would lead to spontaneous childbirth. Apparently the only way to make amends for playing Twister was to walk the aisle during the Sunday night service and confess to the preacher we had inadvertently impregnated the entire youth group.

It was all a bit confusing, but even a thirteen-year-old Southern Baptist kid is smart enough to know you don't mess around with Satan.

Needless to say, we never played Twister again.

Of course, all that trepidation over dancing was for naught, seeing as how in 1996 Baylor University officially lifted the 151-year ban on such activity. Reporters were dispatched to Waco, Texas, to document the first dance of the Baptists—and it was quite an event.[1]

The university issued an edict forbidding pelvic gyrations and excessive closeness, but otherwise it was a gala gathering attended by some seven thousand Baptists. And history records that not a single dancer spontaneously conceived—although there were several dozen young ladies treated for various podiatry issues. And it also exposed the true reason that Baptists don't dance: we were born with two left feet.

A Dance With the Drink

Like most evangelicals, I am a teetotaler. I don't even drink grape juice past its expiration date lest I be tempted by the devil's snares. Jedediah Shubal Starnes learned that lesson the hard way. My great-great-great grandfather was a Methodist circuit-rider by day and a moonshiner by night. He wasn't that great of a preacher, but folks who lived in the Blue Ridge Mountains said he threw one heck of a communion.

I'm a bit of an odd duck in New York City, where just about everyone enjoys the fermented fruit. So I decided to concoct a cosmopolitan beverage for the refined Southern Baptist. It's called a Baptist martini. It's basically a Diet Coke with a wedge of lemon. It's quite refreshing—although after two Baptist martinis I start to feel a bit dizzy.

The fermentation line is what separates high-church Episcopalians from low-church Baptists. High church calls it Eucharist. Low church calls it the Lord's Supper.

I fondly recall those days at the small church I attended as a little boy. I was always partial to Christmas and Easter, when the deacons would break out the Welch's grape juice. During the rest of the year, we got the generic juice.

Actually, it wasn't until I was in college that I realized not all denominations used grape juice. I was dating a girl who happened to be Episcopalian. Needless to say, I was a bit surprised to discover they used real wine. I took one swig of the juice, turned to the parson, and said, "Hit me again, preacher."

And that brings me to what is perhaps one of the more scandalous episodes of my career—the day I got drunk.

It all went down at Mary Mac's Tea Room, one of my favorite Southern restaurants. It's the best place in Atlanta to get classic Southern cooking, from fried green tomatoes to country fried steak and gravy.

At Mary Mac's Tea Room they treat everybody like family. A woman I'll call Miss Labelle sees to that. She's the official ambassador of hospitality at Mary Mac's. She dishes out plenty of hugs and backrubs to the customers—and if you're real nice, she'll sneak you an extra vegetable on your meat-and-three.

The first time I dined at Mary Mac's, Miss Labelle saw I was eating alone and promptly pulled over a chair and joined me for lunch, regaling me with stories of Mary Mac's amazing history.

Over a heaping plate of country fried steak, fresh-cut corn, squash casserole, and sweet potato soufflé, Miss Labelle told me about the time a streaker showed up for lunch. He was a Georgia Tech boy (which seemed to make sense). "He acted just as normal as he could be," she recalled. "He was sitting next to these two older ladies and had all this Elvis memorabilia with him. Then he just got up and pulled everything off."

Apparently the boy wasn't all that much to look at, but one of the cooks popped out of the kitchen and brought the streaker an apron. "It only covered the front," Miss Labelle told me. "And he was just running around the dining room with that little white butt a-shining!"

It just so happened that two detectives from the Atlanta Police Department were in the tea room at the time. They interrupted their lunch long enough to dispatch the young fellow out the door and onto Ponce de Leon Avenue—much to the chagrin of the two little old ladies. They asked the police officers, "Why'd you do that? That's the best thing we've seen in years!"

Now, there's a tradition at Mary Mac's: every first-time guest gets a free bowl of pot likker and a piece of crackling corn bread. Since I'm a Baptist and don't drink, I politely declined the offer—solely on denominational grounds.

Miss Labelle was beside herself. "Let me get this straight. You've never had pot likker?"

"No ma'am," I told her, "I'm a Baptist."

It was as if I had just confessed the most grievous culinary transgression. Miss Labelle got up from the table and marched back to the kitchen. A few minutes later she returned with a piping hot bowl filled to the brim with what I could only assume was pot likker. At Mary Mac's they season it up with salt and pepper and pour it into a little bowl with a few collard greens resting on the bottom.

I looked at the simmering bowl with great trepidation.

"It's OK, honey," she said, "we're family."

My first mistake was trying to eat it like a soup.

"You ain't eating that right, honey," she said.

I'm going to stop here and confess that I am lacking in the way of the collard. But fortunately, Miss Labelle set me straight. "You've gotta take that cracklin' corn bread and plop it in the pot likker," she said. "Then you break it up and pour some hot pepper sauce in there."

I had feasted upon the pot likker, and it was good. Then, after I had slurped the last of the likker, I exclaimed to Miss Labelle that it was not only delicious, but that I felt nary a buzz from my dance with the drink.

And that's when I learned a very interesting lesson about Southern cooking.

"Darlin', pot likker is the leftover juice from a pot of collard greens," she said. "It's likker, not liquor."

Well, if that's the case, hit me again—and make it a double.

Chapter 14

NO GIDEONS ALLOWED

I WAS IN FIFTH grade when I first met the Gideons. I remember Mrs. Folk at Hope Sullivan Elementary School announcing to our class we had special visitors. The men were dressed in suits and came bearing gifts. The Gideons presented each boy and girl in my class with a Bible small enough to fit in our pockets. I carried that Bible for many years, and the verses inside weathered many storms and sustained me through my growing-up years.

That's been the mission of Gideons International for more than a hundred years—to get Bibles in our hands. And through God's grace and blessing, they've been able to share more than 1.8 billion Bibles in public schools and hotels around the world.[1] But these days the good news shared by the Gideons has become unwelcome in the United States.

The story of Walt Tutka of New Jersey illustrates the hostility many public schools have toward the Gideons. Walt was a longtime substitute teacher who was fired after he gave a student a copy of the Bible. The Phillipsburg School District fired Walt because he broke two policies: distributing religious literature on school grounds and remaining neutral when discussing religious material.[2]

Hiram Sasser of the Liberty Institute provided legal advice to Walt, and he believes the man was specifically targeted because he is a member of Gideons International. "Walt was a member of the Gideons, and they were out to get him," Sasser said. "The reason we believe he was fired is because he was a member of the Gideons. They happened to know Walt was somebody they could target."

I obtained a copy of an e-mail from Phillipsburg Middle School assistant principal John Stillo that seems to back up Sasser's claim. The e-mail indicates the school district had an issue with the well-known religious group. "It has been brought to the administration's attention that Gideons may be near our campus to distribute literature to our students," Stillo wrote in a memo to the school's staff. "Please make sure they DO NOT step foot onto our campus at anytime. There will be added police and security presence at dismissal."

It's hard to believe this kind of thing happened in the United States of America. "It's unfortunate the Phillipsburg School District chose the path of religious hostility and intolerance against a retired man serving his community and simply responding to a student's intellectual curiosity," said Sasser. "What's next—are they going to ban Shakespeare because his plays have Bible quotations?"

Joe Imhof has known Walt for years and considers him a close friend. They serve together as Gideons. He said Walt's trouble started when he was standing by a door, waiting on middle-school students to enter the building. One student trailed behind the rest. "Just remember, son," Walt told the tardy student, "the first shall be last, but the last shall be first."

A few days later the student asked about the origins of the quote. Walt told him it was in the Bible. "Over the next few weeks, the young student asked about a half-dozen times where the quote was from in the Bible," Imhof said. "Walt kept forgetting to look it up."

A few days later Walt was eating lunch in the cafeteria when the student approached and brought up the Bible verse. So Walt took out his Bible and showed the student the verse. At some point, the student mentioned he didn't have a Bible. "Walt basically said, 'Would you like mine?'" Imhof said. "The student said yes, and so Walt gave him his personal New Testament."

It's not clear who ratted out Walt, but several days later he was summoned to the principal's office. Walt, who had subbed for twenty-eight out of thirty days, was sent home and never called back.

Walt's friend, Joe, was among dozens of people who turned out to support him at a school board meeting. Joe was not one to mince words. The school board, he said, was basically telling God to "go to hell."

"Just because this guy gave a student a pocket New Testament on his lunch hour—that's enough to throw you out of school," Imhof said. "They have said tonight, 'God, we don't want you in this school.'"

"One of the Gideons in our local camp is from the Soviet Union," Imhof said. "In most countries overseas we are allowed to go into public schools and give Bibles to students. But since this is America, you can't do it here."

Sasser said the board's decision sends a clear message to Christians in New Jersey. "I am sure the school would have celebrated if the issue was a Quran or Hindu text, but this school sent the message that anything associated with the Bible, even good, old-fashioned intellectual curiosity, must be squelched at the source," Sasser said.

I believe Walt's friend Joe summed up the current state of affairs in this nation: Public schools in Russia welcome the Gideons. Public schools in the United States banish them.

Chapter 15

SUFFER NOT THE CHILDREN

CHRISTIAN YOUNG PEOPLE face a daily onslaught of rebuke and ridicule. They have been called bigots and bullies—Jesus freaks. The amount of abuse and bullying they endure at the hands of left-wing teachers and administrators is beyond outrageous. It's as if they are forcing Christian boys and girls to lock their faith in a closet—don't ask, don't tell.

"There is a lot of bullying directed at Christian kids in public schools and the culture at large," said Gary Brown, the founder of an organization called Reach America. He started the group in response to reports of religious censorship in Idaho schools.

In one instance a teacher told students to write an essay titled "I Believe." But there was one caveat: students were not allowed to write anything about God. That act of religious censorship prompted a group of Christian students to create a video highlighting the plight of Jesus followers in today's public school system.

The video features teenagers asking basic questions: Why can't I pray in school? Why do I have to check my religion at the door? Why am I called names because I believe in marriage the way God designed it?[1]

"So many teenagers are being ostracized for being a Christian," Brown told me.

The reports of religious censorship and abuse are widespread:

- A seventeen-year-old member of the National Honor Society was punished because she did community service work at a Virginia church. She was later reinstated after she filed a federal lawsuit, accusing the school district of religious discrimination.[2]

- A Wisconsin teenager who wrote an op-ed in the school newspaper opposing gay adoption was accused of bullying and disrespect. The Shawano School District went so far as to issue a public apology over what it called the "offensive article."[3]

- Students across Massachusetts were warned that they could face punishment if they refused to affirm transgender classmates. An eleven-page directive from the state's Department of Education mandated that transgender students can use the bathroom of their choice.[4] And if little girls took issue with sharing a bathroom with a transgender boy, the state said those little girls could be punished.[5] "If the girl continued to complain, she could be subjected to discipline for not affirming that student's gender identity choice," said Andrew Beckwith, an attorney with the Massachusetts Family Institute, an organization opposed to the rules.

There is a war for the heart and soul of the nation, and it's being waged in classrooms across the country. Following is a compilation of some of the most egregious examples.

"Savage" Gay Activist Bullies Christian Teens

Jake Naman knew something was about to happen. The eighteen-year-old from Redlands, California, was sitting inside a cavernous building in Seattle, waiting to hear from Dan Savage, the founder of the "It Gets Better" anti-bullying campaign.

Savage had been invited to speak to several thousand high school journalists attending a national conference hosted by the National Scholastic Press Association and the Journalism Education Association.

Naman, who was a yearbook photographer at Arrowhead Christian Academy, thought Savage was going to talk about the anti-bullying campaign. But the Christian teenager soon learned Savage had a very different message for the students.

"I hope you're all using birth control," Savage told the teenagers in attendance as he began his remarks. From there he regaled the young people with stories about his husband, describing how he looked in a Speedo. At one point Savage imagined aloud what it would be like to have his husband on stage with him, telling the kids that they would have to pry him off his partner.

Naman was growing increasingly uncomfortable with the tone and tenor of Savage's remarks. There were more lewd comments, profane words, and innuendo. And then Savage said something that made Naman take notice.

"The Bible," Savage said with an elongated pause.

Naman told me, "The very second he said, 'The Bible,' and paused, I knew it was going to get ugly. It was about to be a bashing."

And Naman was absolutely correct.

"We can learn to ignore the [profanity] in the Bible about gay people the same way we have learned to ignore the [profanity] in the Bible about shellfish, about slavery, about dinner, about farming, about menstruation, about virginity, about masturbation," Savage told the young students. "We ignore [profanity] in the Bible about all sorts of things."

Some will say what happened next took courage, but Naman said he was simply following the prompting of the Holy Spirit. And the entire moment was captured on a video that has now gone viral on YouTube.[6]

The eighteen-year-old Eagle Scout and captain of the high school track team rose to his feet and walked out, passing by hundreds of other students who were cheering the anti-bullying advocate's profanity-laced rant.

"I felt like in my heart I couldn't just stay there at all," he said. "It was a really weird feeling. I just had to get out. I didn't want to cause a scene, but I really could not stand to be in that room anymore."

Jake Naman said he felt, well, bullied.

"If Dan Savage had gotten up there and said, 'God hates homosexuals, and they're all going to hell,' there would have been huge outrage from that crowd," he said. "As Christians, we get the other side of that. When our faith is attacked like that, we are ridiculed for taking a stand against it."

Naman thought he was the only person who walked out that day, but when he got to the lobby he learned that was far from the case. Arrowhead's entire yearbook staff followed his lead—including his sixteen-year-old sister. "I was shaking," Julia Naman said. "I saw my brother pop up and leave, and I took off after him."

So did seventeen-year-old Haley Mulder. "I never felt more hurt. [I] felt persecuted," Mulder said. "For me, my faith is what I want to be defined by. For someone to say it was BS is really hurtful. I felt put down and bullied because of my faith."

And then it got worse for the Christian teenagers. Savage directly targeted them with his remarks. "You can tell the Bible guys in the hall they can come back now because I'm done beating up the Bible," he said. "It's funny as someone who's on the receiving end of beatings that are justified by the Bible how pansy-[profanity] people react when you push back."

Naman said a number of the girls began crying. He said the conference seemed like such a safe environment, "but then Dan Savage went off and it didn't seem that way anymore."

"He had a position of power as a speaker, and he was using that against a group of students who had never done anything to him," Naman said. "I would consider that bullying."

"He was completely insulting and degrading our faith," his sister said.

Mulder said Savage needs to practice what he preaches. "I felt it was ironic coming from a person who was talking about not bullying," she said.

In all, about a hundred students walked out of the speech, but Naman said many others wanted to. He said some Christian teenagers felt intimidated and were afraid of what might happen if they had left. Still, the eighteen-year-old said one thing was certainly obvious. "The majority of the students did not support us at all," he said.

Tossed Out of Class

Holly Pope said she was "absolutely stunned" when she received a telephone call from an assistant principal at Western Hills High School informing her that her son, Dakota Ary, had been sent to in-school suspension.

"Dakota is a very well-grounded fourteen-year-old," she said, noting that her son is an honors student, plays on the football team, and is active in his church youth group. "He's been in church his whole life, and he's been taught to stand up for what he believes."

And that's what got him in trouble.

Dakota was in a German class at the high school when the conversation shifted to religion and homosexuality in Germany. At some point during the conversation, he turned to a friend and said that he was a Christian and that "being a homosexual is wrong."

"It wasn't directed to anyone except my friend who was sitting behind me," Dakota said. "I guess [the teacher] heard me. He started yelling. He told me he was going to write me an infraction and send me to the office."

Dakota was sentenced to one day of in-school suspension and two days of full suspension. His mother was flabbergasted, noting that her son had a spotless record.

Officials at the high school did not return calls for comment. However, the Fort Worth Independent School District issued a statement that read, "As a matter of course, Fort Worth ISD does not comment on specific employee or student-related issues. Suffice it to say that we are following district policy in our review of the circumstances and any resolution will likewise be in accordance with district policy."

After a meeting with Pope and her attorney, the school rescinded the two-day suspension so Dakota would be allowed to play in an upcoming football game. "They've righted all the wrongs," said Matt Krause, an attorney with Liberty Counsel. "This should have no lasting effect on his academic or personal record going forward."

Pope contacted Liberty Counsel immediately after her son was punished. "I told the school that he should never have been suspended for exercising his constitutional rights," Krause said. "The principal is sincere in trying to do the right thing and hopefully they will tell the teacher, 'Do not do that anymore.' He won't be pushing his agenda."

Krause called the incident "mind blowing" and said the teacher had frequently brought homosexuality into ninth-grade classroom discussions. "There has been a history with this teacher in the class regarding homosexual topics," Krause said. "The teacher had posted a picture of two men kissing on a wall that offended some of the students."

Krause said the picture was posted on the teacher's "world wall."

"He told the students this is happening all over the world and you need to accept the fact that homosexuality is just part of our culture now," Krause said.

The school district would not comment on why a teacher was discussing homosexuality in a ninth-grade German class. "In German class there should be no talk of being pro-gay or homosexual topics," Krause said.

Dakota's mother said she believes the teacher should apologize. "He should never have been punished," Pope said of her son. "He didn't disrupt the class. He wasn't threatening. He wasn't hostile. He made a comment to his friend, and the teacher overheard it."

"My son knows people that are homosexual," she said. "He's not saying, 'I don't like you.' He's saying, 'I'm a Christian, and I believe that being that way is wrong.'"

Krause said school leaders told Dakota that in the future he should be careful when and where he talks about his opposition to homosexuality, suggesting that he talk about such matters in the hallway instead of the classroom. He said Liberty Counsel will monitor the situation to make sure there is no future retaliation. Meantime, Pope said her son would return to the teacher's classroom.

"I've told him to treat this teacher with respect," she said. "He is your elder. He is your teacher. What his beliefs are or what they are not, outside the school is none of our business."

A Glorious Moment of Righteous Defiance

Roy Costner, a senior at Liberty High School in Pickens, South Carolina, received national attention when he ripped up his pre-approved graduation speech and instead led the crowd in a recitation of the Lord's Prayer.

It was a glorious moment of righteous defiance.

"I think most of you will understand when I say, 'Our Father, who art in heaven,'" he said as the crowd began to cheer.[7]

He concluded his remarks by pointing to the sky and saying, "For thine is the kingdom, the power and the glory, forever and ever. Amen."

The school district had been in a battle over public prayers after the Freedom From Religion Foundation (FFRF) filed a complaint objecting to what it called an "unconstitutional prayer practice."[8]

The FFRF held the school district responsible for Costner's open act of defiance and what it called a string of problematic religious violations. "The valedictorian who so insensitively inflicted Christian prayer on a captive audience at a secular graduation ceremony is a product of a school district which itself set an unconstitutional example by hosting school board prayer," FFRF co-president Annie Laurie Gaylor said in a prepared statement.[9]

Costner told me he has absolutely no regrets. "I'm happy with what I did," he said. "I want this to glorify God. I want to use this as a witnessing tool, and I hope others will stand up for God in our nation."

Costner got the idea to deliver the prayer when he learned he had been selected as the top academic student in the graduating class. He was summoned to the principal's office. "She [the principal] informed us that we could not have anything about religion or talk about God or Allah or whoever we choose to worship," he said. "And they had to approve the speech prior to me going onto stage."

The prayer controversy had gripped the small South Carolina community for quite some time—and many locals took issue with a group from Wisconsin causing problems. "Our community is very passionate about prayer in our schools," Costner said. "I began writing the speech, and I knew from the start that I was going to include prayer."

He talked it over with his father, the youth pastor at Fellowship Community Church. And he also sought the counsel of other pastors in the area. "They wanted me to make sure I was doing it for God and not myself," he said.

So Costner spent the next few days in deep prayer and Bible study. "I asked God exactly what He wanted me to do," Costner explained. "I was trying to think of a prayer that would suit all denominations. That's why I went with the Lord's Prayer."

And on graduation day a very nervous Costner took his place at the ceremony with a serious case of the jitters. "I was extremely nervous," he said. "I didn't know what kind of reaction I was going to get. I didn't know which way it was going to go."

And there was another problem. Costner's speech had already been placed in a binder on the platform. He would not be able to bring a copy of his replacement speech on stage.

What happened will be remembered in Pickens for quite some time—the day an eighteen-year-old boy defied a group of atheists, agnostics, and freethinkers.

"I was always taught to stand for what I believe in," he said. "That's what I believe in. I was thanking my God before everyone. I wanted to give Him a shout-out."

As for his critics, Costner quoted a passage of Scripture from the Gospel of Matthew. "If you deny me among men, I will deny you to the Father," he said.

He also had a special message to give the Freedom From Religion Foundation. "We are not in a country where we have freedom *from* religion," he said. "We have freedom *of* religion."

Take Off That Cross!

A Sonoma State University student was ordered to remove a cross necklace by a supervisor who thought other students might find it offensive, in a case that prompted even one campus official to speculate that "political correctness got out of hand."

Audrey Jarvis, 19, a liberal arts major at the northern California university, said she had no choice but to seek a "religious accommodation" in order to wear the cross. Her lawyer said she deserves an apology, and the school ultimately obliged, but the bigger problem remains.[10]

"It's amazing in this day of diversity and tolerance on university campuses that a university official would engage in this type of obvious religious discrimination," said Hiram Sasser, an attorney with Liberty Institute, which represented Jarvis.

Jarvis was working for the university's Associated Students Productions (ASP) at a student orientation fair for incoming freshmen when her supervisor told her to remove the two-inch-long cross necklace, according to Sasser.

Sasser said the supervisor told her that the chancellor had a policy against wearing religious items and further explained "that she could not wear her cross necklace because it might offend others, it might make incoming students feel unwelcome, or it might cause incoming students to feel that ASP was not an organization they should join."

"My initial reaction was one of complete shock," Jarvis said. "I was thrown for a loop."

Jarvis is a devout Catholic, and she wears the cross as a symbol of her faith in Christ. "I was offended because I believe as a Christian woman it is my prerogative to display my faith any way I like so long as it is not harming anyone else," she said. "I was very hurt and felt as if the university's mission statement—which includes tolerance and inclusivity to all—was violated."

On a second encounter Jarvis's supervisor told her she should hide the cross under her shirt or remove it. At that point Jarvis became so upset she left her student worker job early.

Sasser said the university should apologize for their actions. "It's unfortunate there are university officials out there who think that it's OK to tell Christians to hide their faith but would cringe if somebody said the same thing about hiding someone's pride in whatever political or cultural affiliation they may have," he said.

The law, he said, is clear on the matter: "State employees may wear crosses while they are performing their duties as long as the wearing does not interfere with the employees' duties or harm the employer's business interests."

Audrey's mother, Debbie, was devastated when she heard what happened to her daughter. "She's a strong Christian, a faith-filled young woman who spent her summers at Catholic camp," Jarvis said. "She's just full of the Lord.... She doesn't wear the cross as a fashion statement. It's a statement of her faith."

As she tried to console her daughter, Debbie reminded her, "We are still one nation under God."

Audrey replied, "Mom, it doesn't feel like that here."

Debbie told me, "Our faith was attacked. It's unnerving. I know what's going on in this country. I know Christianity is being attacked. Now, I know it firsthand and it sickens me and saddens me....We need to band together as Christians and fight back."

Flagged for Praying

It's been a season-long tradition for Nicholas Fant to drop to one knee and offer a two-second prayer before his wrestling matches. But that two-second prayer got the Wake Forest-Rolesville High School student in trouble.

Fant was about to compete in the 220-pound class in the first round of the North Carolina playoffs. He jogged to the center of the mat, took a knee, prayed, and was then cited by the referee.

The referee hit Fant with a stalling warning for delaying the match—a charge that cost the high school wrestler a point. The junior wrestler eventually lost the match.

Sam Hershey, the high school's wrestling coach, was not happy with the call—and neither were fans. But the athletic association commissioner, David Whitfield, said the referee made the right call.

"When the referee called them to the center of the mat—at that point it's time to wrestle," he said. "By rule, the official was well within his rights to issue a stall warning."

Whitfield said the warning had nothing to do with religion. "It had nothing to do with prayer or anything related to a faith-based scenario," he said. "It had everything to do with the rules of wrestling."

But Whitfield conceded referees do have some leeway when making these kinds of calls. "You have discretion in all rules as it relates to wrestling," he said. "But in this case, one of the wrestlers was in the circle waiting."

Not all wrestling officials agreed with the call—including David Culbreth of the Southeastern Wrestling Officials Association. "David Culbreth believes in God, and on my mat, God gets two seconds," he said, apologizing for speaking in third-person.

Culbreth said he would have given the teenager time to pray. "I'm not going to call that," he said. "But if it turned into a sixty-second prayer, he'd probably get a verbal warning—or I might try to say 'Amen' for him."

The First-Grader and the Almighty

A North Carolina community is embroiled in controversy after a school ordered a six-year-old girl to remove the word *God* from a poem she was supposed to read during a Veteran's Day ceremony.

The girl was a first-grader at West Marion Elementary School. She was supposed to read the poem during a school assembly marking Veteran's Day. The poem honored her two grandfathers, who had served during the Vietnam War. "He prayed to God for peace, he prayed to God for strength," the poem read.

A parent reportedly found out about the poem and expressed concern about mentioning the word *God* during a school event. The parent did not want the Almighty's name mentioned anywhere in the program, according to one account. "We wanted to make sure we were upholding the school district's responsibility of separation of church and state from the Establishment Clause," Superintendent Gerri Martin told the *McDowell News*.[11]

Martin told the newspaper she made the decision in consultation with the school's principal, Desarae Kirkpatrick, and vice principal, Nakia Carson.

"We jointly decided that we must err on the side of caution to prevent crossing the line on the Establishment Clause of the Constitution," Kirkpatrick said. "As a principal of a public school, I must put aside my personal religious beliefs and follow the law, which upholds that we have freedom of speech and freedom of religion but that we, as public schools, cannot endorse one single religion over another."[12]

Chris Greene, who happens to be employed by the school district, spoke to board members earlier about the situation. "My question is this: When do the rights of one outweigh the rights of another?" he asked in remarks covered by the local newspaper. "I believe that this little girl's rights were violated and that those who worked so hard to prepare this program should receive an apology."[13]

As one pastor told me, "I don't think there's anywhere in the country where you can hide from these issues with the culture changing so quickly."

Fighting Back

Hundreds of Christians in a small Oklahoma town decided to draw a line in the sand and fight back against a national association of atheists and agnostics that want displays of the Ten Commandments removed from local schools.

"It's Christianity under attack within our own country," said Josh

Moore, pastor of First Baptist Church of Muldrow, Oklahoma. "The irony can't be missed by anyone who's lived in this country or grown up in this country."

The controversy surrounds the Ten Commandment plaques that are posted in a number of classrooms at Muldrow High School. It's unclear when the plaques were installed.

Ron Flanagan, superintendent of the local school district, said they had received a complaint about the Ten Commandments from the Freedom From Religion Foundation (FFRF), an organization that has a long history of targeting displays of the Christian faith in public schools.

The complaint was allegedly filed by an anonymous member of the community. "If the facts are as presented to us, and the Ten Commandments are on display throughout Muldrow Public Schools, the displays must be removed immediately," wrote FFRF attorney Patrick Elliott in a letter to the school district.

The FFRF said the displays are a "flagrant violation of the Establishment Clause of the First Amendment."

"Any student will view a Ten Commandments display in school as being endorsed by the school," Elliott wrote. "Muldrow Public Schools promotion of the Judeo-Christian Bible and religion over non-religion impermissibly turns any non-Christian or non-believing student, parent or staff member into an outsider."

But hundreds of students decided to stand up and defend the plaques by launching petitions and raising awareness on social networking sites. And lots of folks around town are wondering why a Wisconsin-based organization is concerned about the affairs of Muldrow, Oklahoma.

"It's a pretty big deal," student Chase Howard told television station KHOG. "One person kind of put it out there on Twitter. A couple of us hashtagged it and asked people to get it trending. After that it just caught on."[14]

Eighteen-year-old Benjamin Hill is one of the students who signed the petition. He said he understands why non-Christians might be upset over the display, but he said students should have the right to express their faith. "I'd really like it if they would leave the Ten Commandments up," he said. "I think they should allow the expression of religion in school."

Pastor Moore said that the local interfaith ministerial association printed a thousand T-shirts emblazoned with the Ten Commandments—and many students planned to wear the shirts to class. "It's not to protest or to be ugly," Moore said. "Legally, they do have First Amendment rights. They can voice what they believe in. We are encouraging them to do that in a way that is respectful of others."

Parent Denise Armer told KHOG she supports the students' efforts to save the Ten Commandment plaques. "If other kids don't want to read the Ten Commandments, then they don't have to," she said. "But that doesn't mean that they have to make everyone else do what they want."[15]

Pastor Moore said it's not surprising the Christian faith is coming under such a fierce attack. "It's promised in Scripture," he said. "As believers and followers, it's a matter of recognizing that and responding in an appropriate manner."

It's one thing for the atheists and secularists to attack grownups, but it really takes a dark kind of evil to go after Christian boys and girls. Jesus once admonished His disciples for rebuking a group of children who sought his attention. "Let the children alone," Jesus told them. "Do not hinder them from coming to Me" (Matt. 19:14, NAS).

I can only imagine what Jesus would tell the likes of Dan Savage and the other Christ-haters—but I think they might want to invest in some fire-retardant underwear and maybe a portable air conditioner.

Chapter 16

SO ABSURD IT COULD BE TRUE: THE HAPPY VALLEY CHURCH OF HARMONIOUS HYPOCRISY

CHURCHES ACROSS THE fruited plain are struggling with how to attract younger Americans into houses of worship. The millennial generation is just not content with robed choirs, organs, and Wednesday fellowship meals. They're searching for something different. The problem facing pastors is trying to define "something different."

I figured the person best able to answer that question was my good pal Harley Buck Twitty, a church-growth specialist based in Nashville. Harley was one of the early pioneers in church growth. He devised a theorem to count souls that is still used by many Southern Baptist deacons and Sunday school superintendents today.

The theorem is $S = a(5) + c$. You count the number of individuals actually sitting in the pews, multiply that number by five, and then add the choir. Any alto or bass weighing more than three hundred fifty pounds must be counted twice. Harley's discovery garnered him praise among Baptist preachers, and he was also awarded an honorary degree from Beaver Lick A&M.

"Harley, are there any churches out there doing some cutting-edge ministry to reach the next generation?" I asked.

"Todd, get yourself on one of those jet planes and get yourself down to Nashvegas," he hollered into the phone. "I know just the place."

The following day I was riding shotgun in Harley's AMC Pacer as we puttered along Interstate 40. Just past the town of Bucksnort is the bedroom community of Laodicia—a breeding ground for Southern hipsters.

"There used to be a tiny church out here called the Happy Valley Baptist Church," Harley said, "but they brought in a new preacher, fired the choir, and changed the name of the church. Now, they're known as the Happy Valley Church of Harmonious Hypocrisy—and brother, they're the biggest church in the state of Tennessee."

"Sweet mercy," I said. "That's pretty impressive."

"Yessir, but they do church a bit different," Harley said. "I ain't gonna lie to ya. The folks down at Happy Valley are a peculiar people."

Harley had piqued my curiosity.

"This here church is what they call hipster," he continued. "They minister exclusively to hipsters—and nobody else."

As we pulled into a massive parking lot filled with Mini Coopers and Priuses, I noticed a long line of well-dressed young people waiting to get inside the building. I felt the slight thumping of a bass line as Harley turned off the ignition.

"This church isn't for everyone," he said. "They really don't like to make folks feel uncomfortable."

Then Harley turned and tossed me a garment bag. Inside was a pair of skinny jeans, a flannel shirt, and a knit cap.

"You'll need to change your clothes," he said. "They don't allow anyone with suits or ties inside the church. And you'll also need to ditch the Bible. They don't allow those either."

"Why not?" I protested.

"It's all about making people feel comfortable," he said. "And by the way, you're going to need a fake ID. They don't allow anyone over thirty-five into the church. They've got bouncers, brother. You can thank me later, but I've got a friend over in Bucksnort who specializes in this kind of work."

Harley handed me the fake ID, and I took one look at it before bursting out in laughter.

"Zac Efron? Do you honestly think these bouncers are going to think I'm Zac Efron?" I asked.

"You're Zac Efron, and I'm one of the Jonas Brothers," he said. "This is going to be like sneaking across the border from Mexico. You'll need to sing something from *High School Musical* to distract them. Got it?"

By a sheer miracle of the Lord, the bouncers allowed us to enter the church, where we were promptly greeted by the head hostess, Miss Jolene Janelle Jones.

"Hey y'all," she crowed. "Welcome to the Happy Valley Church of Harmonious Hypocrisy! I'm Jolene, and I'm just happy, happy, happy! Here at Happy Valley, we love to tell folks it doesn't matter how you feel inside—just fake it when you're in church!"

Think Southern high-school cheerleader hopped up on Red Bull.

Miss Jolene gave us a tour of the sprawling multilevel lobby, where worshippers were lined up to get their late-night fix at the Immaculate Consumption Coffee Shop.

"Try the Laodicea Latte," Miss Jolene told us. "It's not too hot, not too cold."

Happy Valley even has something for the more health-conscious parishioner—a juice bar appropriately named "King of the Juice."

Miss Jolene then escorted us from the lobby to the vast worship center, where the pre-show entertainment had already started. But as soon as Miss Jolene opened the worship center doors, we were met by a tremendous odor. My eyes began to water and my nostrils flared.

"Sweet mercy," I declared. "Why does your worship center smell like...that?"

"Pungent, is it not?" she replied. "Every ten minutes, our worship staff pipes in Old Spice through the church's environmental systems."

Jolene thrust her hands into the air and inhaled a large gulp of air.

"Doesn't it smell just like heaven?" she asked.

If your idea of heaven is a sixteen-year-old preppy drenched in cologne, wearing overpriced skinny jeans and extra-small T-shirts—then yes, I suppose it does smell just like heaven.

A pair of scantily clad hostesses with flowing manes of television evangelist hair escorted us to our seats in a VIP section of the worship center.

"Back in the old days, the 1990s, a relationship with God was about how you looked on the inside," Miss Jolene told us as we walked. "But let's be real. Today's postmodern Christian worships with their eyes. So we focus on how the worshipper looks on the outside."

"How does that work in a practical way?" I inquired.

"For example, instead of ushers we have hostesses," she said. "The girls must have at least some professional dance and cheerleading experience or at least a degree in cosmetology. Each of our worship girls must provide us with an eight-by-ten glossy headshot and undergo weekly weigh-ins."

I was astounded. "It's really that big of a deal that they look right?"

"Oh, yes," Jolene said. "Just a few weeks ago, we had to let a former Dallas Cowboys cheerleader go because she went on a Krispy Kreme binge. She scarfed down three boxes of original glazed and two chocolate éclairs before we could get her to detox. So sad."

Miss Jolene tensed, grabbed me by the hand, and looked directly into my eyes.

"Looks matter," she said. "Everybody loves Jesus, but nobody loves a fatty."

Our conversation was interrupted by a young lady carrying two menus and a round serving tray.

"Good afternoon, gentlemen," the young woman said with a pearly white smile. "Two for communion?"

I was a bit confused until I realized the church was celebrating the Lord's Supper. So I smiled and nodded my head.

"We have a special this evening," she said. "You can either have classic communion or our new high-energy alternative."

"What's the difference?" I asked.

"One is a stale piece of unleavened bread and a cup of generic grape juice," she replied. "The other is a fresh kale chip and a shot of wheatgrass."

Before I could order, the pulsating electronic dance music stopped and the auditorium went dark. The show was about to start.

"Now, I probably shouldn't say anything, but our house band may not exactly be up to our normally high standards," Miss Jolene whispered to us.

"Why's that?"

"Well, a few weeks ago we had to fire our worship pastor," she said in a hushed voice. "We caught him with some very inappropriate books."

"Oh jeez," I said. "Girly magazines?"

"Worse," she said. "We caught him with a copy of the...oh, I can't say it. I just can't say it."

"Go on," I urged her. "I won't say anything."

Miss Jolene composed herself.

"It was the 2010 Baptist hymnal. It was a hardback edition," she said, holding back tears. "Dirk had such promise when we hired him from Urban Outfitters. He was so impeccably dressed."

She said the church had taken out a Craigslist advertisement hoping to find a new worship leader. "We're looking for someone who is both hipster and holey," she said.

"Well, that's a good thing," I offered. "At least you're looking for someone with depth, someone who is leading a holy life. I suspect you're looking for someone with at least several years of seminary training?"

"Oh goodness, no," she said. "I think you misunderstood me. We're looking for someone with holey jeans. People call them destroyed jeans. And, of course, it's also important they have adequate facial stubble, a knit cap, and a sense of irony."

"LADIES AND GENTLEMEN," the announcer thundered, "LET'S GET READY TO WORSHIP!"

Suddenly the auditorium sprang to life. Strobe lights flashed, music pulsed, and smoke rose from the stage. A team of professionally trained worshippers rappelled from the rafters and began jumping over pews.

It was sort of like Bill Gaither meets Circus de Soleil—without the spandex.

Then the entire room was on their feet, dancing, raising their hands, and hollering as fireworks exploded and confetti rained down from on high. A giant sign was unfurled across the length of the stage reading "HOLY C.O.W." It stood for "Celebrating Outrageous Worship."

The worship music was really good. I was quite impressed with the electric guitar riff during "Holy, Holy, Holy," although I felt like the guitarist might have overdone it when he smashed his guitar on the pipe organ.

Then, after about ten minutes of singing, the lights once again dimmed.

"And now, Happy Valley family, it's time for couples worship," the band leader announced. "Couples worship only. You can sing this next song to God or your girlfriend."

It was a bit unusual, honestly—a bit like the television commercial for the Christian dating website where they're singing the worship song "I Want to Fall in Love With You." In their defense, though, I suppose you really could sing that song to either the Almighty or your significant other.

The pastor was a middle-aged man wearing a loud floral shirt, khaki cutoffs, and sandals. He told the congregation to take out their iPhones so they could follow along with his sermon, which was aptly titled "Is Jesus the Hashtag of Your Timelines?" After the ten-minute sermon, there was a cyberspace altar call.

"We really take pride in our state-of-the-art worship center," Miss Jolene said to me as everyone reached for the iPad installed on the pew in front of them. "We discovered that people were insecure about walking the aisle. So we installed touchscreen iPads on every seat. We call them ePads. The *e* stands for *eternity*."

"How do you handle baptisms?" I asked.

"We just tell our new converts to wait until they feel comfortable and then we'll dunk 'em," she said. "Our studies bear out the validity of that argument. We haven't had a baptism in almost ten years. So we turned the baptistry into a Jacuzzi for singles worship night."

After the service, as we wandered the hallways, Miss Jolene told us that one of the key decisions the church made was to end Sunday school. Instead, Happy Valley offers a wide variety of personal enrichment courses.

"For example, our EE class is uber popular," she said.

"Sweet! You guys teach Evangelism Explosion?"

"No—Emitting Emotion," she said. "It's an entry-level class in our Worship 101 series. We teach the fundamentals of worship, from clapping on the down beat to raising your hands. Then we have an advanced class that teaches the proper open-face-palm-at-waist-level technique."

Who knew worship could be so mechanical?

Miss Jolene ran down a litany of other unusual ministries offered by the church, including Keggers for Christ, Tanning for Jesus, and a new aerobics class called Priesthood of the Pilates.

"We used to have a mens group called the Brotherhood," she said. "They would do yard work for widows and repair cars for single moms. Unfortunately, their numbers dwindled. So they decided to rename the group 'The Bros.' Every fifth Sunday, they get together for manis, pedis, and facials."

I noticed, just like Harley said, that I hadn't seen anyone over the age of thirty-five in the church. "Where are all the senior saints?" I asked.

"Oh, we make the elderly enter through the back door of the old chapel," Miss Jolene said. "We really do cherish our white-haired angels, especially since most of our younger members don't have any money."

Then Jolene stopped and looked at me. "My goodness, Mr. Efron, you must be exhausted! Would you like something from King of the Juice? How about a Laodicea Latte?"

"Just a glass of water will be fine," I replied, as I sat down to collect my thoughts. It certainly seemed that in their quest to become culturally relevant, this church—and likely many of our nation's churches—had become spiritually irrelevant.

As I sipped the water Jolene brought me, I was reminded of something the Reverend Anthony George said during a message at First

Baptist Church in Atlanta. "The church is here to preach the cross of Jesus Christ," he declared.

Sadly, the postmodern church seems more interested in hosting a good cocktail party and worship hour.

"I can't tell you how excited we are to have you visit with us, Mr. Efron," Miss Jolene said. "Should you decide to join our fellowship, we have a number of economical worship plans for you to choose from. I trust your water was satisfactory?"

"To be honest," I replied, "it was a bit lukewarm."

Chapter 17

A CLEAR AND PRESENT DANGER

CHRISTIAN CLEANSING OF the military is under way.

That's the assessment of Lieutenant General Jerry Boykin (Retired), an American hero. He's also a vice president of the Family Research Council and an outspoken defender of the faith. "I don't think you can categorize it any other way," he said. "There is a strong effort, led partially by the administration as well as by atheist groups, to destroy the identity of who we are as a nation—and that means robbing us of our history."

There's no disputing that Christian chaplains and military personnel have been marginalized over the past five years. Chaplains are punished for praying in the name of Jesus;[1] crosses have been removed from chapels;[2] military personnel opposed to gay marriage have been rebuked and reprimanded. President Obama has turned the military into a social engineering petri dish, and the Pentagon has become a battleground in the culture war.

In recent years Christian prayers were banned at the funeral services for veterans at Houston's National Cemetery[3]; evangelical leaders such as Franklin Graham, Tony Perkins, and Lieutenant General Boykin were banned from speaking at military events[4]; Catholic chaplains were told not to read a letter to parishioners from their archbishop related to Obamacare[5]; and a war-games scenario in Fort Leavenworth identified Christian groups and evangelicals as potential threats.[6] A group of Army officers was advised to monitor soldiers who belong to what were considered to be anti-gay, anti-Muslim, and anti-immigration organizations, according to a military e-mail. The e-mail was sent by a lieutenant colonel at Fort Campbell in Kentucky to three dozen subordinates, warning them to be on the lookout for any soldiers who might be members of "domestic hate groups." Among the groups the Army listed are well-respected organizations such as the Family Research Council, American Family Association, Atlas Shrugs, and the Federation for American Immigration Reform. The Army listed the groups alongside actual extremist and hate groups such as the Neo-Nazis, the Ku Klux Klan, and other supremacist groups.

"When we see behaviors that are inconsistent with Army values— don't just walk by—do the right thing and address the concern before it becomes a problem," the e-mail advised. "We need to make sure that we maintain our standards—starting with reception and integration."

Perkins said he was stunned by the contents of the e-mail. "It's very disturbing to see where the Obama administration is taking the military and using it as a laboratory for social experimentation and also as an instrument to fundamentally change the culture," he said. "The message is very clear: if you are a Christian who believes in the Bible, who believes in transcendent truth, there is no place for you in the military."

Perkins is not paranoid. He's absolutely correct.

A 2011 US Army College paper written by Colonel Barbara Sherer is a stunning lesson in anti-Christian bias. The paper is titled "Chaplaincy at a Crossroads: Fundamentalist Chaplains in a Pluralistic Army." I should point out the contents of the research paper did not represent the views of the military when it was written—yet.

First, Sherer provided her readers with a working definition of fundamentalism. "A 'fundamentalist' is one who believes the Bible is the inerrant authority on faith and life, salvation is achieved only through faith in Jesus Christ, and he or she has a personal responsibility to share this belief with non-Christians," she wrote.[7] In other words, people like Billy Graham, Sarah Palin, Charles Stanley, and Tim Tebow would be considered fundamentalists under her definition.

Sherer's paper concludes that people like that would be incompatible with military service. "I conclude that in some, but not all cases, fundamentalist views are incompatible with service," she wrote. "A fundamentalist Christian holds very strong beliefs, but like every other American retains the right to the free exercise of those believes. However, certain tenets of fundamentalism, when taken to extreme, are incompatible with other soldiers' rights to free exercise and therefore inappropriate for chaplains. It is not the beliefs themselves which are incompatible with chaplain service, but the practice."[8]

So Billy Graham, America's pastor, would not qualify to be a chaplain in President Obama's progressive military.

Sherer's revelations were made all the more shocking, considering she is the United States Military Academy chaplain.

A Willingness to Cross the Line

You don't have to convince Coast Guard Rear Admiral William Lee that there's a war on Christianity within the military. "This is not a Christian issue," Rear Admiral William Lee told a gathering of Christians in Washington DC. "It is not a Jewish issue or a Muslim issue or a Hindu issue. This is an American issue."[9]

Lee said that religious liberty within the military is being threatened by lawyers and that service members are being told to hide their faith in Christ.

"As one general so aptly put it, they expect us to check our religion in at the door—don't bring that here," Lee said. "Leaders like myself are feeling the constraints of rules and regulations and guidance issued by lawyers that put us in a tighter and tighter box regarding our constitutional right to express our religious faith."

The crowd cheered for nearly a minute when Lee vowed to defy any attempt to curtail religious liberty within the armed forces. "Your armed forces, the sons and daughters of the men and women like you, are being told to hide that light under a basket," Lee said. "I am coming out today to tell you I am not going to run from my religious beliefs, from my right under the Constitution to tell a young man there is hope."

Lee told the audience he had set aside his prepared remarks and instead chose to speak from the heart about the challenges facing Christian service members. "The problem that men and women like me face in uniform who are in senior leadership positions is that the higher you are, the more vulnerable you are to being taken down," he said. "You get in the cross hairs of those people who lay in wait outside the gate, waiting to take us to task for expressing our faith."

Lee told the audience he was not talking about proselytizing. "I am vehemently against that," he said. "I'm talking about gently whispering the gospel."

Lee illustrated his argument that faith is being threatened by telling the story of a young service member who tried to commit suicide but survived. "When I looked at that young man and heard his story, the rules say, 'Send him to the chaplain,'" Lee told the audience. "My heart said, 'Give this man a Bible.'"

Lee said such an act would be a violation of policy. He marveled that he could be reprimanded for "as much as whispering to a young man who is on his last hope that there is hope. That I can just simply whisper, 'Here is the answer; take it home; I'll talk about it if you want to.'"

"The lawyers tell me that if I do that, I'm crossing the line," he said. "I'm so glad I've crossed that line so many times."

Lee said they've been told to "leave that to the chaplains."

"I'm here to tell you there's not enough chaplains to go around," he said.

Boykin said Lee provided evidence of the restrictive rules in place for those who serve. "For those who remain skeptical about the extent of religious hostility in the uniformed services, they should listen to Admiral Lee," he said. "The Admiral's courage in speaking out about the pervasiveness of religious hostility in the military demonstrates that he understands that he is ultimately accountable not to the Pentagon or the Department of Homeland Security but to God."

The Objection of an Administration

Representative John Fleming, the Republican congressman from Louisiana, was so troubled by the attacks on Christianity in the military that he proposed an amendment to the National Defense Authorization Act. It would have required the armed forces to "accommodate the beliefs of a member of the armed forces, reflecting the conscience, moral, principles, or religious beliefs of the member."[10]

But the Obama administration "strongly [objected]" to the proposed amendment to the National Defense Authorization Act that would have protected the religious rights of soldiers, including evangelical Christian service members who are facing growing hostility toward their religion. The administration said the amendment would have a "significant adverse effect on good order, discipline, morale and mission accomplishment."[11]

If nothing else, the Obama administration's reaction to the amendment tipped their hand and forced them to admit what many of us already knew: they are at war with Christians in the armed forces. The president had a chance to protect the religious rights of soldiers, but he declined to do so.

"With its statement, the White House is now endorsing military reprimands of members who keep a Bible on their desk or express a religious belief," Fleming told me. "This administration is aggressively hostile towards religious beliefs that it deems to be politically incorrect."

Tony Perkins called the Obama administration's edict a "chilling suppression of religious freedom."

"The Obama administration has joined forces with those who are attacking the religious freedoms of those who serve in our armed services," Perkins said. "The administration's opposition to Representative Fleming's religious freedom amendment reveals that this administration has gone beyond accommodating the anti-Christian activists who want to remove any vestige of Christianity from the military, to aiding them by blocking this bipartisan measure."

Christians Listed as Examples of Extremism

A US Army training instructor listed evangelical Christianity and Catholicism as examples of religious extremism along with Al Qaeda and Hamas during a briefing with an Army Reserve unit based in Pennsylvania.

The incident occurred during an Army Reserve Equal Opportunity training brief on extremism. Topping the list of extremist groups was evangelical Christianity. Other organizations listed included Catholicism, Al Qaeda, Hamas, the Ku Klux Klan, Sunni Muslims, and Nation of Islam. The military also listed "Islamophobia" as a form of religious extremism.

"We find this offensive to have evangelical Christians and the Catholic Church to be listed among known terrorist groups," said Ron Crews, executive director of the Chaplain Alliance for Religious Liberty. "It is dishonorable for any US military entity to allow this type of wrongheaded characterization."

Army spokesman George Wright said this was an "isolated incident not condoned by the Department of the Army."

"This slide was not produced by the Army and certainly does not reflect our policy or doctrine," he said. "It was produced by an individual without anyone in the chain of command's knowledge or permission."

Wright said after the complaint was lodged, the presenter deleted the slide and apologized. "We consider the matter closed," he said.

The incident was made public by a soldier who attended the briefing. He asked for copies of the presentation and sent them to the Chaplain Alliance. "He considers himself an evangelical Christian and did not appreciate being classified with terrorists," Crews said. "There was a pervasive attitude in the presentation that anything associated with religion is an extremist."

Crews said he is extremely disappointed in the military's handling of the incident and said they need to fix the "gross distortions presented in the briefing."

"Those soldiers who were presented this material—they need to have a new briefing with corrected materials," Crews said. "They need to undo the damage that was done."

Crews also wants the military to consult with chaplains about matters involving religion. "All religious issues of this sort in the US military should be channeled first through the Chiefs of Chaplains offices for review," he said. "Do they really want to classify evangelicals and the Catholic Church as extremist groups?"

Bible Verses Scraped off Army Weapons

The US Army directed troops to remove a Bible inscription that a vendor etched into the serial numbers of weapon scopes. Soldiers at Fort Wainwright in Alaska said they received a directive to turn in their scopes so the Bible references could be removed.

The scopes were made by Trijicon and referenced New Testament passages in John 8:12 and 2 Corinthians 4:6. The verses appeared at the end of the scope serial numbers, reading *JN8:12* and *2COR4:6*.

"The biblical verse (JN8:12) must be removed utilizing a Dremel type tool and then painted black," read instructions on how to remedy the matter.

After the letters and numbers were scraped off, soldiers were directed to apply black paint to ensure the verses were totally covered. "The vendor etched those inscriptions on scopes without the Army's approval," Army spokesman Matthew Bourke said in a written statement. "Consequently, the modified scopes did not meet the requirement under which the contract was executed."

Bourke said the vendor agreed to remove all Bible references on future deliveries. "Some of these scopes had already been fielded," Bourke explained. "Corrective measures were taken to remove inscriptions during the RESET/PRESET process in order to avoid a disruption in combat operations."

Trijicon did not return phone calls seeking comment. A company spokesman told ABC News the inscriptions had always been on the sights and there was nothing wrong or illegal with including them. The company told ABC they believed the issue had been raised by a group that is "not Christian."[12]

One of the Fort Wainwright soldiers who received the order to remove the inscription told Fox News hardly anyone was aware of the religious reference. "It blows my mind," the solider said. "It doesn't help the Army do its mission to take off a biblical reference."

The soldier, who is a Christian, said he had to comply so "someone doesn't get offended.

"We have classes on equal opportunity—things that are clearly irrelevant to our mission, which is to kill the enemy."

Cross Removed From Base Chapel

The US military ordered soldiers to remove a cross and a steeple from atop a chapel and to board up cross-shaped windows at a remote American forward operating base in Afghanistan.

The removal of Christian symbols from the chapel at Forward Operating Base Orgun-E came after a solider complained, leading American Atheists president David Silverman to send a letter to the Pentagon.

"Soldiers with minority religious beliefs and atheists often feel like second-class citizens when Christianity is seemingly officially endorsed by their own base," Silverman told me. "We are very happy the Pentagon and the Army decided to do the right thing."

Silverman said a Christian chapel on an army base in Afghanistan could have put American troops in danger. "It inflames this Muslim versus Christian mentality," he said. "This is not a Muslim versus Christian war, but if the army base has a large chapel on it that has been converted to Christian-only, it sends a message that could be interpreted as hostile to Islam."

An Army spokesman at the Pentagon said that "local command in Afghanistan is aware of this chapel and has taken appropriate action to ensure that it is changed into a neutral facility."

The Army spokesman confirmed doors to the chapel were boarded up because of the cross-shaped windows. "They have already removed the cross from the top of the building," the Army spokesman said. "The primary purpose of making a chapel a neutral, multi-use facility, is to accommodate the free exercise of religion for all faith groups using it."

The Christian cleansing brought condemnation from religious liberty advocates such as Family Research Council president Tony Perkins. "Under this administration, the military has become a Christianity-free zone," Perkins said. "As a veteran, there's an irony here. You put on the uniform to defend freedom—chief among them is freedom of religion. And yet you are stripped of your own freedom to practice your faith."

"This is not about imposing religion on a people we've freed from oppression," Perkins said. "This is about American soldiers having the ability to practice their own faith."

Mikey Weinstein, founder of the Military Religious Freedom Foundation, hailed the military's decision.

"It is the sort of thing that provides a boundless bonanza of terrorist propaganda for the mujahedeen, the insurrectionists, the Taliban, and al Qaeda that we are supposedly fighting to protect our national security," he said. "The message of the cross on the chapel is basically putting out the message in Pashto, Dari, and Arabic to please blow me up because I'm a latter day Christian crusader."

Justin Griffith, military director for American Atheists, said the Christian symbols were sending the wrong message to non-Christians. "The US military is not in the business of building churches in Afghanistan," he said. "A church steeple could easily be seen as 'crusader' imagery to the local population. They got ahead of this one, and by responding to American Atheists' demands, they put the pin back in the grenade."

Griffith also said the Christian imagery was disrespectful to non-Christians. "A military chapel is a shared space, and it must remain religiously neutral," he said. "A Jewish person wouldn't go to a local church to worship in the civilian world. It would be unethical to force a Jewish soldier to worship in a church building, as there is no other designated place."

"Not having it there is really upsetting," one service member told Politico. "I walk by the chapel daily on the way to chow and the gym, and seeing the cross is a daily reminder of my faith and what Jesus accomplished for me. It is daily inspiration and motivation for me to acknowledge my faith and stay on the right path."[13]

Hiram Sasser, director of litigation for Liberty Institute, wondered why Christian soldiers must hide who they are. "Why are we ashamed of one of the major reasons our nation is the most generous and self-sacrificing for the benefit of others that the world has ever known—our inherently Christian benevolence?" he told Fox News. "We have freed the oppressed, fed the hungry, and restored nations throughout the world without anything in particular to show for it other than the satisfaction of making the world better than we found it for the sake of goodness and doing the right thing. Why should we hide a major motivation that compels Americans to do this?"

Boykin said it's no coincidence the Obama administration is using the military, a bastion of traditional American values, to implement social changes.

"You are seeing an assault on the military in an effort to change our society," he said. "The traditional values of the Judeo-Christian beliefs that America was founded upon is a target of the administration."

Group Compares Christian Evangelism to Rape

Religious liberty groups had grave concerns after they learned the Pentagon was vetting its guide on religious tolerance with a group that compared Christian evangelism to rape and advocated that military personnel who proselytize should be court martialed.[14]

Mikey Weinstein, president of the Military Religious Freedom Foundation, and others from his organization met privately with Pentagon officials in April 2013. He said US troops who proselytize are guilty of sedition and treason and should be punished—by the hundreds, if necessary—to stave off what he called a "tidal wave of fundamentalists."

"Someone needs to be punished for this," Weinstein told Fox News. "Until the Air Force or Army or Navy or Marine Corps punishes a member of the military for unconstitutional religious proselytizing and oppression, we will never have the ability to stop this horrible, horrendous, dehumanizing behavior."

Tony Perkins said he was stunned that the Pentagon would be taking counsel and advice from the likes of the Military Religious Freedom Foundation.

"Why would military leadership be meeting with one of the most rabid atheists in America to discuss religious freedom in the military?" Perkins said. "That's like consulting with China on how to improve human rights."

Pentagon officials met with Weinstein and his group to discuss a policy called "Air Force Culture, Air Force Standards," published on August 7, 2012. Section 2.11 requires "government neutrality regarding religion."[15]

"Leaders at all levels must balance constitutional protections for an individual's free exercise of religion or other personal beliefs and the constitutional prohibition against governmental establishment of religion," the regulation states.[16]

Military leaders were admonished not to use their position to "promote their personal religious beliefs to their subordinates or to extend preferential treatment for any religion."[17]

Weinstein said it's time for the Air Force to enforce the regulation— with zeal. "If a member of the military is proselytizing in a manner that violates the law, well, then of course they can be prosecuted," he said. "We would love to see hundreds of prosecutions to stop this outrage of fundamentalist religious persecution."

He compared the act of proselytizing to rape. "It is a version of being spiritually raped, and you are being spiritually raped by fundamentalist Christian religious predators," he told Fox News.

He said there is a time and a place for those in uniform to share their faith, but he took issues with fundamentalism, which he says is causing widespread problems in the military. "When those people are in uniform and they believe there is no time, place, or manner in which they can be restricted from proselytizing, they are creating tyranny, oppression, degradation, humiliation, and horrible, horrible pain upon members of the military," he said.

Perkins said the military regulations have "Weinstein's fingerprints all over it."

"It threatens to treat service members caught witnessing as enemies of the state," he said, referring to a *Washington Post* article highlighting Weinstein's meeting with Pentagon officials.

"Noncompliance, the Pentagon suggests, even from ordained chaplains could result in court-martialing on a case-by-case basis."

Ron Crews, executive director of the Chaplain Alliance for Religious Liberty, warns that the Air Force policy would "significantly impact the religious liberties of Air Force personnel."

"Saying that a service member cannot speak of his faith is like telling a service member he cannot talk about his spouse or children," Crews said. "I do not think the Air Force wants to ban personnel from protected religious speech, and I certainly hope that it is willing to listen to the numerous individuals and groups who protect military religious liberty without demonizing service members."

In an interview with the *Washington Post,* Weinstein called proselytizing a "national security threat."[18]

"And what the Pentagon needs to understand is that it is sedition and treason," he told the newspaper. "It should be punished."[19]

Perkins said it was troubling that the Obama administration would place so much trust in someone like Weinstein. "Unfortunately, it appears our military is on a forced march away from the very freedoms they are sworn to protect," he said. "This language from Weinstein that Christians who share their faith or offer comfort to others from their faith in Jesus Christ is 'sedition and treason' is a treasonous statement in and of itself."

But Weinstein said they count thousands of Protestants among their ranks—and said they are simply going after fundamentalists. "As soon as we find a fundamentalist Muslim, atheist, Jewish person, or anybody else, we will be happy to fight them," he said, "but so far they have been few and far between."

Boykin said he's deeply concerned by what he calls a pattern of attacks on Christianity within the military. "Mikey Weinstein has a very visceral hatred of Christianity and those who are Christians," he said. "He'd like to see it eliminated from the military entirely."

If the Air Force policy is implemented, Boykin said Christians who speak of their faith "could now be prosecuted as enemies of the state."

"This has the potential to destroy military recruiting across the services as Americans realize that their faith will be suppressed by joining the military," Boykin said.

In the meantime Weinstein and his group said they will continue to push for the Pentagon to fully implement its ban on proselytizing. "There is a time, place, and manner in which proselytizing is not only allowed, but it's something we support among our Christian clients," Weinstein said. "However, you can't scream 'Fire!' in a crowded theater, and you can't scream 'Jesus!' in a crowded theater at certain times, places, and in certain manners."

Baptist Chaplains Forced Out for Praying in Name of Jesus

Two Baptist chaplains said they were forced out of a Veterans Affairs chaplain training program after they refused orders to stop quoting the Bible and to stop praying in the name of Jesus.

When the men objected to those demands, they were subjected to ridicule and harassment that led to one of the chaplains leaving the program and the other being ejected, according to a federal lawsuit.

The Conservative Baptist Association of America is suing Secretary of Veterans Affairs Eric Shinseki; the group's suit alleges two of its chaplains were openly ridiculed by the leader of the San Diego-based VA-DOD Clinical Pastoral Education Center program.

"Not only was the treatment these men received inappropriate, it was also a violation of federal law and the religious freedom guarantees of the First Amendment," said John Wells, an attorney representing the Colorado-based denomination.

"No American choosing to serve in the armed forces should be openly ridiculed for his Christian faith," he said, calling it one of the most blatant cases of religious discrimination he has ever seen.

Lieutenant Commander Dan Klender, a Navy chaplain, and Major Steven Firtko, a retired Army chaplain, had enrolled in the VA's Clinical Pastoral Education Center program in San Diego last year. The one-year training program is required for anyone wanting to work as a chaplain in a VA hospital. VA chaplains differ from other military chaplains, in that they are limited to working in VA hospitals.

The program, which has affiliates around the nation, is open to chaplains of all religious faiths. However, applicants must have completed master-level seminary work.

There were seven chaplains enrolled in the San Diego program led by Nancy Dietsch, a Department of Veterans Affairs employee with a history of antagonistic behavior toward evangelicals, Wells said.

"She's been very, very critical of Christians," Wells said in a telephone interview. "Instead of teaching anything dealing with faith issues, she's dealing with a holistic, humanistic approach. It's the idea that the spirit comes from within."

The VA did not want to talk to me, but they did release a statement to NBC San Diego, which said the two men were "bullying other classmates and refusing to honor other faith groups."[20]

Wells said the chaplains were subjected to anti-Christian bigotry.

"And that would be putting it mildly," he said. "A lot of these so-called liberals are very liberal with their own ideas, but when it comes to somebody else's ideas, they don't want to hear it."

Among the allegations listed in the lawsuit[21]:

1. Dietsch told the chaplains that it was the policy of the VA in general and her in particular that chaplains should not pray in the name of Jesus.

2. During a classroom discussion on faith, Firtko said, "Faith is the substance of things hoped for, the evidence of things not seen." Dietsch told the chaplain he was not allowed to quote from the Bible in her classroom.

3. In October 2012 Dietsch told the class she believes God could be either man or woman. When Firtko referred to the Lord's Prayer, Dietsch "angrily pounded her fist on the table and shouted, 'Do not quote Scripture in this class!'"

4. In the aftermath of the Sandy Hook school shooting, Klender mentioned during a group discussion on counseling that he would tell a parent that "there is evil in the world." Dietsch retorted, "You don't actually believe that do you?"

5. In January 2013, Dietsch told the chaplains, "There is no room in the program for those who believe they are right and everybody else is wrong."

6. Later that month she told students there are many ways to heaven and that one religion cannot be right while others are wrong. Firtko objected to that statement by quoting Jesus, who said, "I am the way, the truth, and the life. No one comes to the Father except through Me" (John 14:6). Dietsch told him to stop quoting from the Bible, then stated, "If you believe your beliefs are right, and everyone else's is wrong, you do not belong in this program."

The harassment had become so bad by February that Klender withdrew from the program. A week later Firtko received a letter notifying him he'd been dismissed from the program. In July the pair filed a formal complaint against Dietsch for religious discrimination and violating the Association of Pastoral Continuing Education

Standards. Attorney Wells said it appears the government is trying to establish "a secular humanist-based religion free from any influence of Christian dogma."[22]

"The most egregious part is the VA supervisor told two chaplains that they were not allowed to pray in the name of Jesus and they could not quote Scripture," he said.

Wells feared that unless changes are made, Christian chaplains are going to be discouraged from serving in the military. "Christian chaplains are under a lot of pressure right now and facing a lot of challenges," he said.

The Silencing of the Lambs

They came in the cover of darkness. Airmen. Active duty. Retired. Evangelical Christians, all. They piled out of pickup trucks and SUVs and walked quickly into the church. Old men and young.

The men assembled in the fellowship hall. They congregated around tables. When the tables filled, they brought in plastic chairs. When the chairs filled, the men stood. Nearly eighty airmen in all.

They broke bread together. They ate barbecue and drank sweet tea. Afterward they sipped coffee and waited for the man they had come to hear.

It was Monday, September 16. Village Parkway Baptist Church. San Antonio, Texas. Just a stone's throw from Lackland Air Force Base.

The man they had come to hear was Senior Master Sergeant Phillip Monk. They wanted to hear the story he had told me a few weeks prior.

This is Monk's story.

Monk was a nineteen-year veteran of the Air Force. Just a few weeks before, he was relieved of his duties after he disagreed with his openly gay commander when she wanted to severely punish an underling who had expressed religious objections to homosexuality.

"I was relieved of my position because I don't agree with my commander's position on gay marriage," Monk told me. "We've been told that if you publicly say that homosexuality is wrong, you are in violation of Air Force policy."

Monk had served as a first sergeant at Lackland Air Force Base in San Antonio since 2011. He recently returned from a deployment and discovered he had a new commander—an open lesbian.

"In one of our first meetings she was talking about her promotion and she mentioned something about a benediction," Monk told me. "She said she wanted a chaplain but objected to one particular chaplain that she called a bigot because he preached that homosexuality is a sin."

"She then said, 'I don't know what kind of people actually believe that kind of crap,'" Monk said, recalling the meeting. "I knew I was going to have a rough time in this unit, and I would have to be very careful what I said."

That moment came when Monk was called in to advise the commander on a disciplinary matter involving an Air Force instructor accused of making comments objecting to gay marriage.

The instructor was investigated, and the members of his trainees were asked if the instructor had slandered homosexuals and whether he created a hostile work environment.

Monk said he quickly determined the instructor meant no harm by his public comments, comparing the United States with the fall of the Roman Empire. "He said in spite of our differences, we can't let that happen to the United States," Monk said. "He then used homosexual marriage as an example, saying that he didn't believe in it, but it doesn't matter because he was going to train them the same way."

Seven people filed complaints about the remarks. It then became Monk's job to advise the commander on disciplinary action.

"Her very first reaction was to say, 'We need to lop off the head of this guy,'" Monk said. "The commander took the position that his speech was discrimination."

Monk suggested she use the incident as a learning experience—a way to teach everyone about tolerance and diversity. "I don't believe someone having an opinion for or against homosexuality is discriminatory," Monk told Fox News.

From that point Monk said he was told that he wasn't on the same page as the commander and "if I didn't get on the page they were on, they would find another place for me to work."

"I'm being chastised about what's going on," he said. "I'm told that members of the Air Force don't have freedom of speech. They don't have the right to say anything that goes against Air Force policy."

Monk, who is a devout evangelical Christian, said he met with the young instructor and told him that he was fighting for him. "He was really concerned," Monk said. "He said he felt like he was on an island—that he couldn't be who he is anymore. He didn't understand why somebody would be offended."

The instructor was eventually punished by having a letter of counseling placed in his official file.

Monk soon found himself in a very similar position after his commander ordered him to answer a question about whether people who object to gay marriage are guilty of discrimination.

"She said, 'Sergeant Monk, I need to know if you can, as my first sergeant, if you can see discrimination if somebody says that they don't agree with homosexual marriage,'" he said. "I refused to answer the question."

Monk said to answer would have put him in a legal predicament. "And as a matter of conscience I could not answer the question the way the commander wanted me to," he said.

At that point Monk said that perhaps it would be best if he went on leave. The commander agreed.

"I was essentially fired for not validating my commander's position on having an opinion about homosexual marriage," he said.

Monk said he is brokenhearted over the way the military has treated him. "If this young man would've given a speech and said he was good with homosexuality, we wouldn't be here," he said. "The narrative is that you cannot say anything that contradicts Air Force policy."

Monk said, in essence, Christians are trading places with homosexuals. "Christians have to go into the closet," he said. "We are being robbed of our dignity and respect. We can't be who we are."

Monk said he is scared to speak out and understands he could face severe penalties. "They will make this about me, but I have an impeccable record," he said. "I stand on my own two feet. People have to know what's going on."

Monk told that story to the men gathered in the church fellowship. You could've heard a pin drop. He spoke their language. He talked the talk, but he also walked the walk.

And then something rather extraordinary happened. Other men began to tell their stories. One by one they shared personal experiences of retribution for their religious beliefs.

Pastor Steve Branson presided over the meeting. He told me there was an atmosphere of intimidation at Lackland Air Force Base. "Gay commanders and officers are pushing their agenda on the airmen," Branson told me. "There is a culture of fear in the military, and it's gone to a new level with the issue of homosexuality."

"The religious persecution is happening," the pastor said. "It's getting bigger every day. Gay and lesbian airmen can talk about their lifestyle, but the rest have to stay completely quiet about what they believe."

One airman was told that even thinking homosexuality is a sin is discriminatory. "A commander told him, 'Don't you understand discrimination—that your thought process is discrimination?'" Branson said. "The commander actually pulled up the definition of *discrimination* on Wikipedia and read it to him in front of everyone so he would understand what it was."

The parent of a nineteen-year-old Christian airman said their son was directed to disclose his religion during Basic Training. "What's your religion, little boy?" a master sergeant asked the young man. When he answered "Christian," he had to repeat Basic Training.

One member of the military was written up for having his Bible out, while a Muslim was allowed to publicly display a prayer rug.

A colonel told Branson that officers are being ordered to publicly affirm and promote homosexuality. "The colonel told me he hasn't been asked to do so, but if it did, he would refuse the order," the pastor said. "They're getting mirandized several times a month, but most of the accusations never stick,"

Boykin told me he's not surprised to hear about the assault on religious liberty within the armed forces. "It reinforces what we've been saying," Boykin told me. "There is an orchestrated attack on Christians in the military, and at this stage the Air Force is the worst."

Branson told me he fears there may soon be a mass exodus of Christians from the military. "The consensus at our meeting was that if things don't change, good men will be leaving the military," he said. "It will be a tragedy for our country and our military."

I've had a chance to talk at length with Master Sergeant Monk. He's a soft-spoken man—an introvert, not a religious zealot. He's a good-hearted person with a strong sense of right and wrong.

He told me that he was taking a stand because he wanted his sons to see "a man who stands upright and stands for integrity."

"Every night after dinner we read the Bible together," he said. "I tell the boys we've got a lot of stuff going on in this world and we need people to stand up. My boys know what I'm going through. They are looking at me, wanting to know how I'm going to handle this."

He said the Monks have a "family ethos."

"The Monk family will be strong in mind, strong in soul. They will have strong character and strong work ethic," he said. "That is the ethos of our family. That's what I hope they see in me."

And more importantly, he hopes his young sons will see "a man who stands upright and stands for integrity."

The persecution of Monk and the countless unnamed individuals at Lackland Air Force Base should serve as a warning to all Americans. If the Obama administration's Pentagon can take away their religious liberty, they can take away ours.

For nearly two hours that night Monk shared from his heart. Afterward the men stood to their feet and delivering a thundering ovation. Then they formed a circle around the airman, their fellow brother in Christ, and laid their hands on his shoulders. And they prayed.

It was Monday, September 16, the day Christians had to meet

secretly in a church fearful of government reprisals. It was a sad day. But it was also a day that the Christians decided to fight back, and that made it a good day.

Onward We Go

A few months after that meeting outside Lackland Air Force Base I had the privilege of meeting Monk and his wife, Connie, in Washington DC at the Values Voter Summit. He was just as I imagined: a reserved man with steely determination—the kind of man you'd want fighting alongside you in a fox hole.

He shook my hand and thanked me for telling his story to the nation in my Fox News column. I offered a smile and told him it was an honor.

He then pulled me to the side in the hotel lobby.

"I have something to give you," he said.

The veteran airman pulled out two pieces of cloth and held them in his hands.

"There's a tradition in the Air Force," he said. "The First Sergeant is a prominent position. There is only one First Sergeant in any one unit. The First Sergeant wears a diamond within their chevron to distinguish them from all others. As tradition dictates, when a First Sergeant takes off their diamond, they give their stripes to another; to one who best reflects the character of a First Sergeant. I was not afforded that opportunity."

Sergeant Monk paused for a moment and looked directly into my eyes.

"I want you to have these stripes," he said.

There was an elongated pause as I tried to collect my emotions. I humbly accepted his gift. I swallowed hard. Words failed me. And then he gave me a bear hug.

Brothers in Christ. Onward Christian soldiers.

Chapter 18

ONE NATION UNDER ALLAH

WHEN IT COMES to the world's religions, I'm a pretty easy-going, ecumenical guy, and I have a fairly straightforward religious philosophy: I'm more than happy to fellowship with any denomination that doesn't want to blow me up.

The United States was founded on Judeo-Christian values. We are the greatest nation on the face of the earth because we are a nation that cherishes freedom. And those freedoms are flavored by the Christian faith of our Founding Fathers.

But I'm not too sure the current presidential administration shares my religious philosophy. In recent years we've seen the Christian faith muted in public schools and the public square. Liberals have waged war against our Lord in local, state, and federal courthouses. Polls indicate Christianity is on the decline.

And while the crusade to marginalize Christianity gathers steam, another religious movement is afoot that could radically change the land of the free, the home of the brave. We are now beginning to see the rise of Islam in America, described as a bloodless revolution, a stealth jihad that is being waged in the nation's public school classrooms.

In recent years President Obama has gone out of his way to highlight and promote what he perceives to be Islamic contributions to the United States. He has declared on more than one occasion that the United States is no longer just a Christian nation. He once said that Ramadan "reminds us that Islam is part of the fabric of our nation."[1] He said, "Islam has contributed to the character of our country, and Muslim Americans, and their good works, have helped to build our nation."[2]

And then there's the infamous speech President Obama delivered in 2009 in Turkey.

"We do not consider ourselves a Christian nation or a Jewish nation or a Muslim nation," he said. "We consider ourselves a nation of citizens who are bound by ideals and a set of values."[3]

How ironic that President Obama renounced our Christian heritage in a nation that was once Christian but is now overwhelmingly Muslim.

But not everyone shares President Obama's rosy outlook on Islam. A survey by LifeWay Research indicates two-thirds of the nation's pastors believe Islam is a dangerous religion. The research arm of the Southern Baptist Convention surveyed more than one thousand pastors and found that 66 percent of ministers either somewhat or strongly agreed with the statement: "I believe Islam is a dangerous religion." Seventy-seven percent of evangelical pastors affirmed that statement, while only 44 percent of mainline Protestants agreed.[4]

It's important to note that *dangerous* does not mean "violent." Not every Muslim is a terrorist. And I also know the terrorist attacks have been committed by Muslim extremists. But let's be honest. There sure seem to be a lot of Muslim extremists running around the world blowing stuff up.

Presbyterians did not fly jetliners into the Pentagon or the World Trade Center towers or a field in Pennsylvania. Lutherans did not slaughter soldiers at Fort Hood. A Southern Baptist did not try to blow up a jetliner with his underwear. United Methodists were not responsible for the carnage at the Boston Marathon.

Of course, it's become politically incorrect to remind folks about that. I'm sure I'll be getting a call from the Department of Homeland Security or the Internal Revenue Service.

In 2009 John Brennan, then the White House adviser on Homeland Security and Counterterrorism, delivered a speech declaring the United States is not engaged in a war on terrorism.[5] In

2010 he argued that the term *jihadists* should not be used to describe America's enemies.

"Nor do we describe our enemy as jihadists or Islamists because jihad is a holy struggle, a legitimate tenet of Islam, meaning to purify oneself or one's community, and there is nothing holy or legitimate or Islamic about murdering innocent men, women and children," Brennan said.[6]

Erwin Lutzer, the author of *The Cross in the Shadow of the Crescent*, disputed that notion, arguing the nation is at war with radical Islam and warned that if the government turns a blind eye the long-term implications "will be very chilling."

"Jihad is a holy war," said Lutzer, pastor of the Moody Church in Chicago. "Jihad is a holy war against unbelievers."

Lutzer's book explores Islam's war with Christianity and what it means to the United States.

"In the minds of most Americans, as long as terrorism is under control, they think we are relatively safe," he told Fox News. "What they don't recognize is that we have a stealth jihad in America."

Lutzer said Islam is inserting itself and its views into the federal government as well as the culture at large.

The Federal Bureau of Investigation, for example, was caught purging its anti-terrorism training documents of any material deemed "offensive" to Muslims. That revelation was uncovered by Judicial Watch.[7]

"The FBI is rewriting history in order to help al Qaeda," said Judicial Watch President Tom Fitton. "This shows that the law enforcement agency is in need of serious top-to-bottom reform. As we recently learned from the Boston Marathon terrorist attack, the country is less safe when we allow radical Muslim organizations to tell the FBI how to train its agents and do its job. The FBI's purge of so called 'offensive' material is political correctness run amok, and it puts the nation at risk."[8]

A US attorney in Tennessee warned that it's possible some inflammatory criticism of Muslims posted on social networking sites could violate federal civil rights laws.

"We need to educate people about Muslims and their civil rights, and as long as we're here, they're going to be protected," US attorney Bill Killian told the *Tullahoma News*. "This is also to inform the public about what federal laws are in effect and what the consequences are."[9]

A Colorado high school, for example, came under scrutiny after students were led in an Arabic translation of the Pledge of Allegiance. Instead of one nation under God, students pledged their allegiance to one nation under Allah.[10]

An advanced placement world geography teacher at a Texas high school who encouraged students to dress in Islamic clothing also instructed them to refer to the 9/11 hijackers not as terrorists but as "freedom fighters," according to students who were in the class.

And schoolchildren in Indiana were required to sing a song declaring "Allah is God" during what was supposed to be an inclusive holiday concert.

"The government seems to be turning a blind eye to these kinds of intrusions," Lutzer told Fox News. "It's because of political correctness. I believe it has paralyzed us."

He said the administration's current response to the war on terror is not working.

"In Islam, when you show weakness, it actually invigorates them," he said. "They say to themselves that 'America—the Great Satan—is rolling over and playing dead, and it's happening much more easily and quickly than we ever could have expected.'"

Lutzer noted that countries such as Turkey, Syria, Iran, and Iraq were once Christian strongholds.

"Today, the few Christians who live in these places risk their lives if they attempt to share their faith with others," he wrote in his book. "Could their story be our story?"[11]

He said American Christians should look no farther than Europe to see what happens when Christianity falls and Islam rises.

"What Islam historically has done by force is now being accomplished in Europe through the purchase of churches and other properties, the building of mosques, and the growing insistence that

Europeans respect the rights of Muslims in the name of cultural or religious sensitivity," Lutzer wrote.[12]

Sound familiar?

The *Daily Mail* reported that research indicates Britain may no longer be a Christian country in just twenty years. If trends continue, the number of nonbelievers is set to overtake the number of Christians by 2030. And guess what religion is rapidly gaining ground? Muslims. The *Daily Mail* reports the number of Muslims has surged by 37 percent.[13]

"The non-Muslims of Europe, paralyzed by political correctness and having self-consciously despised their Christian past, are powerless to withstand Islam's growing presence," Lutzer said.[14]

He predicts that Islamic control of Europe will grow and that the region "will experience the exponential expansion of Islam, and the Europe we once knew will come to an end."[15]

The pastor issued a warning to Americans. "We are very naïve as Americans if we judge Islam by its more tolerant American version," he said. "If you really want to understand Islam, you have to go to Egypt and see what the Christians are enduring there. You have to go to Saudi Arabia, Iran, Iraq—this is really Islam and what the religion is once it begins to take over a country."[16]

Lutzer said Islam has two faces—the more tolerant side seen in the United States, and then there's the other kind.

"Many Muslims live in peace and strongly disagree with what the bomber did," he said, referring to the Boston Marathon attacks. "At the same time the bombers are going to point to the Quran for what they do."[17]

Lutzer said pastors need to be preparing their congregations for what could be a very different United States. "I foresee a time in America when Islam is going to have a tremendous amount of effect in our culture," he said. "We must recognize that as not only a distinct possibility, but something that is already happening."[18]

Representative André Carson, a congressman from Indiana, advocated for modeling the nation's public school system after Islamic schools. "America must understand that she needs Muslims," he told a national gathering of the Islamic Circle of North America. "America will never tap into educational innovation and ingenuity without looking at the model that we have in our madrassas—in our schools—where innovation is encouraged—where the foundation is the Quran."[19]

The mainstream media ignored the congressman's declaration. It was only thanks to the investigative efforts of the Media Research Center that we learned an elected official was calling for American children to bow to the Quran.

Could you imagine the mainstream media outrage if the congressman had advocated for American schools to be modeled after the Bible?

Over the past several years significant concerns have been raised by parents who say public schools are indoctrinating students to the Islamic faith. A Prentice world history textbook used in Florida declared Muhammad as the "Messenger of God." The book includes thirty-six pages of study on Islam. The book also instructs students that jihad is a duty that Muslims must follow.

William Saxton, chairman of Citizens for National Security, has studied the promotion of Islam in public school textbooks. Saxton's all-volunteer organization launched a nationwide study in 2009 to root out what they believed to be Islamic bias in American school textbooks. He said they found as many as eighty textbooks that overtly promoted Islam.

He testified before the Brevard, Florida, School Board, warning them the Prentice textbook rewrites Islamic history and presents a biased and incorrect version of the Muslim faith.

"They promote Islam at the expense of Christianity and Judaism," Saxton told me. "It blew my mind to see the kind of propaganda, the pro-Islam information that's in this book—at the expense of Christianity and Judaism."

Saxton said he believes the inclusion is deliberate and that he placed the blame on an organization that was once called Council on Islamic Education. The group works with education officials and publishers to produce chapters on Islam for American textbooks.

But today the Council on Islamic Education is known as the Institute on Religious and Civic Values. It's founder, Shabbir Mansuri, is listed as an academic reviewer on the textbook used in Brevard County.

In 2001 the *OC Weekly* newspaper in California interviewed Mansuri about comments former Second Lady Lynne Cheney made lamenting the amount of time schools were spending teaching cultures that were not American. Mansuri took her comments as a personal attack.

"For the past 11 years, Mansuri has waged what he calls a 'bloodless' revolution: promoting an increased emphasis on world cultures and faiths—including Islam—inside American junior high and high school campuses," the newspaper reported.[20]

Saxton said he is highly suspicious of Mansuri's organization and questioned why they changed their name.

"These people are dedicated to getting this language into the textbooks," he said, noting their new name is "benign and does not sound threatening or Islamic. But the same people are running it."

Saxton said his organization is hearing from concerned parents across the country, and the complaints have generally been the same: public school textbooks that favor Islam over other world religions.

"It's a form of stealth jihad," he said. "[Jihad] is not just blowing up buildings. It's more subtle. I began to understand that one of the ways the bad guys are trying to threaten our way of life is through our children. The Islamists want to get to the hearts and minds of our kids."

Chapter 19

METH ADDICTS ARE FINE
BUT NOT HOMESCHOOLERS?

THE PLIGHT OF the Romeike family represented an ugly chapter in our nation's history. The Romeikes fled their German homeland seeking political asylum in the United States, where they hoped to homeschool their children. In 2010 an immigration judge granted them asylum. But the Department of Homeland Security objected—and launched a lengthy legal battle to have the Southern Baptist family deported.

Just a few months before this book was published, the Obama administration declared victory after the Supreme Court declined to hear the family's case. It meant that Uwe and Hannelore Romeike and their six children could legally be thrown out of our country.

However, in the face of massive outrage from Christians and threats of civil disobedience, the Obama administration decided to let the family stay in the United States indefinitely. The government did not explain why it had a change of heart.

While the nation's Christian community was overjoyed at the administration's last-minute act of mercy, their handling of the case and their arguments against homeschooling should serve as a warning to American Christians.

"The Obama administration is basically saying there is no right to homeschool anywhere," said Michael Farris, founder of the Home School Legal Defense Association (HSLDA). "It's an utter repudiation of parental liberty and religious liberty."

The Justice Department claims the German law banning homeschooling does not violate the family's human rights. By trying to send the family back to a country where they would certainly lose custody of their children, Farris said, "our government is siding with Germany."

Farris said the Germans ban homeschools because "they don't want to have religious and philosophical minorities in their country."

"That means they don't want to have significant numbers of people who think differently than what the government thinks," he said. "It's an incredibly dangerous assertion that people can't think in a way that the government doesn't approve of." He said the Justice Department is backing that kind of thinking by arguing that the Romeikes' human rights weren't being violated.

Farris said he finds great irony in the fact that the Obama administration is releasing thousands of illegal aliens yet wanted to send a family seeking political asylum back to Germany. "Eleven million people are going to be allowed to stay freely, but this one family [was] to be shipped back to Germany to be persecuted," he said. "It just doesn't make any sense."

The fear of persecution is why an immigration judge granted the family political asylum in 2010. German authorities demanded the family stop homeschooling. The family faced thousands of dollars in fines, and the authorities initially took away their children in a police van.

German state constitutions require that children attend public schools. Parents who don't comply face punishment ranging from fines to prison time. The nation's highest appellate court ruled in 2007 that in some cases children could be removed from their parents' care.

"Families that want to have an alternative education can't get it in Germany," Farris said. "Even the private schools have to teach public school curriculum."

After authorities threatened to remove permanent custody of the children from the Christian couple, the family decided to move to the United States. "It was a huge transition," Uwe said. "We had to sell all our possessions. We came here with suitcases and had to start all over."

Uwe, a classically trained pianist, relocated his family to a four-acre farm in the shadow of the Smoky Mountains in eastern Tennessee. And with the help of a generous community, the family adjusted to their new home—complete with chickens, ducks, and a dog named Julie. "We are very happy here to be able to freely follow our conscience and to homeschool our children," he told Fox News. "Where we live in Tennessee is very much like where we lived in Germany."

Danny Thomas, the mayor of Morristown, Tennessee, told me the Romeikes are well-respected members of the community. "They are good citizens without a doubt," he said. "I don't think you'll find anyone with a better work ethic—kind, gentle people. This man walks the walk. He doesn't just talk the talk."

Dean Haun is the pastor of the First Baptist Church of Morristown, where Uwe is an ordained deacon and church pianist. He said the government's assault on the family is an example of what he called a cultural shift. "I think there is without a doubt an incredible drift in our nation and in our government away from God and against Christianity—and against the principles that we have held dear and the freedoms that we've held over the years," he said. "It's an assault in the face of Christianity in America."

While grateful for the last-minute reprieve, Uwe said he was extremely disappointed that their original petition to seek asylum was appealed by the Obama administration. "If we go back to Germany, we know that we would be prosecuted, and it is very likely the Social Services authorities would take our children from us," he said.

Uwe said German schools were teaching children to disrespect authority figures and used graphic words to describe sexual relations. He said the state believed children must be "socialized."

"The German schools teach against our Christian values," he said. "Our children know that we homeschool following our convictions and that we are in God's hands. They understand that we are doing this for their best—and they love the life we are living in America on our small farm."

Mike Donnelly, the HSLDA's director of international affairs, said quite frankly that Germany persecutes homeschoolers. "The court ignored mountains of evidence that homeschoolers are harshly fined and that custody of their children is gravely threatened—something most people would call persecution," he said.

Farris said Americans should be outraged over the way the Obama administration has treated the Romeike family. He believes the case could have repercussions for families who homeschool in this nation. "The right of parents to direct the upbringing and education of their children has been at the pinnacle of human rights," he said. "But not in this country."

Now contrast the plight of the Romeike family with Dennis Vitug, a gay Filipino immigrant who was set to be deported after he was sentenced for drug possession. Vitug came to the United States in 1999 and overstayed his visa, the *Daily Caller* reported. He got addicted to crystal meth and was sent to jail.[1]

Instead of sending Vitug back to his home country, the US Ninth Circuit Court of Appeals overturned the deportation decision and ruled that he should remain in the United States. The judges feared Vitug might suffer persecution because of his sexual orientation.[2]

"Homosexuals, yes, homeschoolers no," Farris told me, noting the Obama administration has a history of granting asylum to LGBT immigrants. "It's disconcerting the lack of equality here. You have to be in one of the favored groups to get any protection by this administration."

So in the eyes of the American courts, meth addicts make more productive members of society than evangelical Christian families who homeschool their children. It's an international version of *Breaking Bad*.

As Farris reflected on his client's long legal ordeal, he said he remains steadfast in his belief that the only reason they were targeted is because of their Christian faith. "I think this is part of the Obama administration's overall campaign to crush religious freedom in this country," he told me. "The [administration's] attitude toward religious freedom, particularly religious freedom for Christians, is shocking. I have little doubt that if this family had been of some other faith that the decision would have never been appealed in the first place."

I'm not sure what to make of the administration's obsession with trying to get this Christian family deported, but I think it's worth noting that neither the Justice Department nor the Department of Homeland Security seemed all that concerned about deporting President Obama's aunt and uncle. Both of them were living here illegally. I'm just saying.

Had the government deported the Romeikes, Farris predicted it would have sparked a movement among religious liberty supporters. He compared it to the moment when "they told courageous Rosa Parks to go to the back of the bus and she wouldn't go."

"I think we may be approaching a similar moment in our country," he said. Could you imagine thousands of Christians engaged in civil disobedience, fighting for religious liberty?

I spoke to nearly a dozen individuals—lawmakers, clergy, citizens—who said they would have been willing to stand on the front porch of the Romeikes' home to block immigration officers from removing the family. Even Pastor Haun told me he was willing to go to jail to protect the sheep he shepherds.

Congressman Phil Roe is a Republican who represents Tennessee's First Congressional District. He was downright furious at the way the Romeikes have been treated. And he was one of the ones who told me that he'd be willing to stand in the gap for the Christian family.

"It may require civil disobedience with this bunch," he said, referring to the Obama administration. "I am furious about this. You've got law-abiding people who did everything right who simply want to homeschool their kids. We used to be that great shining city on a hill. There's some rush on that city if we are doing free people this way."

Farris summed up this sorry chapter in our nation's history by invoking the Pilgrims. "The Pilgrims left England to go to Holland to seek religious freedom," he said. "They came here to seek religious freedom and parental rights for their children. Had this administration been waiting at Plymouth Rock, they would've told the Pilgrims to go back home."

Imagine the scene: Attorney General Eric Holder holding a court order for the Pilgrims. "Just get back on board that boat, turn it around, and head on back to where you came from," he'd say. "You're just not welcome around here."

Chapter 20

THE WAR ON CHRISTMAS

RESIDENT OBAMA ALMOST booted Baby Jesus out of the White House. It happened in 2009 as the Obamas were preparing to celebrate their first Christmas (pardon me, holiday) in the White House. The first family wanted to plan a "non-religious Christmas," according to then-Social Secretary Desirée Rogers.[1]

Rogers told a gathering of former social secretaries that the Obamas did not intend to put the Nativity scene on display—a long-time East Room tradition. The account was reported in the Fashion and Style section of the *New York Times*,[2] not exactly a Jesus-friendly publication.

The White House confirmed to the *Times* there had been internal discussions about making Christmas more inclusive—but in the end, tradition won out, and Mary, Joseph, and Jesus were placed in their traditional spots.

I'd be willing to bet my Sunday tithe that political polling won out. A Rasmussen Reports national survey found that 76 percent of those polled believe the emphasis of the Christmas season should be on the baby born in a manger[3]—that would be the manger President Obama wanted to toss into the White House garbage dumpster.

Just let that sink in for a moment, folks. The president of the United States wanted to throw Baby Jesus out of the White House. What kind of a person does that? What kind of a person *votes* for a kind of person who does that?

There's only one pundit who can adequately parse the president's actions, and that's Bill Donohue, president of the Catholic League. He said the president was trying to "neuter" Christmas.

"It should come as no big surprise that [President Obama] and his wife would like to neuter Christmas in the White House," he told me. "That's their natural step—to ban the public display of Christian symbols."

Religion Mucks It Up?

It's bad enough President Obama is trying to marginalize the reason for the season. Now we're facing an annual assault of yuletide yammering from secularists, atheists, and ill-tempered gadflies prone to take offense at Baby Jesus.

Take the anti-Christmas diatribe delivered by Nancy Snyderman, chief medical editor for the National Broadcasting Company, for example. "I don't like the religion part," Dr. Snyderman said of the holiday on the *Today* show. "I think religion is what mucks the whole thing up."[4]

The "religion" she was referring to is celebrating the birth of Jesus Christ and her outburst came during a panel discussion with Matt Lauer, Star Jones, and Donny Deutsch. Her response came after Jones said she focuses on the religious meaning of Christmas.

"That's the only reason why—that's the only reason for me to have the holiday, quite frankly," Jones said.[5]

Amen, sister.

But Snyderman countered, "No, I don't like the religion part. I think that's what makes the holidays so stressful."[6]

Snyderman said she wanted to focus on green trees during the yuletide season instead—but I believe they already have a holiday for that. It's called Arbor Day. Far be it from me to suggest it, but maybe Dr. Snyderman should stick to treating runny noses and leave the theology to the experts.

Angry Atheists Armed With Attorneys

My friend Sarah Palin, the former governor of Alaska, knows a thing or two about the war on Christmas. (She also knows a thing or two about Christmas Moose Chili. Her recipe is delicious, and it pairs well with a cast iron skillet of cornbread. But I digress.) One afternoon at my office at the Fox News Corner of the World, Palin shared some of her war stories with me.

"When I was mayor of Wasilla," she told me, "I always promoted and participated in our traditional Nativity scene in our public park. I was threatened. People said someone might take offense at the plastic baby doll that represents Jesus sitting in a hay-filled manger."

Unlike many of today's mayors, though, Palin was blessed with a backbone, and she refused to give in to the people she called "angry atheists armed with attorneys."

"In a very jolly, Christmassy way, I'm saying enough is enough of some Scrooge wanting to force Christ out of Christmas and pretend that Jesus isn't the reason for the season," she said. "Christmas is special, and heaven forbid some politically correct Scrooge shouts 'Bah-humbug' at us and tries to take away our constitutional rights to express our faith."

Well said, Governor Palin. Well said.

So here's some ammunition for the next time you run into a naysayer who dismisses the idea of a war on Christmas. The following stories are sure to jingle your bells, and a few of these dispatches might have you ready to deck somebody's halls.

The Dog Days of Christmas

The 2012 White House "holiday card" spotlighted the Obama's family Portuguese water dog—instead of Christmas. The black-and-white illustration was designed by Iowa artist Larassa Kabel and shows Bo the dog wearing a scarf while frolicking in the snow on the South Lawn of a blurred White House.

The inside of the card read, "This season, may your home be filled with family, friends, and the joy of the holidays." The card was signed by the entire first family—along with Bo's paw print. *Vanity Fair* deemed Obama's "holiday card" his best-ever in a posting titled, "Bo Obama: The True Meaning of Christmas."[7]

The 2012 card made no mention of any specific holiday, nor did it include a Bible verse noting the birth of Christ.

The Obama family dog also played a prominent role in yuletide decorations around 1600 Pennsylvania Avenue. For instance, the *Daily Mail* reported that Bo was featured in nearly every room of the White House for Christmas that year, from miniature licorice and marshmallow versions of the canine to a nearly life-size replica of the dog.[8]

A statue of Bo made of marzipan sat outside the massive gingerbread replica of the White House. Additionally, White House Christmas trees were decorated with ornaments made in the dog's likeness—and the newspaper reported holiday visitors would receive a Bo bookmark that would lead them on a scavenger hunt to find Bo-themed decorations throughout the building.

The 2011 card also featured Bo—and made no mention of the word *Christmas*, either. The card showed the dog lounging by a fireplace surrounded by holiday greenery. Presents were placed on a table underneath a poinsettia instead of a Christmas tree. "From our family to yours, may your holidays shine with the light of the season," read the inside of the card, featuring the presidential seal.

Los Angeles-based artist Mark Matuszak told the *Los Angeles Times* he was asked to create the card by the White House social secretary. "They wanted to do an inside shot, something home related," Matuszak told the newspaper. He said one of the ideas was to focus on the Obama's family dog. "So we thought, let's put Bo in front of a fireplace."[9]

Sarah Palin took one look at the card and gave me a telephone call from Wasilla, Alaska. "It's odd," she said, wondering why the president's Christmas card highlighted his dog instead of traditions such as family, faith, and freedom. "Even stranger than that was his first year in office, when the Christmas ornaments included Chairman

Mao," Palin said. "People had to ask that it be removed because it was offensive."

Governor Palin was referring to the 2009 Obama Christmas decorations, which included ornaments saluting Chairman Mao and a drag queen named Hedda Lettuce. Apparently nothing says "Merry Christmas" like a murderous dictator and a man sporting strategically placed produce.

Furthermore, the 2009 greeting card made no reference to Christmas, drawing the ire of Republican Congressman Henry Brown. "I believe that sending a Christmas card without referencing a holiday and its purpose limits the Christmas celebration in favor of a more 'politically correct' holiday," the South Carolina congressman told Fox News Radio in 2009.

Former President Bush's cards did not mention "Merry Christmas" either, but he had a history of including Bible passages on the White House cards. For his final Christmas in office, the president sent a greeting card that included a verse from the Gospel of Matthew. But that was back in the day when Jesus was the reason for the season—not a Portuguese water dog.

Don Your Fun Apparel?

Hallmark, the greeting card people, decided to rewrite the lyrics to "Deck the Halls" over fears it might offend certain people. Instead of donning our "gay apparel," Hallmark wants us to don our "fun apparel."

The lyrics appeared on one of Hallmark's 2013 Christmas ornaments. They said the word *gay* might be misconstrued. "Deck the Halls" was originally written back in the 1880s, when *gay* meant "festive or merry"[10] (instead of which way you butter your biscuit).

Hallmark was sincerely troubled by the prospect of Christmas carolers singing about gay apparel. They feared it might call to mind images of impeccably dressed men draped in scarves and wearing slim-fit cardigans.

Between you and me, I figured Hallmark might've taken issue

with the "fa-la-la-la-la" section. But boy howdy, was I wrong. In my defense, my yuletide gaydar is offline.

Oh, the price one must pay to be politically correct these days. But since they've anointed themselves defenders of tolerance, maybe Hallmark should consider rewriting some other Christmastime favorites. For example, Prancer and Vixen in "Rudolph, the Red-Nosed Reindeer"? Talk about stereotypes! And those lords-a-leaping in the "Twelve Days of Christmas"? If that doesn't scream homophobic, I don't know what does.

And don't even get me started on the gender identity issues associated with Christmas. That's why I've already fired off an e-mail to Hallmark suggesting a remake of the classic yet politically incorrect tune "I Saw Mommy Kissing Santa Claus." How about "I Saw Daddy Kissing Santa Claus" instead?

Somebody's Been Smoking Some Mistletoe

Christmas in Connecticut felt a little less Christmassy in one high school after a teacher told students they could not decorate the classroom door with Santa Claus or Christmas trees.

"This is political correctness run amuck," an outraged mom told me. Her child attends Fairfield Ludlowe High School, where the entire school was involved in a door-decorating contest.

Students in her child's class tossed out some ideas for a Christmas-themed door. One student suggested a Christmas tree, and another student suggested a Santa Claus-inspired fireplace design. Both were rejected.

"She [the teacher] said no reference to Christmas at all can be on the decorations on the door," the parent said. "My son was in disbelief and asked, 'Why can't we decorate for Christmas?'"

That's a great question. So I called Greg Hatzis, the headmaster at the public school.

Hatzis cited a district-wide religion policy that states, "It is the policy of the Board of Education that no religious belief or non-belief will be promoted by the district or its employees, and none will be disparaged."

Hatzis said the teacher may have been misinformed about what is allowed and what is not allowed, but he would not directly say whether or not classroom doors could be decorated with Christmas trees.

"There is room in the policy for classroom and school decorations, but they should have no direct religious meaning," he told me. "If a classroom were to display items of a religious nature, we require the teacher talk about them in a conversation related to diversity and that all religions and cultures are respected."

So, does that mean they promote the Keystone Pipeline on Earth Day? Do they celebrate lumberjacks on Arbor Day? And why does the school district have concerns about Christmas?

"The difficulty is that we want everyone to feel a part of the school community," he said. "Anytime there is a preponderance of any particular holiday, you don't want people to feel excluded. It's really a lesson in respect. It's a lesson in community."

The headmaster said they really do want people to feel festive. Somehow, though, I felt there was a big "but" about to come next. "We want people to be able to have a chance to celebrate," he said, "but just in a way that is not exclusionary."

The dilemma facing the school, he said, is determining what represents a religious holiday decoration and what does not. "Something like a wreath or candy canes or holly have no direct religious meaning, so they would be allowed under the district policy," he said. "But others may say that a Christmas tree would not exist unless you were talking about Christmas, and they make the leap to the religious observance."

Hatzis said the school just wants to be "sensitive."

"We don't want somebody to be offended," he said. "We try to make sure that everybody understands the need for respect and diversity."

The parent who contacted me said it's pretty clear what the school is doing. "Christmas seems targeted for persecution," she said. "If Hanukkah or Kwanzaa were targeted like that, there would be such outrage. We're not allowed to be outraged that Christmas is being taken out of the classroom."

I like the way this mom thinks. "It's angering," she said. "It's frustrating."

I figured I would give the headmaster one last chance to sort all this out. Does the school policy really ban Santa Claus and Christmas?

"It absolutely allows for decorations as long as they are not promoting a particular holiday," he said.

But isn't Christmas a particular holiday? "It comes back to one's personal perspective—and how much it is tied to religion," the headmaster told me.

So, yes or no—are boys and girls allowed to decorate the classroom doors with Christmas trees? "Christmas trees are allowed in the context of showing respect for everybody who's viewing it," Hatzis replied.

Sigh.

This is what happens when you allow the herbal-tea-and-granola crowd to teach our kids. And the sad part is the school district may be too dim-witted to understand that Christmas trees and Santa Claus have absolutely nothing to do with the true reason for the season.

I think I need a cup of egg nog. Better make it a double.

Does ESPN Hate Babies or the Baby Jesus?

ESPN found itself on the naughty list after it banned a Christmas commercial from a Catholic children's hospital because of its religious content—a decision the network eventually reversed after a bit of prodding from your friendly neighborhood scribe.

The sports programming juggernaut had originally passed on the ad for the hospital because it included references to God and celebrating the birth of Christ, officials at the Cardinal Glennon Children's Foundation in Missouri, which provides financial support for the hospital, told me.

"ESPN came back to us and said it was denied due to religious advocacy," said Dan Buck, executive director of the foundation. "We were disappointed and dumbfounded with their decision."

Here's the actual script of the ad that ESPN rejected:

> At SSM Cardinal Glennon Children's Medical Center, we celebrate the birth of Jesus and the season of giving, bringing hope to the many children, parents, and families that we serve. Our patients are filled with hope as they receive a message each day from the treasure chest beneath our tree of hope. Help us reveal God's healing presence this Christmas. Send your message of hope at Glennon.org.

When the foundation learned ESPN had rejected the ad, they asked ESPN to reconsider and then advised them to consult with executive channels at the network. But the network's decision at first remained unchanged.

"They said, 'Yes, it is denied,'" Buck said. "They told us the lines about 'Celebrate the birth of Jesus' and 'Help us reveal God's healing message' are problematic."

Buck told me it's the first time in the history of the organization that anyone has challenged their faith beliefs. "We've been around since 1956," he said. "No one has ever complained or said that our message couldn't be told."

Buck said ESPN is a private entity and has every right to determine what kind of commercials it airs. At the same time he said the children's hospital was not prepared to turn away from its faith. "We do celebrate the birth of Jesus at Cardinal Glennon," he told me. "It's who we are. It's an engrained part of who we are. We're very proud of our faith heritage, and we promote that. We let people know that we pray for our children."

Meanwhile the network's original decision generated a firestorm of criticism from religious liberty supporters. "It's totally ridiculous," said attorney Doug Napier with Alliance Defending Freedom. "To say there's too much Jesus in a Christmas message is like saying there's too much sports in ESPN."

Chicken-Hearted Atheists

A Nativity scene at Shaw Air Force Base in South Carolina was abruptly removed after a group of atheist airmen became frightened at the sight of a plastic Jewish family sitting on the lawn.

The recommendation to remove the Nativity from a Christmas display at the base came from Pentagon lawyers who feared the plastic Baby Jesus could give the appearance the military was endorsing religion.

A spokesperson for the South Carolina base told me Pentagon lawyers were acting on a complaint filed by the Military Religious Freedom Foundation, a radical anti-Christian organization whose leaders appear to hold great sway over President Obama's Pentagon.

Lieutenant Keavy Rake said the Pentagon warned that items that are almost exclusively religious in nature, like a Nativity scene, "could appear to endorse religion" if they are displayed alone and away from chapel grounds. She further said the Pentagon recommended that Baby Jesus either be displayed on chapel grounds or as "part of a larger secular or multicultural display on base."

Ultimately base command made the decision to pull the plug. Rake said volunteers had permission to assemble the Nativity on the chapel grounds. Until then, Mary, Joseph, and the newborn King were to be covered with a tarp.

"It is truly a sad state of affairs when a demilitarized zone has to be created on an Air Force base for Baby Jesus," said my friend Tony Perkins, president of the Family Research Council. "The events in the Air Force alone show that this is much more than a war on Christmas; this is a war on the freedom of religious expression."

The controversy started just a few minutes after the Nativity was erected near the base's Memorial Lake. The Military Religious Freedom Foundation (MRFF) said it was alerted to the event by an undisclosed number of airmen, who said they were emotionally troubled by the sight of the Baby Jesus.

The MRFF claims that because the Nativity scene was not located near a chapel, it was a direct violation of the US Constitution as well as Air Force policy. Mikey Weinstein, president of the group, immediately telephoned the Pentagon, and exactly two hours and fifteen minutes later, the baby wrapped in swaddling clothes had been hauled away.

The Air Force base released a statement explaining all faith-based and secular groups were offered an opportunity to put up holiday displays. The only group to take advantage of the offer was the one that erected the Nativity.

"Based on only one faith group being represented, 20th Fighter Wing officials determined the appropriate course of action was to celebrate the holiday season consistently and elected to remove the nativity scene from Memorial Lake," the statement read.[11]

In other words, to truly celebrate the reason for the season, you have to remove the reason for the season.

Ron Crews, executive director of the Chaplain Alliance for Religious Liberty, said military members have every right to express their faith, even through a nativity scene. "This is yet another example of the Air Force yielding to a phone call from the Military Religious Freedom Foundation," Crews said.

If there is any good news in the controversy, it's that Americans have finally decided to take a stand. Rake told me her office was inundated with thousands of telephone calls from people demanding the Nativity scene be returned.

And that, said Perkins, is great news. "The reason we are hearing about so many of these attacks on Christmas is not necessarily because the number of attacks have increased, but because more and more Americans, both civilians and members of the military, are saying enough is enough," he said.

The Pentagon may privately assure religious liberty groups that Weinstein is nothing more than a gadfly, but the facts prove otherwise. Again, it took just two hours and fifteen minutes for the Pentagon to respond to his query. When the Muslim terrorists attacked the American consulate in Benghazi, it took more than three hours for a military response.

In fact, now that I think about it, it's too bad there wasn't a Nativity on the front lawn in Benghazi. Help might've come a little quicker.

Thou Shalt Not Wear Red or Green

An elementary school in Frisco, Texas, is believed to be the first in the state to violate the "Merry Christmas law" after the school banned Christmas trees and the colors red and green from an upcoming "winter party."

Boys and girls who attended the Nichols Elementary School event were told they would not be able to make any reference to Christmas or any other religious holiday. Christmas trees were also banned— along with the colors red and green. The rules were sent to parents in an e-mail from the school's PTA and reported by a Fox television affiliate in Dallas.

Ironically the school is located in the district of state Representative Pat Fallon, the author of the bill signed into law in June that codifies the fact that students and staff are permitted to discuss winter holidays as they please. Fallon told me he was alerted to the situation by an angry parent.

"When Governor Perry signed the 'Merry Christmas bill,' clearly that didn't solve the issue," Fallon said. "The battle rages on. It's distressing."

"I feel like my calling in life is to protect the students, parents, and teachers," Fallon continued. "They have a constitutional right to express themselves. They have freedom of religion."

So Fallon fired off a letter to every school official in the district, reminding them of their yuletide rights under the law. "Texas law clearly permits Christmas-themed celebrations, events, and displays," Fallon wrote. "The district may also display scenes or symbols associated with traditional winter holidays (e.g. nativity scenes, Christmas trees, menorahs, etc.)."[12]

The lawmaker said he was shocked at the number of calls his office received from nervous teachers and principals, all wondering what they could and could not do. "One teacher wanted to do 'Elf on a Shelf,' and she thought she would get in trouble," he told me.

So this is what it's come to, America. You've got a college-educated teacher terrified to put a toy elf on the shelf because she might get sued by the ACLU or some other left-wing anti-Christmas group.

Unfortunately there are no criminal penalties for violating the "Merry Christmas law." Perhaps Representative Fallon could offer an amendment? In lieu of jail time, violators would be subjected to a lump of coal on Christmas Day.

Helping Poor Kids Is Against the Law

When a national humanist organization threatened to sue SkyView Academy for collecting toys for needy children, students at the Colorado charter school decided to fight back.

Officials at SkyView Academy announced they were dropping its participation in Operation Christmas Child, a ministry of Samaritan's Purse. The project involves stuffing toys, candy, and hygiene items into boxes to send to disadvantaged children around the world. But the American Humanist Association (AHA) said the school's participation in the program violates the US Constitution and sent a letter demanding the school cease and desist.

Meanwhile a small charter school in South Carolina received a similar letter—and complied with the AHA's demands, deciding not to fight it. Renee Mathews, the principal of East Point Academy in West Columbia, South Carolina, said their small school had no choice. "We have a very small budget and very small legal budget. We felt that we could not risk using our school funding for classrooms and teachers to fight a court case."

Even though Operation Christmas Child is connected to an evangelical Christian ministry, Mathews said there were no religious materials included in the boxes. She also pointed out the project was voluntary, non-religious, and not tied to any graded assignments.

Nevertheless, the AHA decided to intervene on behalf of a perturbed parent. This is standing operating procedure for these anti-Christian bullies.

"The boxes of toys are essentially a bribe, expressly used to pressure desperately poor children living in developing countries to convert to Christianity, and are delivered with prayers, sermons, evangelical tracts and pressure to convert," read a letter the AHA sent to Mathews, saying a public school cannot affiliate itself with a group like Operation Christmas Child without violating the Establishment Clause. "Because the purpose and effect of Operation Christmas Child is to induce impoverished children to convert to Christianity, the school's promotion of this program violates the Constitution."[13]

Back in Colorado, even though the project at SkyView was student-initiated and student-led, school officials determined they could not afford to pay for a court battle either. The school's board said they were disappointed by the humanists' threats.

"We know this is a bullying tactic," parent Kendal Unruh told me in a telephone interview. "We know that they target small schools that don't have a budget to defend themselves. In lieu of a fist, they use a letter. We don't have the money to invest in a long, costly legal battle."

Unruh said it's not coincidental that the South Carolina charter school received the exact same letter. "Because they don't like the message that we convey under our religious liberty, they have to shut us down, and that is a tactic of bullying," she said. "They don't believe in equal access. They believe in shutting down anybody who doesn't comply with their view of what society should be—and that is completely godless."

But while the South Carolina school completely shut down its Operation Christmas Child project, the students at SkyView decided to defy the humanists. Hundreds of students and parents and well-wishers staged a grassroots act of defiance.

And while they meant to send a message to the humanists, their stand was really about making sure poor children had toys on Christmas Day. "The young people weren't concerned about the politics of it," Unruh told me. "They were asking, 'What about the kids?'"

Instead of collecting shoe boxes inside the school, the students moved their entire operation outside on a public sidewalk. Volunteers loaded shoe boxes into trucks and vans, while students held a religious liberty rally, hoisting signs condemning the humanists.

"Humanists hate kids," read one sign. Another declared, "You won't steal Christmas from children."

Unruh said the rally was a great life lesson for the young students. "You stand up to bullies," she said. "You don't stand down. You stand up for your belief system."

Some critics have tried to compare the humanists to Ebenezer Scrooge—but that's really unfair. Even Scrooge had a heart.

New Jersey Schools Bans Religious Christmas Music

The angels were not allowed to hark their herald, nor was the little Lord Jesus permitted to sleep on the hay after a New Jersey school district announced a ban on all religious Christmas music.

Constance Bauer, superintendent of the Bordentown Regional School District, posted a message online stating someone had been questioning recent musical selections for the elementary school Christmas concerts.

Pardon me—the school district calls them "winter concerts."

My guess is that a perpetually offended left-winger became unglued when he heard that little boys and girls might be *pa-rum-pum-pum-pum*.

"Religious music should not be part of the elementary program(s)," Superintendent Scrooge wrote in her anti-Christmas screed. "It remains the District's mission to celebrate the rich and wonderful diversity of our children and community and hope that the joy shared through our numerous winter programs will continue to be a cherished part of your family traditions."[14]

So songs about Frosty, Rudolph, and mommy making out with

Santa Claus are fine, but harmonizing about round yon virgin will get you put on the naughty list.

Alliance Defending Freedom, a legal firm specializing in religious liberty cases, fired off a letter to the New Jersey grinches, reminding them it's perfectly constitutional to sing "Joy to the World."

The Alliance Defending Freedom letter explains, "Every federal court to examine the issue has determined that including Christmas carols and other religious music in school choir programs fully complies with the First Amendment."[15] As a result, the First Amendment requires that the district "remains neutral towards religion and refrains from demonstrating an unconstitutional hostility toward songs with religious origins."

And besides, folks love to sing about Baby Jesus as much as they do hauling out the holly. A 2011 Rasmussen poll found that 79 percent of American adults believe public schools should celebrate religious holidays.[16]

"Schools should not have to think twice about whether they can allow students to perform Christmas carols," said legal counsel Matthew Sharp. "Courts have unanimously upheld their inclusion in school productions, even when songs deal with Christian themes that are naturally a part of the holiday."[17]

"Misinformation about the First Amendment is frequently what leads to censorship of constitutionally permissible and culturally significant songs performed during Christmas concerts," added senior legal counsel Jeremy Tedesco. "We urge the Bordentown Regional School District to rescind this new policy and permit religious music to be included among the many non-religious songs performed at school concerts."[18]

How is it possible to have a concert celebrating the Christmas season—pardon me, winter season—without singing about the reason for the season? That's sort of like opening a barbecue joint and telling the customers they can't eat pork.

Perhaps the "enlightened" educators of Bordentown should take a swig or two of egg nog instead of getting their Christmas stockings in a bunch. Pardon me. Ahem. I meant to say *winter* stockings.

It's a Constitutional Crisis, Charlie Brown

The state of Arkansas found itself embroiled in a constitutional crisis over a stage version of *Merry Christmas, Charlie Brown*. The sordid scandal eventually led to a Little Rock church canceling a student matinee performance of the show after critics complained it was too religious and therefore violated the Establishment Clause of the Constitution. Good grief, Charlie Brown!

"It is not our desire to put hard-working, sacrificial teachers and cast members in harm's way," said Happy Caldwell, pastor of Agape Church, in a statement to Fox News. "While we regret the loss of students who will not get this particular opportunity right now, we have taken the school matinees off the table."

The cancellation came as the Arkansas Society of Freethinkers told television station KATV it had received legal advice on pursuing a possible lawsuit against the Little Rock School District. "We're not waging a war," crowed LeeWood Thomas, a spokesman for the group. "We're basically calling a foul against the separation of church and state."[19]

Here's the back story. Students at Terry Elementary School in Little Rock had been invited to attend an upcoming performance of *Merry Christmas Charlie Brown* at Agape Church. The theatrical production is adapted from the popular animated television classic, *A Charlie Brown Christmas*.

A Charlie Brown Christmas was the first prime-time animated television special featuring the Peanuts characters. It touched on the overcommercialization of Christmas and reminded viewers of the true meaning of the season. The show features a poignant moment when Linus recites passages of scripture from the Gospel of Luke noting the birth of Jesus Christ. "And that's what Christmas is all about," Linus said.[20]

The Little Rock School District said students were not required to attend the performance and that as far as the district is concerned, there is no controversy.

"The teachers wanted to provide an opportunity for cultural

enrichment for students through a holiday production and are supported by the principal," spokesperson Pamela Smith told Fox News. "Because it will be held at a church, as some public events often are, a letter was sent home with students so parents who took exception and wished to have their children remain at school could do so."

The Arkansas Society of Freethinkers said they were speaking out on behalf of a parent whose child attends the school. They said the parent felt forced to "choose between maintaining their family religious beliefs versus their child being singled out and possibly ostracized or bullied."[21]

"Merely allowing a child to opt out of a school-sponsored religious activity during the winter holidays is no solution," Anne Orsi, vice president of the group, said in a statement. "Such a situation exposes the children of minority faiths and outlooks to majority pressure and victimization. Thus the religious rights of children are being violated along with their right to privacy."[22]

The society said public schools should not take students to churches to see plays with religious content. "This isn't about Charlie Brown or Christmas," Orsi said in her statement. "It's about the separation of church and state.... We must be sensitive to that and never allow public schools to promote one brand of religion over any other."[23]

But attorneys with Alliance Defending Freedom said the secular group is way off base. "An overwhelming majority of Americans agree that it's okay to celebrate Christmas in schools and in the public square," attorney Matt Sharp said.[24]

The ADF sent a letter to the Little Rock School District offering their legal services should anyone sue over the performance. "Schools should not have to think twice about whether they can allow students to watch a classic Christmas production simply because a Bible verse is mentioned in it," Sharp said. "Are atheist groups going to start demanding that students be blocked from attending other classic productions just because they contain religious references?"[25]

The atheists refused to reveal the complainant over fears they might be singled out and bullied—much like how the atheists are singling out and bullying Christians.

The pastor of Agape Church said it was clear *Merry Christmas Charlie Brown* did not pose a constitutional issue. "Christmas is a Christian holiday—hence its name, Christmas," the pastor wrote in a statement. "Our program addresses its origins with light-hearted songs and theatre. The context of the birth of Christ is broadly described in both Old and New Testament texts."[26]

For the life of me I just don't understand why atheists get their britches in a bunch over something they don't even believe in.

The Day They Took Down the Christmas Crosses

One Christmas cross was perched high atop an Illinois water tower. Another was erected on the top of a hose tower at a Massachusetts fire station. Both were taken down after legal threats, leaving residents heartbroken and angry. It's another example of how atheists and secularists and their ilk are targeting small towns and communities.

For nearly seventy years a cross erected on the top of the hose tower at the Central Street fire station served as a beacon of the Christmas season. But that changed in 2004 when the Holliston Board of Selectmen ordered the cross removed over fears of a lawsuit. "Signs of the season are fine," Selectmen Chairman Andy Porter told the local newspaper. "But a cross is a symbol of religion versus a symbol of a holiday."[27]

But that wasn't good enough for the firefighters, who argued that the cross was a cherished tradition within the volunteer department. So over the past few years firefighter Gregg Lewis said they've been conducting a sort of covert operation—erecting the cross—and then taking it down once someone complained.

Finally, Lewis decided to make it official. He appealed to the Board of Selectmen for permission to legally resume the fire department's longtime tradition. The firefighters said they were frustrated by the lack of respect for the cross and what it means to the volunteers.

"A lot of history, a lot of tradition with the cross," Lieutenant Mark

Dellicker told me. "It's been handed down from generation to generation. We feel like we're letting all of the past firefighters down by letting it go. We're not trying to offend anybody, but it means a lot to us."

Not to everyone, though. The firefighters said there was one complaint filed, and that led to the trouble. "We talked to the guy," Dellicker said. "It [the cross] offended him for whatever reason. One out of 14,000—we aren't doing too bad."

Dellicker said it doesn't have anything to do with politics or religion, although he acknowledged the cross has a deeper meaning in his life. "When we go into a fire, we say prayers, and we hope that everyone is safe," he said. "And this is all part of it. Maybe the next thing is we can't even say prayers to our fellow firemen. I don't know where it's going to lead next."

And in Alsip, Illinois, officials were originally contacted by the Freedom From Religion Foundation (FFRF) and told their cross violated the so-called "separation of church and state." The Wisconsin-based group warned the village that unless the cross was removed, it could face a long legal battle.

"We work to keep religion out of government," FFRF co-president Annie Laurie Gaylor told the *Southtown Star.* "Towns can't put crosses on public structures such as water towers because we have separation between religion and government."[28]

The FFRF said they were acting on a complaint they allegedly received from a resident of the village. However, Mayor Patrick Kitching told local media that no one has ever complained about the cross, which was first erected atop the water tower in 1973. He said he was offended by the outcome.

"It's a tradition—and our tradition has been slapped down," he told the newspaper. "They told me an anonymous person complained. I doubt that. I think they were driving down the toll way and saw our cross."[29]

The Christmas cross is not too hard to miss. The lighted symbol is nineteen feet tall and is hoisted atop the water tower every holiday season. Kitching said he feared a possible lawsuit and the amount of money it would take to fight the out-of-state group. "In these economic times, the village cannot afford to waste any tax dollars on a lawsuit that simply cannot be won," he wrote in a letter to local residents and businesses. Kitching said they plan on replacing the cross with a tree. He said they won't call it a "Christmas" tree to avoid problems.[30]

"I thought about putting up a thirty-foot Grinch, but I couldn't find one," Kitching told the newspaper.[31]

If he can't find a Grinch, a thirty-foot devil would work just as well.

Neither Rain, Nor Sleet, Nor Hail, Nor Christmas Carols

A group of Christmas carolers was thrown out of a US Post Office in Silver Spring, Maryland, after the post office manager told them they were not allowed to sing Christmas carols on government property.

A spokesman for the US Postal Service confirmed the incident occurred at a branch office in the Aspen Hill Shopping Center. A trio of carolers walked into the building dressed in attire reminiscent of Charles Dickens and began singing.

"They were only a few notes into their carol when suddenly, out of the corner of my eye, I saw a scowling postal manager rushing to confront them," said J. P. Duffy, who was standing in a line with his wife and two-year-old daughter.

Duffy, who also happens to be a staff member of the Family Research Council, said he was stunned by what happened next. "He [the postal manager] told them that they had to leave immediately because they were violating the post office's policy against solicitation," Duffy said. "He told them they couldn't do this on government property. He said, 'You can't go into Congress and sing and you can't do it here either.'"

A spokesman for the US Postal Service's Capital Metro Area said the carolers had beautiful voices but were told they could not perform in the lobby. "Public assembly and public address, except when conducted or sponsored by the Postal Service, are prohibited in lobbies and other interior areas open to the public," the spokesperson told me.

"We have rules and regulations governing conduct on postal property," the spokesman added. "The only reason you should be inside is for postal business."

The carolers explained they had been performing at businesses in the shopping center for several years—including the post office—and had never encountered any problems. But the post office employee refused to budge and ordered them to leave. Duffy said that customers standing in line began to boo the postal worker.

"Over the last several years we have watched militant secularists team up with federal bureaucrats in the effort to sterilize the public square of anything remotely connected to anything religious," Duffy said. "This postal manager has clearly received the memo which has led him to stamp out Christmas caroling. But I have my own memo to all the Christmas carolers out there: let's not surrender to the secularist version of Christmas future."

I recall the words of Benjamin Franklin, the founder of the United States Post Office, who once wrote, "So shalt thou always live jollily; for a good conscience is a continual Christmas."[32]

"This is good advice that the US Post Office and all of us would do well to heed," Duffy said.

I suspect if Franklin were alive today, he'd use FedEx.

They Banned a Plant

Controversy embroiled Stockton, California, over allegations that elementary school teachers have been told they could not display poinsettias or Santa Claus in their classroom for fear it might offend people.

Yes, dear readers, they banned a plant.

"District office would like to remind everyone when displaying holiday decorations in and around school to be mindful no association to any religious affiliation i.e. Santa, poinsettias, Christmas trees, etc.," read a document obtained by News 10 in Sacramento that was reportedly sent to teachers at Claudia Landeen Elementary School. The same document said holiday decorations like snowmen and snowflakes were appropriate for grade school classrooms.[33]

Tom Uslan, superintendent of the Lincoln Unified School District, told News 10 that because there are "a myriad of religious affiliations [in the community].... We don't want a pervasive theme of a class to be representing one religious affiliation."[34]

Now, I must confess that I have a Kudzu League education as opposed to an Ivy League one, so I'm just going to be honest and say I don't have a clue what the superintendent was talking about. I picked up the phone and called the school district's spokesperson, hoping to set the record straight.

So, does that mean teachers can decorate their classrooms with Santa Claus and poinsettias?

"Not if that's going to be the pervasive theme," a school district spokesperson told me. "That's the operative word. If you're going to have a pervasive theme of one culture over another, unless it's part of the core curriculum, then we would encourage that not to be so."

Then the spokesperson said Stockton is a "very, very diverse community." She specifically mentioned the first Sikh temple in the West is located in the city.

"We want to be respectful of all of our community," she said. "To promote one over another in a public space or as a pervasive theme in a classroom would be inappropriate. Always be respectful."

Still, the school district fell back to their last line of defense: blaming the news reporter's "sloppy" reporting.

"The encouragement was not to be Christmas cops, not to be Menorah monitors, but to be sensitive and to be sure that people are respected," the spokesperson said.

Something tells me they aren't too jolly about holly either.

School District Expels Santa Claus

Students and parents in Fort Worth, Texas, were outraged after the school district declared Christmas celebrations—including visits from Santa Claus—would no longer be allowed during the school day.

The Fort Worth Independent School District also banned students exchanging Christmas gifts after they determined public schools could no longer "endorse or sponsor any religious activity or doctrine."

Apparently these poor misguided educators are under the impression that Jolly Old Saint Nick was present at the birth of Jesus.

I figured there must be a misunderstanding, so I called the school district. It turns out there was no misunderstanding. They told me that "in an effort to be politically correct," teachers are not allowed to "post something that would foster or promote or impugn one doctrine or religion over another—or even give that impression."

Seasonal decorations are still allowed, but they have to comply with the district's ban on decorations that are "religious in nature." In other words, don't expect to see any virgins round yonder.

"We have people of different races and religions, and to them this particular time of year may not be celebratory," school district spokesman Clint Bond told me. "Because of their religious beliefs, they may not choose to celebrate anything at this time of year."

But what about students and teachers who *do* celebrate Christmas?

It seemed a bit silly that a war on Christmas was being waged in Texas, so I called up my good friend Robert Jeffress, senior pastor of First Baptist Church in Dallas. He was just as upset as I was. He said it's time for Christians to rise up and put a stop to what he called "political correctness gone awry."

"America is a Christian nation," Jeffress said. "It's time for Americans to stand up and push back against this increasing encroachment upon our First Amendment rights."

Parents like Brandon Brewer are outraged. He has three children at Ridglea Hills Elementary School.

"In their effort to be PC, they've achieved the absurd," Brewer wrote in an e-mail to the *Fort Worth Star-Telegram.* "They've taken legality out of the equation, insisting that holiday traditions (secular or religious) are suddenly too much of a distraction, and besides, if we let Santa in, maybe a Voodoo Witch Doctor will want to visit the classrooms, and gee, we'd have to let 'em."[35]

Bond said the policy has been blown out of proportion and disputed the notion that they've "killed Santa," arguing instead that the values of all students must be considered. He blamed the controversy on a "cheap headline that was in the newspaper" that "unfortunately looks around the reality of the facts." He said many schools still have Santa artwork on the walls and display Christmas trees "with stars on top."

"We're not killing off the Great Pumpkin," he said. "We're not killing off Valentine's Day. We're not killing off the Easter Bunny. Those holidays are welcome in our school—at the appropriate time."

There are just three problems with Mr. Bond's logic: There's no such thing as a Great Pumpkin, Cupid, or the Easter Bunny.

I'll let Pastor Jeffress put the Santa ban in perspective: "We all agree [Santa] is not the reason for the season. However, it is a more insidious attempt to remove acknowledgement of Christmas from our mind-set. The bottom line is Christmas is a day to remember Christ's birth—and yes, we live in a pluralistic society, but we were still founded as a Christian nation, and I believe as Americans we have every right to exchange Christmas gifts and, in the school district, to celebrate Christmas."

Library Bans Nativity Scene

A Louisiana library banned a local church youth group from performing a living Nativity scene on its property because of its religious overtones. "They told us it was because they couldn't have anything with a religious tone or message," said Letha Dew, chairperson of SpringHill's annual Christmas celebration. "They had a problem with the Nativity."

The living Nativity was supposed to be set up at the SpringHill branch of the Webster Parish Library. It was just one part of a large Christmas celebration planned for the town's Main Street—a family-friendly holiday event.

"I was very, very surprised," Dew told me. "But this is the time we live in, and public entities have to be very careful. They are scrutinized. People threaten to sue over every little thing, and they have to do what they can to keep themselves out of trouble."

Rev. Patricia Stroud, the children's minister at First Assembly of God, told me she was very disappointed the young people would not be allowed on library property. "I think our Christian faith is being attacked," Stroud said. "Our nation was founded—in God we trust. Now when we try to share our faith, we're being questioned. That disturbs me."

Stroud said the living Nativity includes children and teenagers dressed as Mary, Joseph, and the wise men. Depending on the weather, she said they might even have a real baby portray Jesus. "We do have a couple of babies that are in consideration," she said.

She said it was hardly controversial. "We wanted to share Christ's love with our community. People could drive by and watch what happened on that wonderful Christmas night."

But the issue was the religious component of Christmas, and that has many people wondering what's really going on. "What could you even have if there's no religious message?" Dew wondered. "The only thing I could think of is Santa. Pretty much everything to do with Christmas has a religious message."

"Christ is the whole reason for Christmas, and we're getting away from that," Stroud agreed. "We're trying to be politically correct in everything we do."

For what it's worth, the library hasn't banned the Bible. But there's always next year.

Those are just a sampling of the battles being waged in the war on Christmas. But perhaps the most egregious happened during the lighting of the National Christmas Tree in 2013.

It was quite a festive December night. Great songs of the season filled the air. There was lots of yuletide cheer—until, that is, President Obama rose to speak. He told the audience Christmas is a time to celebrate the birth of a child that remained nameless. Then he made the following comments about the birth of that nameless child: "It's a message both timeless and universal—no matter what God you pray to, or if you pray to none at all."[36]

With one sentence, the president managed to deconstruct Christmas into a secular holiday free-for-all. Why does he do that? Why does President Obama always, and I mean *always*, marginalize Christian holidays?

In 2011 he failed to release a statement or a proclamation recognizing the national observance of Easter Sunday, Christianity's most sacred holiday. By comparison, the White House has released statements recognizing the observance of major Muslim holidays and released statements in 2010 on Ramadan,[37] Eid-ul-Fitr,[38] Hajj, and Eid-ul-Adha.[39]

The White House also failed to release a statement marking Good Friday. However, they did release an eight-paragraph statement heralding Earth Day.[40] In 2010 President Obama was criticized for releasing an all-inclusive Easter greeting. He reached out to Jews, Muslims, Hindus, and people of no faith at all in a statement about a holiday that is uniquely Christian.

"All of us are striving to make a way in this world; to build a purposeful and fulfilling life in the fleeting time we have here," Obama said in his 2010 "Easter" message. "A dignified life. A healthy life. A life, true to its potential. And a life that serves other. These are aspirations that stretch back through the ages—aspirations at the heart of Judaism, at the heart of Christianity, at the heart of all the world's great religions."[41]

When the White House released statements about Muslim holidays, no attempts were made to include Christianity or to mention a spirit of inclusivity. For example, in his 2010 statement on Hajj and Eid-ul-Adha, Obama made no references to Christianity or any other religion.[42]

By contrast, former President Bush traditionally included Scripture passages in his Easter messages and made a point to explain what Easter is about. In 2007 he said, "The resurrection of Jesus Christ is the most important event of the Christian faith.... On this powerful day, let us join together and give thanks to the Almighty for the glory of His grace."[43]

In his 2008 Easter message President Bush said, "The Resurrection of Jesus Christ reminds people around the world of the presence of a faithful God who offers a love more powerful than death. Easter commemorates our Savior's triumph over sin, and we take joy in spending this special time with family and friends and reflecting on the many blessings that fill our lives. During this season of renewal, let us come together and give thanks to the Almighty who made us in His image and redeemed us in His love."[44]

Yet in 2011 President Obama redefined the meaning of Christmas during his weekly address to the nation, calling on Americans to "remember the spirit of service"—whatever they believe.[45]

The president told Americans that Christmas is specifically about "giving of ourselves."

"Service to others—that's what this season is all about," Obama said. "For my family and millions of Americans, that's what Christmas is all about."[46]

That's not what Christmas is about for the Starnes family.

There were absolutely no mentions of Jesus, wise men, or even so much as a manger in the Obamas' address.

"So whatever you believe, wherever you're from, let's remember the spirit of service that connects us all this season—as Americans," he said. "Each of us can do our part to serve our communities and our country, not just today, but every day."[47]

The president also made the Christmas message all-inclusive, noting that "part of what it means to love God is to love one another, to be our brother's keeper and our sister's keeper."[48]

"But that belief is not just at the center of our Christian faith; it's shared by Americans of all faiths and backgrounds," Obama said.[49]

I don't know, folks. Maybe we should give President Obama the benefit of the doubt. Maybe he's simply unintentionally slighting his own religion. Maybe he doesn't really understand the true meaning of the Christian holidays.

So in the spirit of goodwill and patriotism, I'm going to help out the president. And I'll attempt to do so using a punctuation mark the president is so fond of using.

Christmas is about celebrating the birth of Jesus, Mr. President. Period.

Chapter 21

NAZIS, COMMUNISTS, AND THE USA

ITLER WAS NOT a big fan of the Baby Jesus. Neither were the communists. And apparently some American government employees and schoolteachers share an equal disdain for the little Lord Jesus.

You are about to read about some recent attempts to silence Christmas in the United States. These incidents illustrate chilling similarities to incidents that occurred during the regimes of the Nazis in Germany and the communists in the former Soviet Union and Vietnam.

In Long Island, New York, a school district came under fierce criticism from parents after educators removed all religious references in the traditional Christmas carol "Silent Night."

"It's kind of insulting," parent Robert Dowd told television station WCBS. His child attends Ralph J. Osgood Intermediate School in Kings Park, Long Island.[1]

Many parents and concert goers were stunned when the children sang the familiar Christmas carol—sans the references to Jesus. The words "holy infant," "round yon virgin" and "Christ the Savior" were taken out. Instead, the phrase "sleep in heavenly peace" was used.

School Superintendent Susan Agruso told the *Kings Park Patch* that the words were removed to prevent non-Christians from being offended. "The chorale director thought it was an appropriate way to represent the song without offending those of other faiths," Agruso told the newspaper.[2]

The outrage was so severe, the board of education apologized. They said the words were censored without approval from the district administration or the board of education. In other words, this was a case of passing the yuletide log.

A similar incident occurred in 2005 when educators at Ridgway Elementary School in Dodgeville, Wisconsin, secularized "Silent Night" for a school holiday program, drawing the ire of columnist Matt Barber. The secularized version of the song went something like this: "Cold in the night, no one in sight, winter winds, whirl and bite, how I wish I were happy and warm, safe with my family out in the storm."[3]

The Nazis also secularized "Silent Night." Their version went something like this:

> Silent night! Holy night!
> All is calm. All is bright.
>
> Only the Chancellor steadfast in fight
> Watches o'er Germany by day and by night.
> Always caring for us.
>
> Silent night! Holy night!
> All is calm. All is bright.
> Adolf Hitler is Germany's wealth,
> Brings us greatness, favor and health.
> Oh, give us Germans all power![4]

The great writer Jonah Goldberg noted that in 1938 Christmas carols and Nativity plays were entirely banned.[5]

Children's choirs in the Vietnamese province of Dak Lak were forbidden from singing "Silent Night," *Christianity Today* reported. There must be something about round yon virgins that terrifies the anti-Christian crowd.[6]

And that brings me to the quartet of incidents that rocked VA hospitals across the nation. Hospitals in four states placed restrictions on Christian volunteers, including a group of school children who were told they could only perform Christmas carols from a government-approved list.

In Iowa City American Legion members were told they could not hand out presents to veterans if the wrapping paper said Merry Christmas.[7] In Augusta, Georgia, the VA told a group of students from a Christian school that they could not sing religious-themed Christmas carols in the hospital's public places. Instead, the students were presented with a list of government-approved secular songs.[8] In Montgomery, Alabama, a woman was told she could not deliver goodie bags to patients because they were decorated with "Merry Christmas" wrapping paper. And in Dallas the VA hospital refused to allow children to distribute Christmas cards to patients because the cards included phrases such as "Merry Christmas" and "God Bless You."

Boys and girls from Grace Academy in Prosper, Texas, were planning on hand delivering the cards to wounded veterans at a VA hospital in Dallas. Math teacher Susan Chapman called the hospital to make final arrangements and that's when she learned there was a problem.

"I told him my students made cards, we'd like to bring them down for the veterans," Chapman told MyFoxDFW.com. "And he said, 'That's great. We're thrilled to have them, except the only thing is, we can't accept anything that says 'Merry Christmas' or 'God bless you' or any scriptural references because of all the red tape.'"[9]

A VA official quoted the policy which is in the Veterans Health Administration handbook:

> In order to be respectful of our Veterans' religious beliefs, all donated holiday cards are reviewed by a multi-disciplinary team of staff led by chaplaincy services and determined if they are appropriate (non-religious) to freely distribute to patients.... We regret this process was not fully explained to this group and apologize for any misunderstanding.[10]

"It really didn't occur to me there would be a problem with distributing Christmas cards," said Chapman. She is married to a veteran and is a volunteer with the American Legion and other veterans' organizations.[11]

Hiram Sasser, director of litigation for Liberty Institute, said it was a new low "even for the Scrooges and Grinches at the VA."

"Targeting the benevolent work of little children for censorship is disgusting," Sasser told me. "Do the Grinches in the administration of the VA really believe our bravest warriors need protection from the heartfelt well wishes of small children saying Merry Christmas?"

High school students from the Alleluia Community School were told they could sing about Frosty the Snowman but not Baby Jesus at the Charlie Norwood VA Medical Center in Augusta, Georgia.

Instead, when they arrived to perform, the students were given a list of twelve Christmas songs provided by the hospital's pastoral service that had been "deemed appropriate for celebration within the hearing range of all veterans." In other words, all secular, nothing sacred, the *Augusta Chronicle* reported.[12]

"Military service veterans, male and female, represent people of all faiths," hospital spokesman Brian Rothwell said in a statement to the newspaper. "It is out of respect for every faith that The Veterans Administration gives clear guidance on what 'spiritual care' is to be given and who is to give it."[13]

Dan Funsch, the school's principal, told me this is the first year they've been told not to perform religious carols. "Have we gotten to the point where there are approved Christmas songs?" he asked. "What concerns me is using our government to apply an agenda of aggressive secularization, systematically removing any reference to the Christian underpinnings of western civilization." The students opted not to deviate from their prepared selections and left without singing any carols.

The incidents reminded me of a story Ronald Reagan told on a radio program he hosted back in the 1970s. Reagan recounted a story about Christmas in the Ukraine before and after communism. The Communist leaders secularized a popular Ukrainian Christmas carol, "Joyous News Has Come to Us." Religious lyrics were replaced with references to the revolution and Lenin.[14]

The Liberty Counsel noted that the communists eventually banned Christmas celebrations, including Christmas trees and Santa Claus. But Christians there exhibited bravery and courage in confronting Communism's anti-Christmas campaign. Liberty Counsel went on to explain that young people would go out in the streets and sing Christmas carols, knowing full well that if the police heard their voices, they would be arrested and thrown into jail.[15]

The similarities are a bit chilling, eh? I can't help but think about those Christian boys and girls in Augusta, Georgia, who showed up at a VA hospital and were told they could only sing songs from a government-approved Christmas carol list. This is Obama's America, comrades.

Chapter 22

IT'S TIME TO TAKE A STAND

OUR NATION STANDS on a precipice. We are a people in grave danger. Freedom hangs in the balance. We live in a post-modern and post-God world that has increasingly become post-intelligent.

Tony Perkins, president of Family Research Council, and Kelly Shackelford, president of Liberty Institute, penned an open letter to the American people in 2013. Hostility against religious liberty has reached an all-time high, they warned. The freedom of religion is being pushed out of public life, schools, and even churches.

"Our Founding Fathers considered religious liberty our 'first freedom,' and the bedrock upon which all other freedoms rest," the men wrote. "They understood that one's right to worship God and follow his conscience according to the principles of his religious faith was foundational to civic tranquility. A man whose religious faith was repressed could never be a loyal citizen since the state was usurping his first allegiance and costing him his primary freedom. This is one of the most important distinctions that makes America an exceptional nation—if not the most important."[1]

Both groups document more than six hundred recent examples of religious hostility. *Six hundred.* American stories. Our stories. Their documentation included many stories I have covered during my career at Fox News Channel.

The Obama administration is trying to force religious organizations to provide insurance for birth control and abortion-inducing drugs in direct violation of their religious beliefs. The administration banned Bibles from Walter Reed Medical Center. The Internal Revenue Service launched investigations into pro-life organizations, demanding to know the contents of their prayers. They ordered a Wyoming church to turn over its membership rolls.

This is happening right here, right now, in the United States of America. We are under attack from within.

Billy Graham penned a letter expressing his dismay over the moral decline of the nation, declaring that his "heart aches for America and its deceived people."[2]

The man known as America's pastor delivered his concerns in the form of a prayer letter released by the Billy Graham Evangelistic Association just days after a gunman massacred a dozen people and injured many more at a movie theatre in Aurora, Colorado.

"The farther we get from God, the more the world spirals out of control," Graham wrote, noting that the nation seems to be going out of its way to remove God from the public arena.[3]

"Just a few weeks ago in a prominent city in the South, Christian chaplains who serve the police department were ordered to no longer mention the Name of Jesus in prayer," he wrote, noting that officers were only allowed to pray to "the being in the room."[4]

"Our society strives to avoid any possibility of offending anyone—except God," he continued.[5]

He likened the United States to the Old Testament cities of Sodom and Gomorrah and Nineveh.

"In Jonah's day, Nineveh was the lone world superpower—wealthy, unconcerned, and self-centered," Graham wrote. "When the Prophet Jonah finally traveled to Nineveh and proclaimed God's warning, people heard and repented. I believe the same thing can happen once again, this time in our nation."[6]

Of Sodom and Gomorrah, Graham recounted a conversation he had with his late wife, Ruth, while she was reading the draft of a book he was writing. The book dealt with the "terrible downward spiral of our nation's moral standards and the idolatry of worshiping false gods such as technology and sex."[7]

"She startled me by exclaiming, 'If God doesn't punish America, He'll have to apologize to Sodom and Gomorrah,'" Graham related.[8]

"I wonder what Ruth would think of America if she were alive today," he wrote. "In the years since she made that remark, millions of babies have been aborted and our nation seems largely unconcerned. Self-centered indulgence, pride, and a lack of shame over sin are now emblems of the American lifestyle."[9]

We ask God to bless America, but we elected a president whose pastor asked God to damn America. We ask God to bless America, but we slaughter millions of unborn babies. We ask God to bless America, but we silence His children.

God bless America? We should be on our knees asking for His mercy instead.

Here We Raise Our Ebenezer

Early on in this book I told you about those summers I spent at Rabbit Ridge in Byhalia, Mississippi. Oh, how I remember those good days! While the grownups gathered in the open-air tabernacle for an all-night singing, the boys and girls would run among the pine and sweet gum trees. But not me! I would sneak into the tabernacle and try to harmonize on the rip-roaring hymns.

There was one song that always perplexed me: "Come Thou Fount of Every Blessing." It was written by Robert Robinson in 1758. There was one particular line in the second verse I never understood: "Here I raise my Ebenezer."[10] Who was Ebenezer? Why did he need to be lifted? Was he heavy? Oh, the questions my young mind did ponder.

The phrase references a passage of Old Testament scripture, in 1 Samuel 7. The Israelites had once again found themselves in a pickle. So they summoned the prophet Samuel to intercede on their behalf. As the story goes, Samuel offered a sacrifice to God and prayed for His protection against the Philistines. The Philistines eventually lost the fight and retreated back to their own land. The Bible notes that Samuel took a stone and set it up between Mizpah and Shen. He called its name Ebenezer. "Thus far the LORD has helped us," Samuel said (v. 12).

In Hebrew, the word *Ebenezer* is translated "stone of help."[11] In the context of Mr. Robinson's song, it's a reminder to thank God for those moments He's come to our rescue. "Here I raise my Ebenezer; Hither by Thy help I'm come."

The time has come for people of faith to rise up and claim their Ebenezer. We need patriots who will take back this land. We need patriots who will say we are still one nation under God.

The storm clouds are gathering. The winds of revolution are blowing, friends. Religious liberty is under attack.

Will you, church member, be a sunshine citizen or an all-weather patriot?

Will you, pastor, be willing to take unpopular positions in the pulpit?

One pastor who's taken a stand is Robert Jeffress, senior pastor of the historic First Baptist Church in Dallas. I've mentioned him a few times in this book already, and that's because I count Pastor Jeffress among the men of God who preach the truth without fear or intimidation. He appeared on Fox News Channel awhile back and took his fellow ministers to task for shying away from tough topics.

"Wimpy pastors produce wimpy Christians—and that is why we are losing this culture war," he told Fox News Channel host Bill O'Reilly.[12]

He went on to say many Christian leaders are timid about addressing hot-button issues because they have the wrong idea about Jesus.

"They see Jesus as this little, wimpy guy who walked around plucking daisies and eating birdseed and saying nice things, but never doing anything controversial," the pastor said. "The fact is, Jesus did confront His culture with truth—and He ended up being crucified because of it."[13]

In today's society there is a price to be paid for taking a stand, the pastor said.

"I believe it's time for pastors to say, 'You know, I don't care about controversy, I don't care whether I'm going to lose church members, I don't care about building a big church. I'm going to stand for truth regardless of what happens,'" he said.[14]

Years ago the Christian songwriter Steve Green penned a song titled, "Find Us Faithful." It was a prayer that all who came after us would find this generation of believers faithful. The call still rings true today.

In these early days of the twenty-first century, the fire is flickering and the footprints are few. Storm clouds are gathering. The winds of persecution are blowing. But friends, no matter how difficult these days have become, let not your heart be troubled.

The sovereign Lord is our strength. And I believe He is raising up a new generation of believers—young people who are fervent in their faith, a new generation of Billy Grahams and Billy Sundays. Young men like Roy Costner and Jake Naman and young ladies like Audrey Jarvis who have raised their Ebenezer. They considered the cost, they took a stand, and God honored their faithfulness.

The time has come, brothers and sisters, my fellow countrymen. Who among you is willing to take a stand for religious liberty? Who among you is will to risk everything for the cause of Christ? Who among you is willing to rise up and declare that we are still one nation under God?

"If my people who are called by My name will humble themselves, and pray and seek My face, and turn from their wicked ways, then I will hear from heaven, and will forgive their sin and heal their land," the Scriptures declare (2 Chron. 7:14).

The most pressing problem facing America can't be solved in Washington DC. True hope and change can't be found at 1600 Pennsylvania Avenue. It can only be found at the foot of the cross on Calvary.

When militant homosexual activists launched attacks on Chick-fil-A and the *Duck Dynasty* family, millions of Christians rose up and took a stand. Remember what happened when Cracker Barrel announced they would no longer sell *Duck Dynasty* merchandise?

Within twenty-four hours of their announcement, the restaurant chain reversed their decision—and apologized for offending Christians.

We saw firsthand what could happen when people of faith mobilize. Hollywood and the mainstream media would have you believe we are the minority in this country. But I disagree. The outcry over Chick-fil-A and Obamacare and *Duck Dynasty* has proven them wrong.

Together we are a mighty force.

So, what are you going to do about it? We need men and women willing to stand firm in the faith. We need patriots willing to defend religious liberty. As I have outlined in these pages, we are in the midst of a culture war. American values are under attack. They may spy on our phone lines. They may throw us in jail. They may take away our shops and bakeries. They may demand to know the content of our prayers. But we will not be bullied. We will not be intimidated. We will not be silenced.

It's time for a new generation of believers to raise an Ebenezer. And as I write these final words from my home in Brooklyn, I issue this call to you, my fellow countrymen: Onward, Christian soldiers. Onward.

NOTES

Epigraph

1. As quoted in William J. Federer, *Treasury of Presidential Quotes* (St. Louis, MO: Americsearch, Inc., 2004), 373.

Introduction
God Bless America?

1. YouTube.com, "Obama in Turkey 'We Do Not Consider Ourselves a Christian Nation,'" http://www.youtube.com/watch?v=QIVd7YT0oWA (accessed January 28, 2014).

2. CBN News, "Obama to CBN News: We're no Longer Just a Christian Nation," http://www.cbn.com/cbnnews/204016.aspx (accessed January 28, 2014).

3. Sheryl Gay Stolberg, "The Spotlights Bright Glare," *New York Times*, December 4, 2009, http://www.nytimes.com/2009/12/06/fashion/06desiree .html?pagewanted=all&_r=0 (accessed February 4, 2014).

4. Andrew Silow-Carroll, "In Proclamation for Jewish Heritage Month, Obama Edits Out Standard Reference to Jesus," May 6, 2010, http://www .jweekly.com/article/full/57999/in-proclamation-for-jewish-heritage-month -obama-edits-out-standard/ (accessed January 28, 2014).

5. Kara Rowland, "White House Says Actions Louder Than Words on Lack of Easter Proclamation," *Washington Times*, April 25, 2011, http:// www.washingtontimes.com/blog/inside-politics/2011/apr/25/white-house -defends-obama-lack-easter-proclamation/ (accessed January 28, 2014).

6. Nicholas D. Kristof, "Obama:" Man of the World," March 6, 2007, http://www.nytimes.com/2007/03/06/opinion/06kristof.html?_r=0 (accessed January 28, 2014).

7. NBC Washington, "Whoops! Walter Reed Temporarily Bans Bibles," December 19, 2011, http://www.nbcwashington.com/news/local/Whoops -Walter-Reed-Temporarily-Bans-Bibles-135853463.html (accessed January 28, 2014).

8. James Dao, "Final Resting Place, and Battleground," *New York Times*, August 30, 2011, http://www.nytimes.com/2011/08/31/us/31funerals.html (accessed March 4, 2014).

9. WSOCTV.com, "CMPD Chaplains Told to Stop Invoking Jesus at Public Events," http://www.wsoctv.com/news/news/local/cmpd-chaplains -told-stop-invoking-jesus-public-eve/nPZdq/ (accessed January 28, 2014).

10. Liberty Institute, "Liberty Institute Defends Airman Persecuted for His Faith," October 12, 2013, http://www.libertyinstitute.org/pages/issues/in-the-public-arena/liberty-institute-defends-airman-persecuted-for-his-faith? (accessed January 28, 2014).

11. YouTube.com, "Jeremiah Wright: 'God Damn America,'" http://tinyurl.com/nxulqhn (accessed January 28, 2014).

12. Richard D. Land, "An Appeal to Christian Authenticity," CP Editorials, October 8, 2013, http://m.christianpost.com/news/an-appeal-to-christian-authenticity-106173/ (accessed January 28, 2014).

13. Stoyan Zaimov, "Richard Land Calls on Evangelicals to Reclaim Culture From Satan," *Christian Post*, October 13, 2013, http://www.christianpost.com/news/richard-land-calls-on-evangelicals-to-reclaim-culture-from-satan-106523/ (accessed January 28, 2014).

14. Library of Congress, "Thomas Paine Write 'The American Crisis,' December 1776," http://www.loc.gov/teachers/classroommaterials/presentationsandactivities/presentations/timeline/amrev/north/paine.html (accessed January 28, 2014). Regan.utexas.edu, "Inaugural Address," January 5, 1967, http://www.reagan.utexas.edu/archives/speeches/govspeech/01051967a.htm (accessed January 29, 2014).

15. Henry Wadsworth Longfellow, "Paul Revere's Ride," http://www.poemhunter.com/i/ebooks/pdf/henry_wadsworth_longfellow_2004_9.pdf (accessed March 4, 2014).

16. Ibid.

Chapter 1
The War on Christianity

1. CBN News, "Obama to CBN News: We're no Longer Just a Christian Nation."

2. Hank De Zutter, "What Makes Obama Run?", *Chicago Reader*, December 7, 1995, http://www.chicagoreader.com/chicago/what-makes-obama-run/Content?oid=889221 (accessed January 29, 2014).

3. Lindsay Goldwert, "Barack Obama: Faith Has Been 'Hijacked,'" CBS News, June 24, 2007, http://www.cbsnews.com/news/barack-obama-faith-has-been-hijacked/ (accessed January 29, 2014).

4. Ibid.

5. Jake Tapper and Amy Bingham, "Dems Quickly Switch to Include 'God,' 'Jerusalem,'" September 5, 2012, http://abcnews.go.com/Politics/OTUS/democrats-rapidly-revise-platform-include-god/story?id=17164108 (accessed January 29, 2014).

6. Ibid.; see also YouTube.com, "Democrats Boo God—Vote Him Out of Platform Before They Put Him Back In," http://www.youtube.com/watch?v=QxA_ZzPZleI (accessed January 29, 2014).

7. Mayhill Fowler, "Obama: No Surprise That Hard-Pressed Pennsylvanians Turn Bitter," *Huffington Post*, April 11, 2008, http://www

.huffingtonpost.com/mayhill-fowler/obama-no-surprise-that-ha_b_96188
.html (accessed January 29, 2014).

8. Lachlan Markay, "Defense Department Classifies Catholics, Evangelicals as Extremists," *Washington Times*, April 5, 2013, http://www
.washingtontimes.com/news/2013/apr/5/dod-presentation-classifies
-catholics-evangelicals/?page=1 (accessed January 30, 2014); Catholic News
Agency, "Military archdiocese objects to Catholic 'extremist' label," April 9,
2013, http://www.catholicnewsagency.com/news/military-archdiocese
-objects-to-catholic-extremist-label/ (accessed January 30, 2014).

9. Wesley Brown, "Augusta VA Won't Let Carolers Sing Religious Songs,"
Augusta Chronicle, December 23, 2013, http://chronicle.augusta.com/life/
your-faith/2013-12-23/augusta-va-wont-let-carolers-sing-religious-songs
(accessed January 30, 2014).

10. Associated Press, "Religious Groups: IRS Scrutinized Us," May 15,
2013, http://www.cbsnews.com/news/religious-groups-irs-scrutinized-us/
(accessed January 31, 2014).

11. Baptist Press, "IRS Affirms Biblical Recorder Tax," September 25,
2013, statushttp://www.bpnews.net/bpnews.asp?ID=41163 (accessed January
31, 2014).

12. Todd Starnes, "IRS Caught on Tape Telling Nonprofit: 'Keep Your
Faith to Yourself,'" Fox News, http://nation.foxnews.com/2013/06/10/irs
-caught-tape-telling-nonprofit-keep-your-faith-yourself (accessed January 31,
2014).

13. Mark Becker, "CMPD chaplains told to stop invoking Jesus at public
events," WSOCTV, June 19, 2012, http://www.wsoctv.com/news/news/local/
cmpd-chaplains-told-stop-invoking-jesus-public-eve/nPZdq/ (accessed January 31, 2014).

14. First Amendment Center, "Meal Prayer at Ga. Senior Center Stopped,
Then Restored," May 11, 2010, http://www.firstamendmentcenter.org/meal
-prayer-at-ga-senior-center-stopped-then-restored (accessed January 31,
2014).

15. *Christa Schultz, et al., v. Medina Valley Independent School District*,
United States District Court Western District of Texas, http://www.txwd
.uscourts.gov/Opinions/Cases/schultz/default.asp (accessed January 31, 2014).

16. Gerry Tuoti, "Taunton Second-Grader Sent Home Over Drawing of
Jesus," *Taunton Daily Gazette*, December 15, 2009, http://www.taunton
gazette.com/x1903566059/Taunton-second-grader-suspended-over-drawing
-of-Jesus (accessed January 31, 2014).

17. Mark Oppenheimer, "Astronomer Sues the University of Kentucky,
Claiming His Faith Cost Him a Job," December 18, 2010, http://www
.nytimes.com/2010/12/19/us/19kentucky.html (accessed January 31, 2014).

18. NBC Washington, "Whoops! Walter Reed Temporarily Bans Bibles."

19. American Freedom Law Center, "Christian Teacher Sues New York
Public School District for Restricting Her Religious Speech," January 10,

2013, http://www.americanfreedomlawcenter.org/press-release/christian
-teacher-sues-new-york-public-school-district-for-restricting-her-religious
-speech/ (accessed January 31, 2014).

20. Elisabeth Meinecke, "TH Magazine: Persecution of Christians... in
America," *Townhall Magazine*, August 6, 2013, http://townhall.com/
tipsheet/elisabethmeinecke/2013/08/16/th-magazine-persecution-of
-christians-in-america-n1662288 (accessed January 31, 2014).

21. Alliance Defending Freedom, "Evicting a Widow's Prayer," October
19, 2012, http://www.alliancedefendingfreedom.org/News/PRDetail/7706
(accessed January 31, 2014).

22. Ibid.

23. Ibid.

24. Ibid.

25. Becker, "CMPD chaplains told to stop invoking Jesus at public events."

26. The Rutherford Institute, "Ariz. Man Jailed for 60 Days for Home
Bible Study to Appear in Court for Violating Probation by Holding Additional Bible Studies on His Property," July 16, 2012, https://www.rutherford
.org/publications_resources/on_the_front_lines/ariz_man_jailed_for_60_
days_for_home_bible_study_to_appear_in_court_for_vio (accessed January
31, 2014).

27. Katherine T. Phan, "Phoenix Officials Release 'Fact Sheet" in Jailed
Pastor's Home Bible Study Case," July 12, 2012, http://www.christianpost
.com/news/city-of-phoenix-release-fact-sheet-in-michael-salman-jail-pastor
-home-bible-study-case-78153/ (accessed January 31, 2014).

28. 9News.com, "Sterling cemetery 'Jesus' controversy," October 18, 2013,
http://www.9news.com/news/article/360364/339/Sterling-cemetery
-backtracks-after-Jesus-ban?chrisitian_persecution_complex_again (accessed
January 31, 2014).

29. The Salem News, "Park Service Rescinds Permit Requirement for
Baptisms," August 20, 2010, http://www.thesalemnewsonline.com/news/
local_news/article_ccc35038-09a8-11e3-9ce3-001a4bcf6878.html (accessed
January 31, 2014).

30. Ibid.

31. Ibid.

32. Department of the Interior National Park Service, http://jasonsmith
.house.gov/sites/jasonsmith.house.gov/files/Park%20Service%20Letter_0.pdf
(accessed January 31, 2014).

33. Ibid.

34. Ibid.

35. Drew Mikkelsen, "Olympia Church May Sue State Over Baptism
Dispute," King5.com, August 15, 2011, http://www.king5.com/news/cities/
olympia/Olympia-church-may-sue-state-over-baptism-dispute-127794213
.html (accessed January 31, 2014).

36. Tamar Lewin, "Some U.S. Universities Install Foot Baths for Muslim Students," August 7, 2007, http://www.nytimes.com/2007/08/07/world/americas/07iht-muslims.4.7022566.html?_r=0 (accessed January 31, 2014).

37. Ibid.

38. USA Today, "Sky Harbor Installs Cleanup Station for Muslim Drivers," May 20, 2004, http://usatoday30.usatoday.com/travel/news/2004-05-20-muslims-airport_x.htm (accessed January 31, 2014).

39. *Phil Matier and Andy Ross*, "Airport's Garage Now Muslim House of Worship," SF Gate, June 9, 2013, http://blog.sfgate.com/matierandross/2013/06/09/airports-garage-now-muslim-house-of-worship/ (accessed January 31, 2014).

40. Ibid.

41. John H. Hutson, *The Founders on Religion: A Book of Quotations* (Princeton, NJ: Princeton University Press, 2009).

42. Mackenzie Zaragoza, "Controversy Still Surrounds a Cross-Shaped Flowerbed in Local Park," WTVM, July 25, 2012, http://www.wtvm.com/story/19105137/controversy-still-surrounds-a-cross-shaped-flower-bed (accessed January 31, 2014).

43. Ibid.

44. Cindy Stauffer, "Atheist Files Complaint Over Restaurant's Sunday Promotion," *York Daily Record*, July 15, 2012, http://www.ydr.com/ci_20996278/atheist-files-complaint-over-restaurants-sunday-promotion (accessed January 30, 2014).

45. Freedom From Religion Foundation, "About the Foundation FAQ," http://ffrf.org/faq/item/14999-what-is-the-foundations-purpose (accessed January 31, 2014).

46. LanscasterOnline, "Atheist Files Complaint Over Restaurant's Sunday Promotion," July 2, 2012, http://lancasteronline.com/news/atheist-files-complaint-over-restaurant-s-sunday-promotion/video_3e384646-fcf7-5445-8bf8-f7631e31dfd9.html (accessed March 4, 2014).

47. John Rutter, "Columbia Restaurant Gets OK to Give Discounts to Patrons With Church Bulletins," LancasterOnline, November 28, 2012, http://lancasteronline.com/article/local/787132_Columbia-restaurant-gets-OK-to-give-discounts-to-patrons-with-church-bulletins.html (accessed January 31, 2014).

48. Ephesians 6:12, NIV.

49. Stuart Hughes, "The Greatest Motivational Poster Ever?", BBC News, February 4, 2009, http://news.bbc.co.uk/2/hi/uk_news/magazine/7869458.stm (accessed January 31, 2014).

Chapter 2
From the Annals of God-Blessed Living:
Baptists, Bagels, and Brooklyn

1. Nicholas D. Kristof, "Obama:" Man of the World," March 6, 2007, http://www.nytimes.com/2007/03/06/opinion/06kristof.html?_r=0 (accessed January 31, 2014).

Chapter 3
Chick-fil-A: The Gospel Bird

1. Sarah Arathun, "Chick-fil-A Wades Into a Fast-Food Fight Over Same-Sex Marriage Rights," July 28, 2012, http://www.cnn.com/2012/07/27/us/chick-fil-a-controversy/ (accessed January 31, 2014).

2. Tim Craig, "Gray Opposes Chick-fil-A Expansion; Calls It 'Hate Chicken,'" *Washington Post*, July 28, 2012, http://www.washingtonpost.com/blogs/dc-wire/post/gray-opposes-chick-fil-a-expansion-calls-it-hate-chicken/2012/07/27/gJQA8SlREX_blog.html (accessed January 31, 2014).

3. Jan Ransom, "Kenney Tells Chick-fil-A President to Take a Hike," Philly.com, July 25, 2012, http://www.philly.com/philly/blogs/cityhall/Kenney-tells-Chick-Fil-A-president-to-take-a-hike.html#FlvrYD7uj72D3dzH.99 (accessed January 30, 2014).

4. Anna Susman, "Chick-fil-A Controversy: University of Louisville Students Protest to Remove On-Campus Fast-Food Joint," *Huffington Post*, July 27, 2012, http://www.huffingtonpost.com/2012/07/27/college-students-protest-chick-fil-a_n_1711001.html (accessed January 31, 2014); Timothy Sandoval, "In Gay-Rights Protest, Students Try to Push Chick-fil-A Off Campuses," *The Chronicle of Higher Education*, August 1, 2012, http://chronicle.com/article/In-Gay-Rights-Protest/133347 (accessed January 31, 2014); Zack Ford, "Emory University Students Aren't Backing Down Campaign Against Campus Chick-fil-A," Think Progress, January 30, 2013, http://thinkprogress.org/lgbt/2013/01/30/1517621/emory-university-students-arent-backing-down-campaign-against-campus-chick-fil-a/ (accessed January 31, 2014).

5. Hal Dardick, "Alderman to Chick-fil-A: No Deal," Chicago Tribune, July 25,m 2012, http://articles.chicagotribune.com/2012-07-25/news/ct-met-chicago-chick-fil-a-20120725_1_1st-ward-gay-marriage-ward-alderman (accessed January 31, 2014).

6. Ibid.

7. Ibid.

8. National Association of Evangelicals, "Chick-fil-A Clashes Threaten Religious Freedom," July 30, 2012, http://www.nae.net/resources/news/792-press-release-chick-fil-a-clashes-threaten-religious-freedom (accessed January 31, 2014).

9. *Huffington Post*, "Maryland Chick-fil-A Vandalized in Overnight Incident," August 13, 2012, http://www.huffingtonpost.com/2012/08/13/maryland-chick-fil-a_n_1772443.html (accessed January 31, 2014); *Los Angeles Times*, "Gay Artist Arrested in Chick-fil-A 'Hate' Vandalism Incident," August 10, 2012, http://latimesblogs.latimes.com/lanow/2012/08/gay-artist-arrested-in-chick-fil-a-hate-vandalism-incident.html (accessed January 31, 2014).

10. Anne Sorock, "Chicago Chick-fil-A Kiss-In Protesters 'Chalk' Homeless Street Preacher," August 4, 2012, http://legalinsurrection.com/2012/08/chicago-chick-fil-a-kiss-in-protesters-chalk-homeless-street-preacher/ (accessed January 31, 2014); Examiner.com, "Chicago Values: Gay Activists Harass, Chalk Black Street Preacher at Chick-fil-A," August 5, 2012, http://www.examiner.com/article/chicago-values-gay-activists-harass-chalk-black-street-preacher-at-chick-fil-a (accessed January 31, 2014).

11. *Journal*, "Chick-fil-A in Martinsburg Re-Opens After Bomb Threat," August 1, 2012, http://www.journal-news.net/page/content.detail/id/582561/Bomb-threat-called-in-to-Chick-f---.html (accessed January 30, 2014).

12. Tanya Eiserer, "Dallas Police Sergeant Transferred Over Chick-Fil-A Incident," August 8, 2012, http://crimeblog.dallasnews.com/2012/08/dallas-police-sergeant-transferred-over-chick-fil-a-incident.html/ (accessed January 31, 2014).

13. YouTube.com, "Adam M Smith at Chick Fil A drive thru," August 2, 2012, http://www.youtube.com/watch?v=VFdPBtxzT6k (accessed January 31, 2014).

14. Ibid.

15. Ibid.

16. ArmitageChurch.org, "An Appeal to Mayor Rahm Emanuel," http://armitagechurch.org/_pdf/appealtomayor.pdf (accessed January 31, 2014).

17. Ibid.

Chapter 4
No Christian Left Behind

1. Rebecca Shimoni Stoil, "Saeed Abedini, DC's Other Iran Issue, Comes to the Fore," *Times of Israel*, November 10, 2013, www.timesofisrael.com/saeed-abedini-dcs-other-iran-issue-comes-to-the-fore/ (accessed January 30, 2014).

2. Jordan Sekulow, "An Appalling Betrayal of American Pastor Saeed Abedini," American Center for Law and Justice, November 24, 2013, http://aclj.org/iran/appalling-betrayal-american-pastor-saeed-abedini (accessed February 1, 2014); David French, "The American Pawns of the American Government," American Center for Law and Justice, December 13, 2013, http://aclj.org/iran/the-american-pawns-of-the-american-government (accessed February 7, 2014).

3. Cruz.senate.gov, "Cruz on Iranian Prisoner Abedini: Unconscionable That Top American Diplomats Did Not Mention His Name," December 5, 2013, http://www.cruz.senate.gov/?p=press_release&id=694 (accessed February 1, 2014).

4. Leah Barkoukis, "Wife of US Pastor Held in Iran: 'I Never Thought I'd Have to Battle My Own Gov't for My Husband's Freedom,'" Townhall.com, December 12, 2013, http://townhall.com/tipsheet/leahbarkoukis/2013/12/12/naghmeh-abedini-i-never-thought-id-have-to-battle-my-own-government-for-my-husbands-freedom-n1762235 (accessed February 1, 2014)

5. President Obama, Remarks at National Prayer Breakfast, Washington Hilton, February 6, 2014, http://www.whitehouse.gov/the-press-office/2014/02/06/remarks-president-national-prayer-breakfast (accessed February 7, 2014).

6. Glenn Kessler, "During Visit by Bill Clinton, North Korea Releases American Journalists," *Washington Post*, August 5, 2009, http://www.washingtonpost.com/wp-dyn/content/article/2009/08/04/AR2009080400684.html (accessed February 1, 2014).

7. The White House, Office of the Press Secretary, "Statement of President Barack Obama on the Unjust Detention of Sarah Shourd, Shane Bauer, and Josh Fattal," July 30, 2010, http://www.whitehouse.gov/the-press-office/statement-president-barack-obama-unjust-detention-sarah-shourd-shane-bauer-and-josh (accessed February 1, 2014).

8. Federal Bureau of Investigations, "Meeting With President Obama," http://www.fbi.gov/news/stories/2012/march/levinson/press-conference-gallery/meeting-with-president-obama/view (accessed February 1, 2014).

9. Samaritan's Purse, "Billy Graham Calls for Pastor Saeed's Release," September 26, 2013, http://www.samaritanspurse.org/article/billy-graham-calls-for-pastor-saeeds-release/ (accessed February 1, 2014).

Chapter 5
So Absurd It Could Be True:
The Gospel According to Barack Obama

1. Frank Newport, "Many Americans Can't Name Obama's Religion," Gallup Politics, http://www.gallup.com/poll/155315/many-americans-cant-name-obamas-religion.aspx (accessed February 1, 2014).

2. YouTube.com, "Barack Hussein Obama Mmm Mmm Mmm," http://www.youtube.com/watch?v=9Ty7WU872Lk (accessed February 1, 2014).

3. Real Clear Politics, "Jamie Foxx: "Our Lord And Savior Barack Obama," http://www.realclearpolitics.com/video/2012/11/26/jamie_foxx_our_lord_and_savior_barack_obama.html (accessed February 1, 2014).

4. *Daily Caller*, "Book compares Obama to Jesus Christ and Martin Luther King," http://dailycaller.com/2012/11/09/book-compares-obama-to-jesus-christ-and-martin-luther-king/ (accessed February 1, 2014).

5. Sasha Johnson and Candy Crowley, "Winfrey tells Iowa crowd: Barack Obama is 'the one,'" CNNPolitics.com, December 8, 2007, http://www.cnn.com/2007/POLITICS/12/08/oprah.obama/ (accessed February 1, 2014).

6. Jake Tapper and Amy Bingham, "Dems Quickly Switch to Include 'God,' 'Jerusalem.'"

7. The Lonely Conservative, "Newsweek Inauguration Special—The Second Coming Of Obama," January 19, 2013, http://lonelyconservative.com/2013/01/newsweek-inauguration-special-the-second-coming-of-obama/ (accessed February 1, 2014).

8. Matthew Breen, "In Obama We Trust," *Advocate*, http://www.advocate.com/print-issue/cover-stories/2012/07/13/obama-we-trust (accessed February 1, 2014).

9. *Newsweek* cover, November 22, 2010.

10. Kyle Drennen, "*Newsweek*'s Evan Thomas: Obama Is 'Sort of God,'" June 5, 2009, http://newsbusters.org/blogs/kyle-drennen/2009/06/05/newsweek-s-evan-thomas-obama-sort-god (accessed February 1, 2014).

11. Ibid.

12. Lynn Elber, "Spike Lee Takes Jackson to Task for Obama Comments," *USA Today*, July 9, 2011, http://usatoday30.usatoday.com/life/people/2008-07-10-spike-lee-obama_N.htm (accessed February 1, 2014).

13. Billy Hallowell, "Obama to accompany Baby Jesus & Wise Men in Italian Nativity Scenes (Yes, Really)," TheBlaze, November 9, 2012, http://www.theblaze.com/stories/2012/11/09/obama-to-accompany-baby-jesus-wise-men-in-italian-nativity-scenes-yes-really/ (accessed February 1, 2014).

14. WND Faith, "Video Stunner: Boy Prays to Obama," August 12, 2013, http://www.wnd.com/2013/08/video-stunner-boy-prays-to-obama/ (accessed February 1, 2014).

15. Hot Air, "Michelle Obama: This President Has Led Us Out of the Darkness and Into the Light," April 17, 2012, http://hotair.com/archives/2012/04/17/michelle-obama-baracks-led-us-out-of-the-darkness-and-into-the-light/comment-page-2/ (accessed February 1, 2014).

16. Jonathan Alter, *The Promise: President Obama, Year One* (New York: Simon & Schuster, 2010), 102.

Chapter 6
Are You Now or Have You Ever Been a Christian?

1. Ali Weinberg and Andrew Mach, "Pastor Nixed From Obama Inaugural Over Anti-Gay Remarks," January 10, 2013, http://usnews.nbcnews.com/_news/2013/01/10/16449097-pastor-nixed-from-obama-inaugural-over-anti-gay-remarks?lite (accessed February 1, 2014).

2. Jonathan Karl, "Pastor Backs Out of Obama Inauguration Over Previous Anti-Gay Comments," ABC News, January 10, 2013, http://abcnews.go.com/blogs/politics/2013/01/obama-inauguration-pastor-steps-down-over-previous-anti-gay-comments/ (accessed February 1, 2014).

3. John Nolte, "Memory Holed: New York Times Reported White House Forced Pastor to Quit Inauguration," Breitbart.com, January 14, 2013, http://www.breitbart.com/Big-Journalism/2013/01/14/NYTs-Reports-White-House-Forced-Pastor-Out (accessed February 1, 2014).

4. Natalie Jennings, "Louie Giglio Pulls Out of Inauguration Over Anti-Gay Comments," *Washington Post*, January 10, 2013, http://www.washingtonpost.com/blogs/post-politics/wp/2013/01/10/louie-giglio-pulls-out-of-inaugural-over-anti-gay-comments/ (accessed February 1, 2014); Billy Hallowell, "Pastor Louie Giglio Withdraws From Obama Inauguration Following Furor Over Past Sermon about Gays," TheBlaze, January 10, 2013, http://www.theblaze.com/stories/2013/01/10/pastor-withdraws-from-obamas-inauguration-after-furor-following-past-comments-about-homosexuality/ (accessed February 1, 2014).

5. Ruth Malhotra and Jennifer Keeton, "Tolerance Tyrants Strike Again: Louie Giglio, the Inaugural Uproar, and a Marketplace of Ideas" *Christian Post*, January 21, 2013, http://www.christianpost.com/news/tolerance-tyrants-strike-again-louie-giglio-the-inaugural-uproar-and-a-marketplace-of-ideas-88590/ (accessed February 1, 2014).

6. AlbertMohler.com, "The Giglio Imbroglio—The Public Inauguration of a New Moral McCarthyism," January 10, 2013, http://www.albertmohler.com/2013/01/10/the-giglio-imbroglio-the-public-inauguration-of-a-new-moral-mccarthyism/ (accessed February 1, 2014).

7. Ibid.

8. Ibid.

9. Ibid.

10. Hallowell, "Pastor Louie Giglio Withdraws From Obama Inauguration Following Furor Over Past Sermon about Gays."

11. United States Senate, "'Have You No Sense of Decency?'," http://www.senate.gov/artandhistory/history/minute/Have_you_no_sense_of_decency.htm (accessed February 1, 2014).

Chapter 8
Gay Rights vs. Religious Rights

1. Charles C. Haynes, "For Most Americans, Gay Equality Trumps Religious Objections," First Amendment Center, August 8, 2013, http://www.firstamendmentcenter.org/for-most-americans-gay-equality-trumps-religious-objections (accessed February 1, 2014).

2. Ibid.

3. David Brody, "Brody File Video Exclusive: Ted Cruz Warns That Charging Pastors With Hate Speech Is Next Step," The Brody File, July 23, 2013, http://blogs.cbn.com/thebrodyfile/archive/2013/07/23/brody-file-video-exclusive-ted-cruz-warns-that-charging-pastors.aspx (accessed February 1, 2014).

4. Scott Sloan, "Hands On Originals T-shirt Company Accused of Discrimination," Kentucky.com, March 26, 2012, http://www.kentucky.com/2012/03/26/2127245/hands-on-originals-t-shirt-company.html (accessed February 1, 2014).

5. Mike Adams, "The Cisco Kid," Townhall.com, June 16, 2011, http://townhall.com/columnists/mikeadams/2011/06/16/the_cisco_kid/page/full (accessed February 1, 2014).

6. Liberty Counsel, "Virginia Employee Fired for Supporting Marriage Amendment," October 20, 2006 http://www.lc.org/index.cfm?PID=14100&PRID=243&printpage=y (accessed February 1, 2014).

7. Alliance Defense Fund, "ADF Files Suit After North Carolina High School Suspends Student for Distributing Day of Truth Card," May 4, 2006, http://www.alliancedefendingfreedom.org/News/PRDetail/1297 (accessed February 1, 2014).

8. Dave Bohon, "School District Sued for Punishing Student's Opposition to 'Gay' Lifestyle," The New American, December 21, 2011, http://www.thenewamerican.com/culture/education/item/378-school-district-sued-for-punishing-students-opposition-to-gay-lifestyle (accessed February 1, 2014).

9. Joshua Rhett Miller, "Indianapolis Bakery Declines Order for Rainbow Cupcakes, Sparking City Inquiry," FoxNews.com, September 29, 2010, http://www.foxnews.com/us/2010/09/29/city-officials-launch-inquiry-cupcake-denial-gay-student-group/ (accessed February 1, 2014).

10. Jesse McKinley, "Theater Director Resigns Amid Gay-Rights Ire," New York Times, November 12, 2008, http://www.nytimes.com/2008/11/13/theater/13thea.html?_r=0 (accessed February 1, 2014).

11. Washington Blade, "Who Signed the Md. Anti-Gay Marriage Petition?", July 25, 2012, http://www.washingtonblade.com/2012/07/25/who-signed-the-md-anti-gay-marriage-petition/ (accessed February 1, 2014).

12. YouTube.com, "Anti-Gay Preacher Gets Beat-Up at Seattle Pride," http://www.youtube.com/watch?v=bEcilTcjk9g (accessed February 1, 2014).

13. Ivan Moreno, "Colorado's Masterpiece Cakeshop Must Serve Gay Couples Despite Owner's Religious Beliefs, Judge Rules," Huffington Post, December 6, 2013, http://www.huffingtonpost.com/2013/12/06/colorado-baker-gay-ruling-_n_4401050.html (accessed February 1, 2014).

14. Charlie Craig and David Mullins v. Masterpiece Cakeshop, Inc., American Civil Liberties Union, https://www.aclu.org/sites/default/files/assets/initial_decision_case_no._cr_2013-0008.pdf (accessed February 1, 2014).

15. American Civil Liberties Union of Colorado, "Court Rules Bakery Illegally Discriminated Against Gay Couple," December 6, 2013, http://aclu-co.org/news/court-rules-bakery-illegally-discriminated-against-gay-couple (accessed February 1, 2014).

16. American Civil Liberties Union, https://www.aclu.org/sites/default/files/assets/initial_decision_case_no._cr_2013-0008.pdf (accessed February 1, 2014).

17. American Civil Liberties Union of Colorado, "Court Rules Bakery Illegally Discriminated Against Gay Couple."

18. Alliance Defending Freedom, "Colo. Court Denies Baker's Freedom in Same-Sex Ceremony Suit," December 6, 2013, http://www.alliancedefendingfreedom.org/News/Detail?ContentID=71948 (accessed February 1, 2014).

19. Ibid.

20. Maxine Bernstein, "Lesbian Couple Refused Wedding Cake Files State Discrimination Complaint," *Oregonian*, August 14, 2013, http://www.oregonlive.com/gresham/index.ssf/2013/08/lesbian_couple_refused_wedding.html#incart_m-rpt-2 (accessed February 1, 2014).

21. KPTV.com, http://www.kptv.com/video?clipId=9265800&autostart=true (accessed February 1, 2014).

22. *Elane Photography, LLC, v. Vanessa Willock*, Alliance Defending Freedom, http://www.adfmedia.org/files/ElanePhotoNMSCopinion.pdf (accessed February 1, 2014).

23. Ibid.

24. Ibid.

25. Ibid.

26. Ibid.

27. Alliance Defending Freedom, NM Supreme Court to Christians: There Is a 'Price' for Your Beliefs," August 22, 2013, http://www.alliancedefendingfreedom.org/News/PRDetail/8465 (accessed February 1, 2014).

28. Fox News, "DC Comics Faces Boycott Over Anti-Gay Superman,." http://radio.foxnews.com/toddstarnes/top-stories/dc-comics-faces-boycott-over-anti-gay-superman-writer.html (accessed January 30, 2014).

29. GLAAD.org, "Orson Scott Card," http://www.glaad.org/cap/orson-scott-card (accessed February 1, 2014).

30. All Out, "DC Comics: Drop Orson Scott Card!", https://www.allout.org/en/actions/dccomics-osc (accessed February 1, 2014).

31. Queerty, "Why Did DC Comics Hire Rabid Homophobe Orson Scott Card to Write 'Superman'?" http://www.queerty.com/why-did-dc-comics-hire-rabid-homophobe-orson-scott-card-to-write-superman-20130212/ (accessed February 1, 2014).

32. Dominic Rushe, "DC Comics Under Fire for Hiring Anti-Gay Writer to Pen Superman," *Guardian*, February 11, 2013, http://www.theguardian.com/culture/2013/feb/11/dc-comics-homophobic-writer-superman (accessed February 1, 2014).

33. Ibid.

34. Michael Hartney, "I Just Wrote This to DC Comics," Tumblr.com, http://michaelhartney.tumblr.com/post/42809859391/i-just-wrote-this-to-dc-comics (accessed February 1, 2014).

35. *Linda M. Ozum v. Lamar University and Judith Sebesta*, http://www.courthousenews.com/2012/03/29/45140.htm (accessed February 1, 2014).

36. Ibid.

37. Ibid.

38. Ibid.

39. Ibid.

40. Ibid.

41. Ibid.

42. Ibid.

43. *Star Ledger*, "Union Township School Officials Investigate Teacher Who Allegedly Made Anti-Gay Remarks on Facebook," NJ.com, October 13, 2011, http://www.nj.com/news/index.ssf/2011/10/union_township_school_official.html (accessed February 1, 2014).

44. CBS New York, "NJ Teacher's Husband Defends Wife As Rally Is Held Condemning Alleged Anti-Gay Comments," October 13, 2011, http://newyork.cbslocal.com/2011/10/18/activists-to-demand-union-high-teacher-be-fired-for-alleged-anti-gay-comments-on-facebook/ (accessed February 1, 2014).

45. Jenna Johnson, "Gallaudet Diversity Officer on Paid Leave after Signing Petition on Same-Sex Marriage Law," *Washington Post*, October 10, 2012, http://www.washingtonpost.com/local/education/gallaudet-diversity-officer-accuses-university-of-discrimination-in-lawsuit/2013/09/30/2c8268be-2a07-11e3-b139-029811dbb57f_story.html (accessed February 1, 2014).

46. Ibid.

47. Lee P. Washington, "Press Release: Dr. Angela McCaskill," Reidtemple.org, http://www.reidtemple.org/pages/page.asp?page_id=236814 (accessed February 1, 2014).

48. Ibid.

49. Ibid.

50. PRN Newswire, "Gallaudet University Punishes Official for Signing Marriage Ballot Petition" October 10, 2012, http://www.prnewswire.com/news-releases/gallaudet-university-punishes-official-for-signing-marriage-ballot-petition-173590901.html (accessed February 1, 2014).

51. Ibid.

52. *Washington Post*, "Gallaudet's Mistake," October 13, 2012, http://www.washingtonpost.com/opinions/gallaudets-mistake/2012/10/13/86dbad96-148e-11e2-bf18-a8a596df4bee_story.html (accessed February 1, 2014).

53. Liberty Counsel, "LGBT Inclusion at Work: The 7 Habits of Highly Effective Managers," http://libertycounsel.com/wp-content/uploads/2013/05/LGBT_tips_for_managers.pdf (accessed February 1, 2014).

54. Ibid.

55. Ibid.

56. Chloé Sorvino, "Students Mobilize to Remove Priest," *GW Hatchet*, April 4, 2013, http://www.gwhatchet.com/2013/04/04/students-mobilize-to -remove-priest/ (accessed February 1, 2014).

57. Ibid.

58. Ibid.

59. Jeff Weinsier, "School District Looks to Evict Controversial Pastor," Local10.com, July 16, 2012, http://www.local10.com/news/School-district -looks-to-evict-controversial-pastor/-/1717324/15563548/-/11etoovz/-/index .html (accessed February 1, 2014).

60. Jeff Weinsier, "Controversial Sermons at Public School Questioned," Local10.com, July 15, 2012, http://www.local10.com/news/Controversial -sermons-at-public-school-questioned/-/1717324/15505984/-/1073igjz/-/index .html (accessed February 1, 2014).

61. Bob Unruh, "Judge: Following Christian Beliefs Wrong," WND Faith, January 12, 2012, http://www.wnd.com/2012/01/judge-says-following -christian-beliefs-wrong/ (accessed February 1, 2014).

62. American Civil Liberties Union of New Jersey, "Judge Rules in Favor of Same-Sex Couple in Discrimination Case," January 13, 2012, http://www .aclu-nj.org/news/2012/01/13/judge-rules-in-favor-of-same-sex-couple-in -discrimination-case/ (accessed February 4, 2014).

63. Lori Culbert, "Gay Couple Wins Human Rights Battle After Reserva- tion Cancelled at B.C. B&B," *Vancouver Sun*, July 18, 2012, http://www .vancouversun.com/travel/couple+wins+human+rights+battle+after+ reservation+cancelled/6953044/story.html (accessed February 1, 2014).

64. Jason St. Amand, "Gay Canadian Couple Win B&B Discrimination Case," *Edge*, July 19, 2012, http://www.edgeboston.com/index.php?ch =&sc=&sc3=&id=135244&pf=1 (accessed February 1, 2014).

65. Charlie Butts, "Lost the Business but Counting the Blessings," *One News Now*, July 20, 2012, http://www.onenewsnow.com/legal-courts/2012/ 07/20/lost-the-business-but-counting-the-blessings (accessed February 1, 2014).

66. Queerty.com, "Canadian B&B Owners Fined For Turning Away Gay Couple," http://www.queerty.com/canadian-bb-owners-fined-for-turning -away-gay-couple-20120720/ (accessed February 1, 2014).

67. Butts, "Lost the Business but Counting the Blessings."

68. Pacific Justice Institute, "PJI Warns Community College Officials Not to Stifle Free Speech," September 12, 2012, http://www.pacificjustice.org/1/ post/2012/09/pji-warns-community-college-officials-not-to-stifle-free -speech.html (accessed February 1, 2014).

69. Matt Krupnick, "Peralta Settles Lawsuit Over Student Prayer," *San Jose Mercury News*, May 6, 2010, http://www.mercurynews.com/breaking -news/ci_15033286 (accessed January 30, 2014).

70. Erica Rodriguez, "Buell lawyer: District Believes Teacher Violated Church-State Provision," *Orlando Sentinel*, August 25, 2011, http://articles .orlandosentinel.com/2011-08-25/features/os-jerry-buell-facebook-rally -20110825_1_church-and-state-ethics-policy-facebook-posts (accessed February 1, 2014).

Chapter 9
Macy's Kinky Thanksgiving Day Parade

1. Dallasvoice.com, "Conservatives blast 'Kinky Boots' performance in Macy's Thanksgiving Day Parade," November 29, 2013, http://www .dallasvoice.com/conservatives-blast-kinky-boots-performance-macys -thanksgiving-day-parade-10162331.html (accessed February 3, 2014).

2. WND.com, "Moms: Famous Store Can't Be Trusted with Kids," December 5, 2013, http://mobile.wnd.com/2013/12/moms-famous-store -cant-be-trusted-with-kids/ (accessed February 3, 2014).

3. Ibid.

4. Ibid.

5. "Kinky Boots Outrage," *Huffington Post*, December 2, 2013, http:// www.huffingtonpost.com/news/kinky-boots-outrage (accessed February 3, 2014)

6. Facebook.com, https://www.facebook.com/ToddStarnesFNC, November 28, 2013, 1:11 p.m.

7. Page Six, "'Kinky Boots' Walks Tall in Macy's After Parade Controversy," November 30, 2013, http://pagesix.com/2013/11/30/kinky-boots -walks-tall-in-macys-after-thanksgiving-parade-controversy/ (accessed February 3, 2014).

8. Theresa Walsh Giarrusso, "Did You Explain 'Kinky Boots Performance in Macy's Parade?", *Atlanta Journal-Constitution*, December 1, 2013, http:// blogs.ajc.com/momania/2013/12/01/did-you-explain-kinky-boots -performance-in-macys-parade/ (accessed February 3, 2014).

9. Ibid.

10. Michael Gioia, "Following Twitter Stir, Tony Winner Harvey Fierstein Issues Statement Regarding Kinky Boots Thanksgiving Day Performance," Playbill, November 29, 2013, http://tinyurl.com/nwgn22z (accessed February 3, 2014).

11. Parents Television Council, "MTV Serves Sex to 14-Year-Olds at MT"'s Video Music Awards," August 26, 2013, http://w2.parentstv.org/Main/ News/Detail.aspx?docID=2910 (accessed February 3, 2014).

12. Ibid.

Chapter 10
The Day the Gays Tried to Cook Duck Dynasty's Goose

1. James Hibberd, "Holy Duck! A&E's 'Duck Dynasty' Return Shatters Cable Record," *Entertainment Weekly*, August 15, 2013, http://insidetv.ew .com/2013/08/15/holy-duck-aes-duck-dynasty-return-shatters-cable-record/ (accessed February 3, 2014).

2. TheBlaze, "'Duck Dynasty' Brother Reveals Why He Was Kicked Out of a New York City Hotel This Week," April 15, 2013, http://www.theblaze .com/stories/2013/08/15/duck-dynasty-brother-reveals-why-he-was-kicked -out-of-a-new-york-city-hotel-this-week/ (accessed February 3, 2014).

3. Ibid.

4. Foxnews.com, "'Duck Dynasty' star Phil Robertson suspended by A&E," December 19, 2013, http://www.foxnews.com/entertainment/2013/ 12/18/phil-robertson-suspended-after-comments-about-homosexuality/ (accessed February 3, 2014).

5. Dana Ford, "'Duck Dynasty' Star Suspended for Anti-Gay Remarks," CNN.com, December 18, 2013, http://www.cnn.com/2013/12/18/showbiz/ duck-dynasty-suspension/ (accessed February 3, 2014).

6. Drew Magary, "What the Duck?", *GQ*, January 2014, http://www .gq.com/entertainment/television/201401/duck-dynasty-phil-robertson (accessed January 30, 2014).

7. Ross Murray, "Duck Dynasty's Phil Robertson Uses Vile stereotypes to Tell GQ His Thoughts on LGBT People," GLAAD.org, December 18, 2013, http://www.glaad.org/blog/duck-dynastys-phil-robertson-uses-vile -stereotypes-tell-gq-his-thoughts-lgbt-people (accessed February 3, 2014).

8. Lesley Messer and Kevin Dolak, "'Duck Dynasty' Puts Star Phil Robertson on Hiatus After Anti-Gay Comments," ABC News, December 18, 2013, http://abcnews.go.com/blogs/entertainment/2013/12/duck-dynasty -puts-star-phil-robertson-on-hiatus-after-anti-gay-comments/ (accessed February 3, 2014).

9. Magary, "What the Duck?"

Chapter 12
Why Does the NFL Hate Tim Tebow?

1. Ben Boychuk and Joel Mathis, "Should Tim Tebow Be so Flamboyant about His Faith?", *Times Herald*, December 10, 2011, http://www.times herald.com/article/JR/20111210/OPINION03/111219990 (accessed January 30, 2014).

2. Ibid.

3. Dan Bernstein, "Acquiring Tebow a Bad Idea," CBSChicago.com, March 21, 2012, http://chicago.cbslocal.com/2012/03/21/bernstein -acquiring-tebow-a-bad-idea/ (accessed February 3, 2014).

4. Mark Kizsla, "Broncos Need New Meaning for Tim Tebowing," *Denver Post*, October 30, 2011, http://www.denverpost.com/ci_19228711 (accessed January 30, 2014).

5. Gregg Rosenthal, "Tebow's Pre-Wonderlic Prayer Request Falls Flat," NCB Sports, March 23, 2010, http://profootballtalk.nbcsports.com/2010/03/23/tebows-pre-wonderlic-prayer-request-falls-flat/ (accessed February 3, 2014).

6. Meghan Keneally, "'Christ Comes First in My Life': Tim Tebow Hits Back after Ex-Broncos Quarterback Urges Him to 'Shut Up About God,'" *Daily Mail*, http://www.dailymail.co.uk/news/article-2065302/Tim-Tebow-hits-ex-Broncos-quarterback-Jake-Plummer-says-shut-God.html (accessed February 3, 2014).

7. Anthony Bradley, "Tim Tebow's Self-Inflicted Criticism," *WORLD Magazine*, November 9, 2011, http://www.worldmag.com/2011/11/tim_tebow_s_self_inflicted_criticism (accessed February 3, 2014).

8. Dan Bickley, "Kurt Warner to Tim Tebow: Let Your Actions Be Your Words," *Arizona Republic*, November 26, 2011, http://www.azcentral.com/sports/cardinals/articles/2011/11/26/20111126nfl-kurt-warner-tim-tebow-advice.html?nclick_check=1 (accessed February 3, 2014).

Chapter 13
From the Annals of God-Blessed Living:
The Seven Deadly Sins Minus Five

1. *New York Times*, "After 151 Years, Dance Ban Ends at Baylor," April 19, 1996, http://www.nytimes.com/1996/04/19/us/after-151-years-dance-ban-ends-at-baylor.html (accessed January 30, 2014).

Chapter 14
No Gideons Allowed

1. Wikipedia.org., "Gideons International," http://en.wikipedia.org/wiki/Gideons_International (accessed February 3, 2014).

2. Todd Petty, "Phillipsburg Teacher Allegedly Fired for Giving Bible to Student, Files Complaint Against School District," April 11, 2013, http://tinyurl.com/cbpp5dk (accessed February 3, 2014).

Chapter 15
Suffer Not the Children

1. Reach America, *The Thaw*, http://letsreachamerica.org/ (accessed February 3, 2014).

2. *Donna Stites v. Fairfax County School Board*, Alliance Defending Freedom, http://www.adfmedia.org/files/SScomplaint.pdf (accessed February 3, 2014).

3. Patti Zarling, "High School Newspaper Column Sparks Controversy," *USA Today*, January 15, 2011, http://usatoday30.usatoday.com/news/nation/story/2012-01-15/gay-parenting-shawano/52567228/1 (accessed February 3, 2014).

4. Jay Lindsay, "Mass. Education Department Issues Rules On Transgender Students," February 16, 2013, WBUR.org, http://www.wbur.org/2013/02/16/mass-education-transgender (accessed February 3, 2014).

5. Ibid.

6. YouTube.com, "Dan Savage discusses Bible at High School Journalism Convention," http://www.youtube.com/watch?v=ao0k9qDsOvs (accessed February 3, 2014).

7. YouTube.com, "Valedictorian, Roy Costner IV, Tears Up Speech on Stage, Recites The Lord's Prayer at Graduation," http://www.youtube.com/watch?v=SofwwWkWkC4 (accessed February 3, 2014).

8. Freedom From Religion Foundation, "FFRF Calls Out Pickens County Schools Multiple Religious Offenses," June 6, 2013, http://ffrf.org/news/news-releases/item/17877-ffrf-calls-out-pickens-county-schools-multiple-religious-offenses (accessed February 3, 2014).

9. Ibid.

10. Sonoma State University, Office of the President, July 18, 2013, http://www.libertyinstitute.org/document.doc?id=92 (accessed February 3, 2014).

11. *Landdis Hollifield*, "'God' Removed From Student's poem," *McDowell News*, http://www.mcdowellnews.com/news/article_b44b1b0a-acd4-5c48-91a5-ef547a31a9d5.html (accessed March 4, 2014).

12. Ibid.

13. Ibid.

14. Emily Maher, "Student Speaks Out Against Banning Religious Plaques From School," 4029tv.com, May 13, 2013, http://www.4029tv.com/news/arkansas/oklahoma/high-school-students-speak-out-against-banning-religious-plaques-from-school/-/13003784/20091512/-/l7wyw7z/-/index.html (accessed February 3, 2014).

15. Ibid.

Chapter 17
A Clear and Present Danger

1. *Washington Times*, "Military Chaplains Told to Shy From Jesus," December 21, 2005, http://www.washingtontimes.com/news/2005/dec/21/20051221-121224-6972r/?page=all (accessed February 3, 2014).

2. Karis, Huus, "Steeple, Cross at US Army Base on Afghan Frontier Raise Hackles," NBC News, January 24, 2013, http://worldnews.nbcnews.com/_news/2013/01/24/16647516-steeple-cross-at-us-army-base-on-afghan-frontier-raise-hackles?lite (accessed February 3, 2014).

3. James Dao, "Final Resting Place, and Battleground," *New York Times*, August 31, 2011, http://www.nytimes.com/2011/08/31/us/31funerals

.html?pagewanted=all&_r=0 (accessed February 3, 2014); Lindsay Wise, "VA Defends Houston National Cemetery Staff," *Houston Chronicle*, July 18, 2011, http://www.chron.com/news/houston-texas/article/VA-defends -Houston-National-Cemetery-staff-2079035.php (accessed February 3, 2014).

4. David Waters, "Franklin Graham Cut From Pentagon Prayer Event for Anti-Islam Remark," OnFaith, http://www.faithstreet.com/ onfaith/2010/04/22/cnn-army-rescinds-franklin-grahams-invitation-to -speak-at-prayer-event-at-pentagaon/9025 (accessed February 3, 2014); Jennifer Wishon, "Tony Perkins 'Disinvited' to National Prayer Luncheon." CBN News, February 25, 2010, http://www.cbn.com/cbnnews/politics/ 2010/February/Tony-Perkins-Uninvited-to-National-Prayer-Luncheon/ (accessed February 3, 2014); Ken Blackwell, "Gen. Boykin Blocked at West Point," CNSNews.com, February 1, 2012, http://cnsnews.com/node/508665 (accessed February 3, 2014).

5. Gerard O'Connell, "U.S. Army Prevented Catholic Chaplains From Reading Bishop's Pastoral Letter at Mass," Vatican Insider, February 5, 2012, http://vaticaninsider.lastampa.it/en/world-news/detail/articolo/12347/ (accessed February 3, 2014).

6. Fox News "Army E-mail Labels Christian Ministries as 'Domestic Hate Groups,'" http://radio.foxnews.com/toddstarnes/top-stories/army -e-mail-labels-christian-ministries-as-domestic-hate-groups.html (accessed February 3, 2014).

7. Barbara Sherer, "Chaplaincy at a Crossroads," March, 3, 2011, http:// www.dtic.mil/dtic/tr/fulltext/u2/a547386.pdf (accessed February 3, 2014).

8. Ibid.

9. Fox News, "Admiral Says Christians Told to Hide Their Faith," http:// radio.foxnews.com/toddstarnes/top-stories/admiral-says-christians-told-to -hide-their-faith.html (accessed February 3, 2014).

10. National Defense Authorization Act for Fiscal Year 2013, Sec. 533, http://docs.house.gov/billsthisweek/20121217/CRPT-112HRPT-705.pdf, (accessed February 5, 2014).

11. Bruce Alpert, "Fleming Proposal to Require Free Religious Expression in Military Draws White House Objections," Nola.com, June 12, 2013, http://www.nola.com/politics/index.ssf/2013/06/fleming_proposal_to_ require_fr.html (accessed February 3, 2014).

12. Joseph Rhee, Tahman Bradley, and Brian Ross, "U.S. Military Weapons Inscribed With Secret 'Jesus' Bible Codes," ABC News January 18, 2010, http://abcnews.go.com/Blotter/us-military-weapons-inscribed-secret -jesus-bible-codes/story?id=9575794 (accessed January 30, 2014).

13. Tim Mak, "Cross Removed at Base in Afghanistan," Politico, November 23, 2011, http://www.politico.com/news/stories/1111/69039.html (accessed February 4, 2014).

14. Billy Hallowell, "Is the US Military Really Planning to Court Martial Christian Soldiers Who Proselytize? TheBlaze Explores the Stunning

Allegations," TheBlaze, May 8, 2013, http://www.theblaze.com/stories/2013/05/
08/is-the-u-s-military-really-planning-to-court-martial-christian-soldiers
-who-proselytize-theblaze-explores-the-stunning-allegations/

15. Department of the Air Force, "Air Force Culture, Air Force Standards," August 7, 2013, http://static.e-publishing.af.mil/production/1/af/
publication/afi1-1/afi1-1.pdf (accessed February 3, 2014).

16. Ibid.

17. Ibid.

18. Sally Quinn, "Military Should Put Religious Freedom at the Front,"
OnFaith, April 26, 2013, http://www.faithstreet.com/onfaith/2013/04/26/us
-military-should-put-religious-freedom-at-the-front (accessed January 30, 2014).

19. Ibid.

20. Andie Adams and Steven Luke, "Men Accuse VA of Religious Persecution," NBC San Diego, November 8, 2013, http://www.nbcsandiego.com/
news/local/Men-Accuse-VA-of-Religious-Persecution-231216811.html
(accessed February 3, 2014).

21. *Conservative Baptist Association of America, Inc., v. Eric Shinseki*,
John Wells Law, http://johnwellslaw.com/files/CBAmericaComplaint.a13.pdf
(accessed February 3, 2014).

22. Ibid.

Chapter 18
One Nation Under Allah

1. WhiteHouse.gov, "Statement by the President on the Occasion of
Ramadan," July 20, 2012, http://www.whitehouse.gov/the-press-office/
2012/07/20/statement-president-occasion-ramadan (accessed February 3,
2014).

2. Whitehouse.gov, Remarks by the President at Iftar Dinner," July 26,
2013, http://www.whitehouse.gov/the-press-office/2013/07/25/remarks
-president-iftar-dinner (accessed February 3, 2014).

3. YouTube.com, "Obama in Turkey 'We Do Not Consider Ourselves a
Christian Nation.'"

4. Lifeway.com, "Research: Most American Pastors Say 'Islam Is a Dangerous Religion,'" http://www.lifeway.com/Article/LifeWay-Research-finds
-most-American-pastors-say-Islam-is-a-dangerous-religion (accessed February 3, 2014).

5. *Washington Times*, "White House: 'War on Terrorism' Is Over,"
August 6, 2009, http://www.washingtontimes.com/news/2009/aug/06/white
-house-war-terrorism-over/?feat=home_headlines (accessed February 3,
2014).

6. Fox News, "Counterterror Adviser Defends Jihad as 'Legitimate Tenet
of Islam,'" May 27, 20110, http://www.foxnews.com/politics/2010/05/27/

counterterror-adviser-defends-jihad-legitimate-tenet-islam/ (accessed January 30, 2014).

7. Judicial Watch, "JW Report: "U.S. Government Purges of Law Enforcement Training Material Deemed 'Offensive' to Muslims," December 9, 2013, http://tinyurl.com/lhvqn3r (accessed January 30, 2014).

8. Judicial Watch, "Documents Obtained by Judicial Watch Reveal FBI Training Curricula Purged of Material Deemed 'Offensive' to Muslims," June 3, 2013, http://tinyurl.com/lwtoye7 (accessed February 3, 2014).

9. Brian Justice, "Group Sets Meeting to Increase Tolerance of Muslims, Culture," *Tullahoma News*, May 21, 2013, http://www.tullahomanews.com/?p=15360 (accessed February 3, 2014).

10. Nick McGurk, "Fort Collins Students Read Pledge of Allegiance in Arabic," 9News.com, January 29, 2013, http://www.9news.com/rss/article/313505/188/Students-read-pledge-in-Arabic (

11. Erwin Lutzer, *The Cross in the Shadow of the Crescent* (Eugene, OR: Harvest House Publishers, 2013), 53.

12. Ibid.

13. Daniel Martin, "2030: The Year Britain Will cease to be a Christian Nation With the March of Secularism," *Daily Mail*, March 2, 2012, http://www.dailymail.co.uk/news/article-2109488/2030-The-year-Britain-cease-Christian-nation-march-secularism.html

14. Lutzer, *The Cross in the Shadow of the Crescent*, 53–54.

15. Ibid., 54.

16. Fox News, "Pastor Says America Is at War With Radical Islam," http://radio.foxnews.com/toddstarnes/top-stories/pastor-says-america-is-at-war-with-radical-islam.html (accessed February 3, 2014).

17. Ibid.

18. Ibid.

19. Laura Hibbard, "André Carson, Indiana Congressman, Says U.S. Public Schools Should Be Modeled After Islamic Schools," *Huffington Post*, July 6, 2012, http://www.huffingtonpost.com/2012/07/06/andre-carson-schools-should-be-modeled-after-madrassa_n_1654510.html (accessed February 3, 2014).

20. Nick Schou, "Pulling His Cheney," *OC Weekly*, October 11, 2001, http://www.ocweekly.com/2001-11-01/news/pulling-his-cheney/ (accessed February 4, 2014).

Chapter 19
Meth Addicts Are Fine but Not Homeschoolers?

1. Eric Owens, "Meth Addict Gets Asylum; Christian Homeschoolers Get the Boot," *Daily Caller*, July 26, 2013, (accessed February 3, 2014).

2. Ibid.

Chapter 20
The War on Christmas

1. Sheryl Gay Stolberg, "The Spotlights Bright Glare," *New York Times*, December 4, 2009, http://www.nytimes.com/2009/12/06/fashion/06desiree .html?pagewanted=all&_r=0 (accessed February 4, 2014).

2. Ibid.

3. Rasmussen Reports, "76% Think Christmas Should Be About Jesus, Not Santa," December 9, 2012, ttp://www.rasmussenreports.com/public_ content/lifestyle/holidayshristmar_2012/76_think_christmas_should_be_ about_jesus_not_santa (accessed February 4, 2014).

4. *Today*, "No Time to Pick a Tree? Outsourcing Christmas To-Dos," December 11, 2012, http://www.today.com/video/today/50158256#50158256 (accessed February 4, 2014).

5. Ibid.

6. Ibid.

7. Juli Weiner, "Bo Obama: the True Meaning of Christmas," Vanity Fair, December 6, 2012, http://www.vanityfair.com/online/daily/2012/12/Bo -Obama-the-True-Meaning-of-Christmas (accessed February 4, 2014).

8. *Daily Mail*, "First Look at Adorable New White House Holiday Card (and Guess Who Makes a Special Appearance," December 8, 2012, http:// www.dailymail.co.uk/news/article-2245087/Christmas-2012-First-look -adorable-new-White-House-holiday-card-guess-makes-special-appearance .html (accessed February 4, 2014).

9. *Los Angeles Times*, "Obama Family's White House Holiday Card Is L.A. Artist's Design," December 15, 2011, http://latimesblogs.latimes.com/ culturemonster/2011/12/obama-family-white-house-holiday-card.html (accessed February 4, 2014).

10. Rande Iaboni, "Hallmark Ornament has 'Deck the Halls'—Without the Gay Apparel," October 30, 2013, http://www.cnn.com/2013/10/30/us/ hallmark-deck-the-halls-ornament/ (accessed February 4, 2014).

11. Shaw Air Force Base, "Nativity Scene Removal at Shaw AFB," December 11, 2013, http://www.shaw.af.mil/news/story.asp?id=123373981 (accessed February 4, 2014).

12. House of Representatives, Pat Fallon, November 14, 2013, http:// txvalues.org/wp-content/uploads/2013/11/Merry-Christmas-BillREpFallon FriscoISDLtr.pdf (accessed February 4, 2014).

13. Appignani Humanist Legal Center, http://americanhumanist.org/ system/storage/2/23/7/4719/letter_re_Operation_Christmas_Child_ Columbia_SC.pdf (accessed February 4, 2014).

14. Bordentown Regional School District, "Winter Concert Information," October 18, http://www.bordentown.k12.nj.us/news.cfm?story=73029 &school=0 (accessed February 4, 2014); David Matthau, "Bordentown Bans Religious Christmas Songs at School Concerts," New Jersey 101.5, October

30, 2013, http://nj1015.com/bordentown-bans-religious-christmas-songs-at-school-concerts/ (accessed February 4, 2014).

15. Alliance Defending Freedom, http://www.adfmedia.org/files/BordentownLetter.pdf (accessed February 4, 2014).

16. Rasmussen Reports, "79% Say Religious Holidays Should Be Celebrated in Public Schools," December 7, 2011, http://www.rasmussenreports.com/public_content/lifestyle/holidays/december_2011/79_say_religious_holidays_should_be_celebrated_in_public_schools (accessed February 4, 2014).

17. Alliance Defending Freedom, "NJ School District Bans Religious Christmas Carols," October 29, 2013, http://www.adfmedia.org/News/PRDetail/8615 (accessed February 4, 2014).

18. Ibid.

19. Matt Johnson, "Church Will Not Do 'Charlie Brown' School Shows Due to Controversy," KATV, November 29, 2012, http://www.katv.com/story/20222656/athiest-group-gets-legal-help-for-charlie-brown-school-controversy (accessed February 4, 2014).

20. *A Charlie Brown Christmas* directed by Bill Melendez (Burbank, CA: Warner Home Video, 2008), DVD.

21. Arkansasmatters.com, "Arkansas Society of Freethinkers Denies 'War on Christmas' Charge," November 21, 2012, http://www.arkansasmatters.com/story/arkansas-society-of-freethinkers-denies-war-on-chr/d/story/h5AhwpXJGEGX1Sns9-TIlw (accessed February 4, 2014).

22. Ibid.

23. Ibid.

24. Alliance Defending Freedom, "Good Grief! Atheist Group Disgruntled With 'A Charlie Brown Christmas,'" November 26, 2012, http://www.alliancedefendingfreedom.org/News/PRDetail/7819 (accessed February 4, 2014).

25. Ibid.

26. Johnson, "Church Will Not Do 'Charlie Brown' School Shows Due to Controversy."

27. Kendall Hatch, "Holliston Firefighters Ticked at Town for Banning Cross Atop Fire Station," *Metro West Daily News*, December 10, 2009, http://www.metrowestdailynews.com/x1758134651/Holliston-firefighters-ticked-at-town-for-banning-cross-atop-fire-station (accessed February 4, 2014).

28. Steve Metsch, "Lawsuit Threat Means Alsip Christmas Tradition Gets Crossed Off," *Southtown Star*, December 21, 2012, http://southtownstar.suntimes.com/news/16491738-418/lawsuit-threat-means-alsip-christmas-tradition-gets-crossed-off.html (accessed February 4, 2014).

29. Ibid.

30. Ibid.

31. Ibid.

32. Benjamin Franklin, *Poor Richard's Almanac* (New York: Barnes & Noble Publishing, Inc., 2004), 92.

33. Tim Daly, "Stockton School Christmas Décor 'Ban' Explained," News 10, December 6, 2011, http://host-37.242.54.159.gannett.com/news/watchdogs/166743/449/Stockton-school-Christmas-decor-ban-explained (accessed February 4, 2014).

34. Tim Daly, "Holiday Decorations Off Limits at Stockton School," News 10, December 2, 2011, http://www.news10.net/news/article/165912/2/Holiday-decorations-off-limits-at-Stockton-school (accessed February 4, 2014).

35. Jessamy Brown, "Texas School District Bans Santa Claus, Gift Exchanges in Classrooms," *Fort Worth Star-Telegram*, December 2, 2011, http://www.mcclatchydc.com/2011/12/02/131944/texas-school-district-bans-santa.html (accessed February 4, 2014); *Sun Journal*, "Fort Worth Schools Ban Santa, Gifts in Classroom," December 3, 2011, http://www2.sunjournal.com/pdfs/2011/12/03/A08SJD-120311_1.pdf (accessed February 4, 2014).

36. Norma Cook Everist, "President Obama Cut Short His Vacation?", *Huffington Post*, December 27, 2013, http://www.huffingtonpost.com/norma-cook-everist/president-obama-vacation_b_4507967.html (accessed February 4, 2014).

37. Whitehouse.gov, "Statement by the President on the Occasion of Ramadan," August 11, 2010, http://www.whitehouse.gov/the-press-office/2010/08/11/statement-president-occasion-ramadan (accessed February 4, 2014).

38. Whitehouse.gov, "Statement by the President on the Occasion of Eid-ul-Fitr," September 9, 2010, http://www.whitehouse.gov/the-press-office/2010/09/09/statement-president-occasion-eid-ul-fitr (accessed February 4, 2014).

39. Whitehouse.gov, "Statement by the President on the Occasion of Hajj and Eid-ul-Adha," November 15, 2010, http://www.whitehouse.gov/the-press-office/2010/11/15/statement-president-hajj-and-eid-ul-adha (accessed February 4, 2014).

40. Whitehouse.gov, "Presidential Proclamation—Earth Day," April 22, 2011, http://www.whitehouse.gov/the-press-office/2011/04/22/presidential-proclamation-earth-day-2011 (accessed February 4, 2014).

41. Whitehouse.gov, "Weekly Address: President Obama Extends Holiday Greeting," April 3, 2010, http://www.whitehouse.gov/the-press-office/weekly-address-president-obama-extends-holiday-greeting (accessed February 4, 2014).

42. Whitehouse.gov, "Statement by the President on the Occasion of Hajj and Eid-ul-Adha."

43. George W. Bush, "Presidential Message: Easter 2007," April 6, 2007, http://georgewbush-whitehouse.archives.gov/news/releases/2007/04/20070406-2.html (accessed February 4, 2014).

44. George W. Bush, "Presidential Message: Easter 2008," March 21, 2008, http://georgewbush-whitehouse.archives.gov/news/releases/2008/03/ 20080321.html (accessed February 4, 2014).

45. Whitehouse.gov, "Weekly Address: The President and First Lady Thank Our Troops for Their Service This Holiday Season," December 24, 2011, http://www.whitehouse.gov/photos-and-video/video/2011/12/23/ weekly-address-president-and-first-lady-thank-our-troops-their-ser# transcript (accessed February 4, 2014).

46. Ibid.

47. Ibid.

48. Ibid.

49. Ibid.

Chapter 21
Nazis, Communists, and the USA

1. WCBS 880, "Some Parents Upset After L.I. School Removes Religious References From 'Silent Night,'" December 29, 2013, http://newyork.cbslocal .com/2013/12/19/some-parents-upset-after-l-i-school-removes-religious -references-from-silent-night/ (accessed February 4, 2014).

2. *Kings Park Patch*, "School Chorus Sings Altered 'Silent Night,' Removes Religious References," December 19, 2013, http://kingspark.patch .com/groups/schools/p/video-rjo-chorus-performs-altered-silent-night (accessed February 4, 2014).

3. J. Matt Barber, "The War on Christmas: It's a Commie Thing," http:// old.worldviewweekend.com/worldview-times/print.php?&ArticleID=5696 (accessed February 4, 2014).

4. Robert G. L. Waite, *The Psychopathic God: Adolf Hitler* (New York: Basic Books, 1977), 31–32.

5. Jonah Goldberg, *Liberal Fascism* (New York: Doubleday, 2007), 365.

6. Liberty Counsel, "Christmas According to Marx and Lenin, by Ronald Reagan," December 24, 2010, http://www.lc.org/index.cfm?PID =14100&PRID=1019 (accessed February 4, 2014).

7. The American Legion, "VA Christmas Card Ban Defies Law," December 26, 2013, http://www.legion.org/news/218127/va-christmas-card -ban-defies-law (accessed February 4, 2014).

8. Ibid.

9. Calvert Collins, "Students, Parents Upset That Christmas Cards Won't Go to Local Veterans Due to Policy," Students," MyFoxDFW.com, December 24, 2013, http://www.myfoxdfw.com/story/24293539/students -parents-upset-that-religious-christmas-cards-wont-go-to-north-texas -veterans (accessed February 4, 2014).

10. Ibid.

11. Ibid.

12. Wesley Brown, "August VA Won't Let Carolers Sing Religious Songs," *Augusta Chronicle*, December 23, 2013, http://chronicle.augusta.com/life/ your-faith/2013-12-23/augusta-va-wont-let-carolers-sing-religious-songs (accessed February 4, 2014).

13. Ibid.

14. Liberty Counsel, "Ronald Reagan's Radio Program on Christmas Under Communism," http://www.lc.org/misc/reagan_christmas.htm (accessed February 4, 2014).

15. Liberty Counsel, "Christmas According to Marx and Lenin, by Ronald Reagan," December 24, 2010, http://www.lc.org/index.cfm?PID =14100&PRID=1019 (accessed February 4, 2014).

Chapter 22
It's Time to Take a Stand

1. Liberty Institute, "An Open Letter to the American People," http:// downloads.frc.org/EF/EF12H60.pdf (accessed February 4, 2014).

2. Billy Graham, "My Heart Aches for America," Billy Graham Evangelistic Association, July 19, 2012, http://billygraham.org/story/billy-graham -my-heart-aches-for-america/ (accessed February 4, 2014).

3. Ibid.

4. Ibid.

5. Ibid.

6. Ibid.

7. Ibid.

8. Ibid.

9. Ibid.

10. "Come Thou Fount of Every Blessing" by Robert Robinson. Public Domain.

11. Blue Letter Bible, "Dictionary and Word Search for *Ebenezer*," http:// www.blueletterbible.org/search/dictionary/viewTopic.cfm?topic=NT0001512 ,BT0001237 (accessed February 4, 2014).

12. YouTube.com, "Bill O'Reilly: Why Aren't Christian Leaders More Outraged Over the War on Christmas?", December 11, 2013, http://www .youtube.com/watch?v=SSnT-sYgHGs (accessed February 4, 2014).

13. Ibid.

14. Ibid.

CREDIBLE,
RELEVANT COVERAGE
of the issues that **matter most to you**

FrontLine brings you books, e-books, and other media covering current world affairs and social issues from a Christian perspective. View all of FrontLine's releases at the links below and discover how to bring your values, faith, and biblical principles into today's marketplace of ideas.

FRONT LINE

WWW.CHARISMAHOUSE.COM

TWITTER.COM/CHARISMAHOUSE • FACEBOOK.COM/CHARISMAHOUSE

FREE NEWSLETTERS
TO HELP EMPOWER YOUR LIFE

Why subscribe today?

☐ **DELIVERED DIRECTLY TO YOU.** All you have to do is open your inbox and read.

☐ **EXCLUSIVE CONTENT.** We cover the news overlooked by the mainstream press.

☐ **STAY CURRENT.** Find the latest court rulings, revivals, and cultural trends.

☐ **UPDATE OTHERS.** Easy to forward to friends and family with the click of your mouse.

CHOOSE THE E-NEWSLETTER THAT INTERESTS YOU MOST:

- Christian news
- Daily devotionals
- Spiritual empowerment
- And much, much more

SIGN UP AT: **http://freenewsletters.charismamag.com**

8178